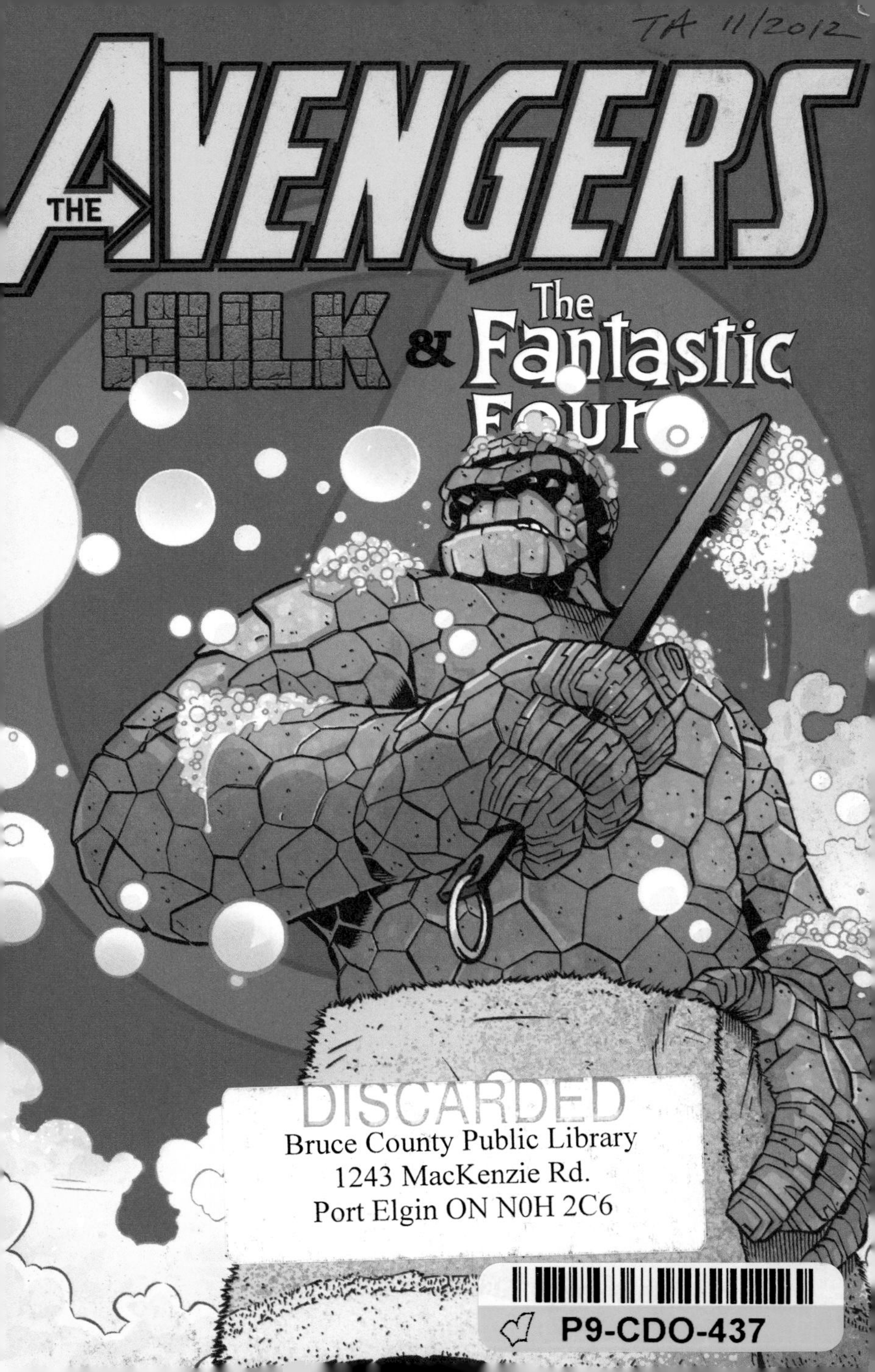
THE AVENGERS
HULK & The Fantastic Four

AVENGERS

HULK & The Fantastic Four

"The Big Idea"
Writer: **J.M. DeMatteis**
Penciler: **Wellinton Alves**
Inker: **Nelson Pereira**
Colorist: **Bruno Hang**

"Super Troupers"
Writer: **Jen Van Meter**
Artist: **Pepe Larraz**
Color Artist: **Andres Mossa**

"The Hulk"
Writer: **Steve Niles**
Penciler: **Leonard Kirk**
Inker: **Kris Justice**
Colorist: **Lee Loughridge**

"King of the Mole Men"
Writer: **Brian Reed**
Penciler: **Ray-Anthony Height**
Inker: **Walden Wong**
Colorist: **Jordie Bellaire**

"The Rise and Fall of the Super-Skrull"
Writer: Mark Sable
Penciler: Tim Levins
Inker: Jaime Mendoza
Colorist: Chris Sotomayor

"A Mountain from an Anthill"
Writer: Marc Sumerak
Penciler: Ig Guara
Inker: Norman Lee
Colorist: Ulises Arreola

Letterers: Dave Sharpe & Blambot's Nate Piekos
**Cover Artists: Carlo Pagulayan with Jeff Huet
& Chris Sotomayor (Issue #21);
and Ale Garza with Chris Sotomayor (Issue #23)**
**Editors: Tom Brennan, Ellie Pyle, Nathan Cosby,
Mark Paniccia & Rachel Pinnelas**
Senior Editor: Stephen Wacker

Collection Editor: Cory Levine
Assistant Editors: Alex Starbuck & Nelson Ribeiro
Editors, Special Projects: Jennifer Grünwald & Mark D. Beazley
Senior Editor, Special Projects: Jeff Youngquist
Senior Vice President of Sales: David Gabriel
SVP of Brand Planning & Communications: Michael Pasciullo

Editor in Chief: Axel Alonso
Chief Creative Officer: Joe Quesada
Publisher: Dan Buckley
Executive Producer: Alan Fine

MARVEL UNIVERSE AVENGERS: HULK & FANTASTIC FOUR. Contains material originally published in magazine form as SUPER HEROES #21-24. First printing 2012. ISBN# 978-0-7851-6559-0. Published by MARVEL WORLDWIDE, INC., a subsidiary of MARVEL ENTERTAINMENT, LLC. OFFICE OF PUBLICATION: 135 West 50th Street, New York, NY 10020. Copyright © 2011 and 2012 Marvel Characters, Inc. All rights reserved. $ 9.99 per copy in the U.S. and $10.99 in Canada (GST #R127032852); Canadian Agreement #40668537. All characters featured in this issue and the distinctive names and likenesses thereof, and all related indicia are trademarks of Marvel Characters, Inc. No similarity between any of the names, characters, persons, and/or institutions in this magazine with those of any living or dead person or institution is intended, and any such similarity which may exist is purely coincidental. **Printed in the U.S.A.** ALAN FINE, EVP - Office of the President, Marvel Worldwide, Inc. and EVP & CMO Marvel Characters B.V.; DAN BUCKLEY, Publisher & President - Print, Animation & Digital Divisions; JOE QUESADA, Chief Creative Officer; TOM BREVOORT, SVP of Operations & Procurement, Publishing; RUWAN JAYATILLEKE, SVP & Associate Publisher, Publishing; C.B. CEBULSKI, SVP of Creator & Content Development; DAVID GABRIEL, SVP of Publishing Sales & Circulation; MICHAEL PASCIULLO, SVP of Brand Planning & Communications; JIM O'KEEFE, VP of Operations & Logistics; DAN CARR, Executive Director of Publishing Technology; SUSAN CRESPI, Editorial Operations Manager; ALEX MORALES, Publishing Operations Manager; STAN LEE, Chairman Emeritus. For information regarding advertising in Marvel Comics or on Marvel.com, please contact Niza Disla, Director of Marvel Partnerships, at ndisla@marvel.com. For Marvel subscription inquiries, please call 800-217-9158. **Manufactured between 8/20/2012 and 9/24/2012 by SHERIDAN BOOKS, INC., CHELSEA, MI, USA.**

10 9 8 7 6 5 4 3 2 1

#21

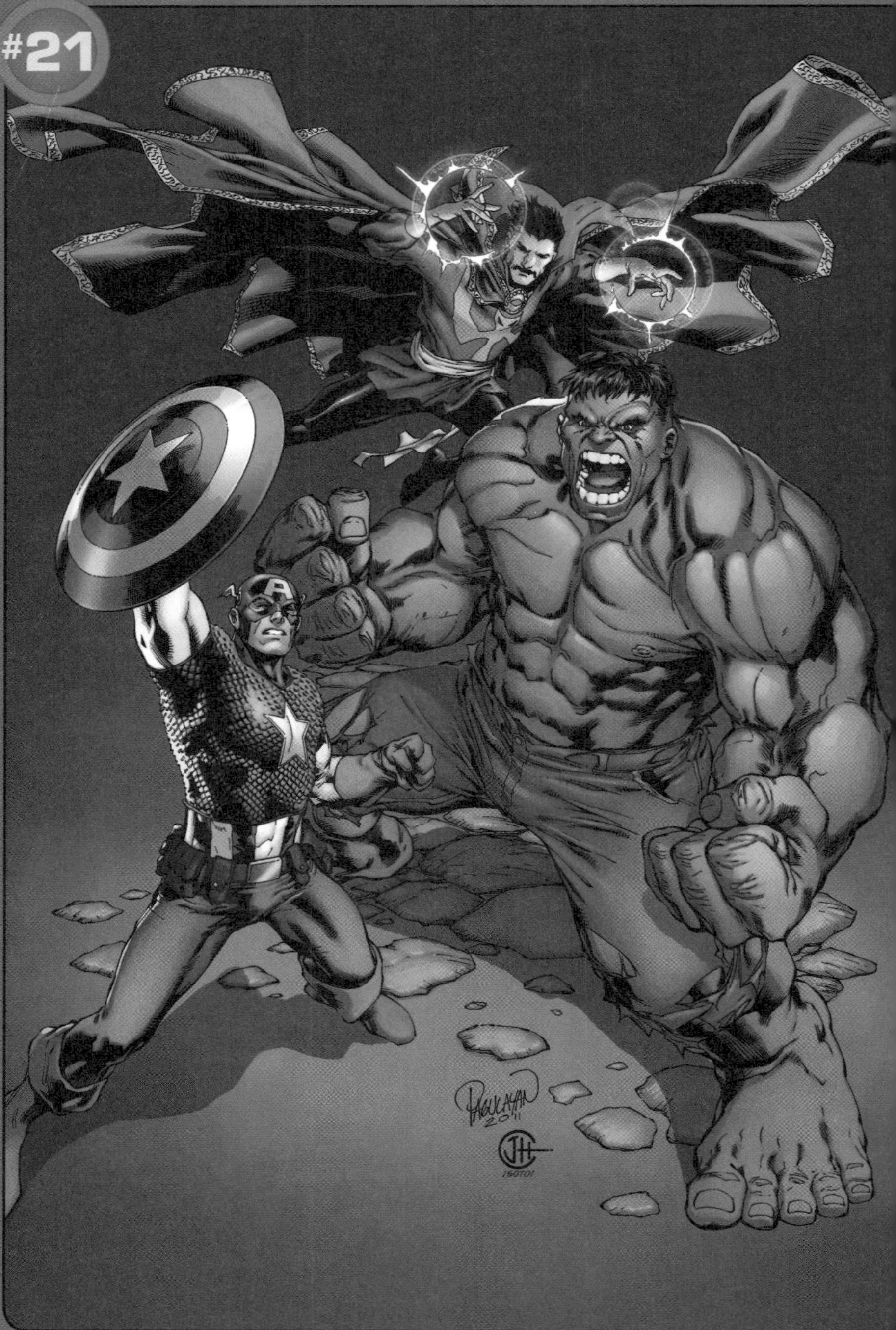
PAGULAYAN 2011

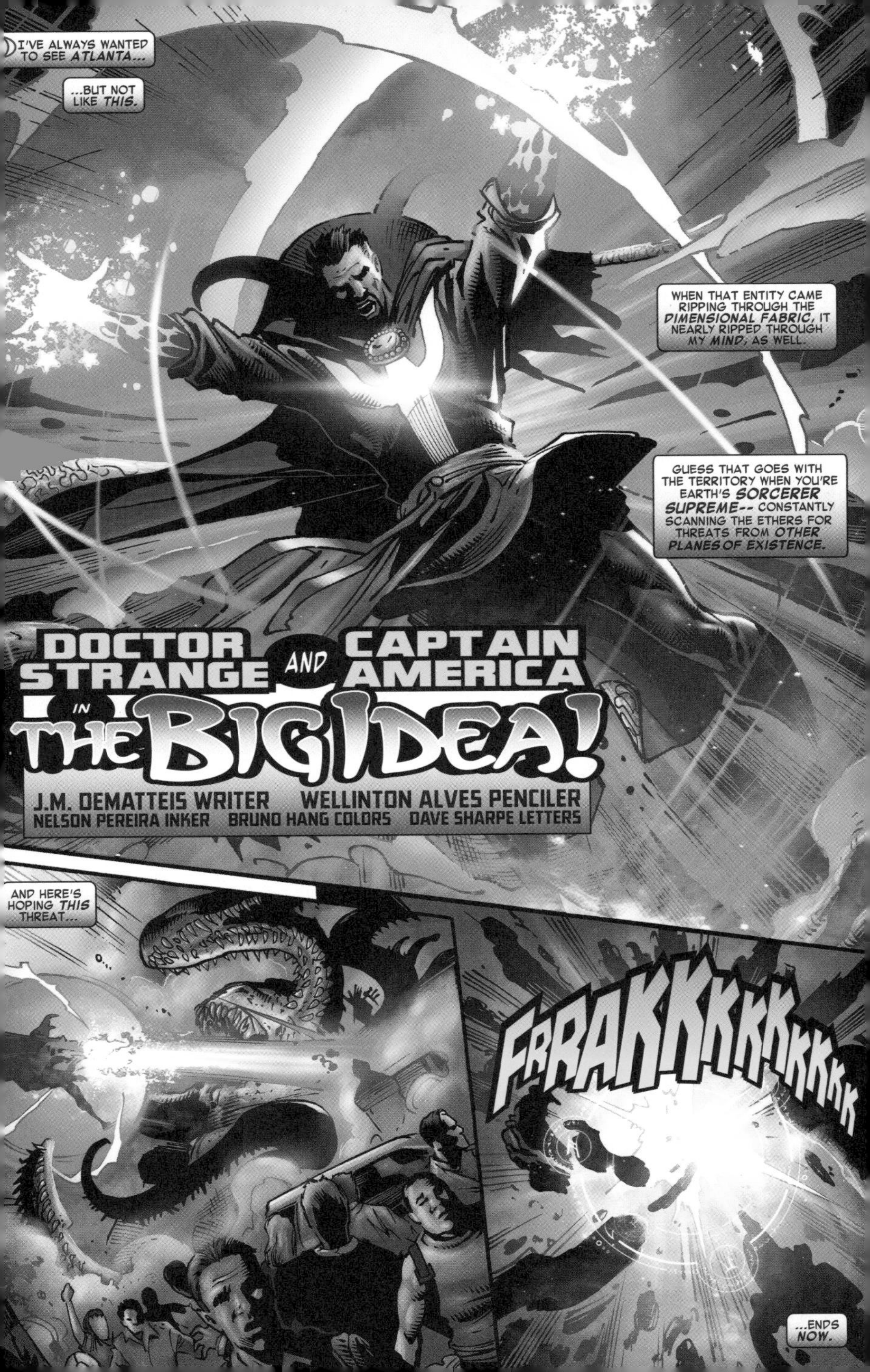
I'VE ALWAYS WANTED TO SEE ATLANTA...
...BUT NOT LIKE THIS.
WHEN THAT ENTITY CAME RIPPING THROUGH THE DIMENSIONAL FABRIC, IT NEARLY RIPPED THROUGH MY MIND, AS WELL.
GUESS THAT GOES WITH THE TERRITORY WHEN YOU'RE EARTH'S SORCERER SUPREME-- CONSTANTLY SCANNING THE ETHERS FOR THREATS FROM OTHER PLANES OF EXISTENCE.
DOCTOR STRANGE AND CAPTAIN AMERICA
IN THE BIG IDEA!
J.M. DEMATTEIS WRITER WELLINTON ALVES PENCILER
NELSON PEREIRA INKER BRUNO HANG COLORS DAVE SHARPE LETTERS
AND HERE'S HOPING THIS THREAT...
FRRAKKKKKKKK
...ENDS NOW.

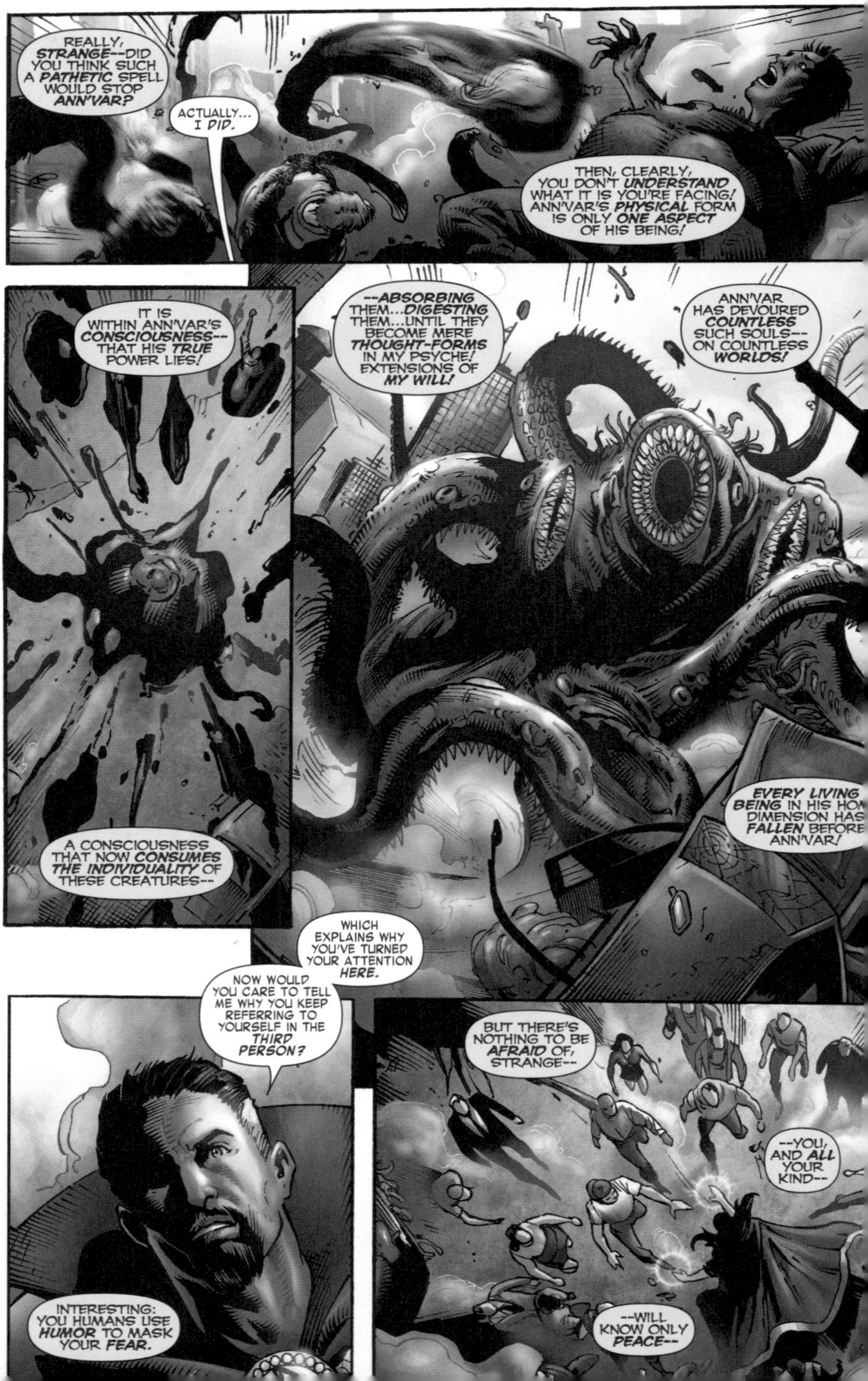
REALLY, STRANGE--DID YOU THINK SUCH A PATHETIC SPELL WOULD STOP ANN'VAR?
ACTUALLY... I DID.
THEN, CLEARLY, YOU DON'T UNDERSTAND WHAT IT IS YOU'RE FACING! ANN'VAR'S PHYSICAL FORM IS ONLY ONE ASPECT OF HIS BEING!
IT IS WITHIN ANN'VAR'S CONSCIOUSNESS--THAT HIS TRUE POWER LIES!
A CONSCIOUSNESS THAT NOW CONSUMES THE INDIVIDUALITY OF THESE CREATURES--
--ABSORBING THEM...DIGESTING THEM...UNTIL THEY BECOME MERE THOUGHT-FORMS IN MY PSYCHE! EXTENSIONS OF MY WILL!
ANN'VAR HAS DEVOURED COUNTLESS SUCH SOULS--ON COUNTLESS WORLDS!
WHICH EXPLAINS WHY YOU'VE TURNED YOUR ATTENTION HERE.
NOW WOULD YOU CARE TO TELL ME WHY YOU KEEP REFERRING TO YOURSELF IN THE THIRD PERSON?
INTERESTING: YOU HUMANS USE HUMOR TO MASK YOUR FEAR.
BUT THERE'S NOTHING TO BE AFRAID OF, STRANGE--
--YOU, AND ALL YOUR KIND--
--WILL KNOW ONLY PEACE--

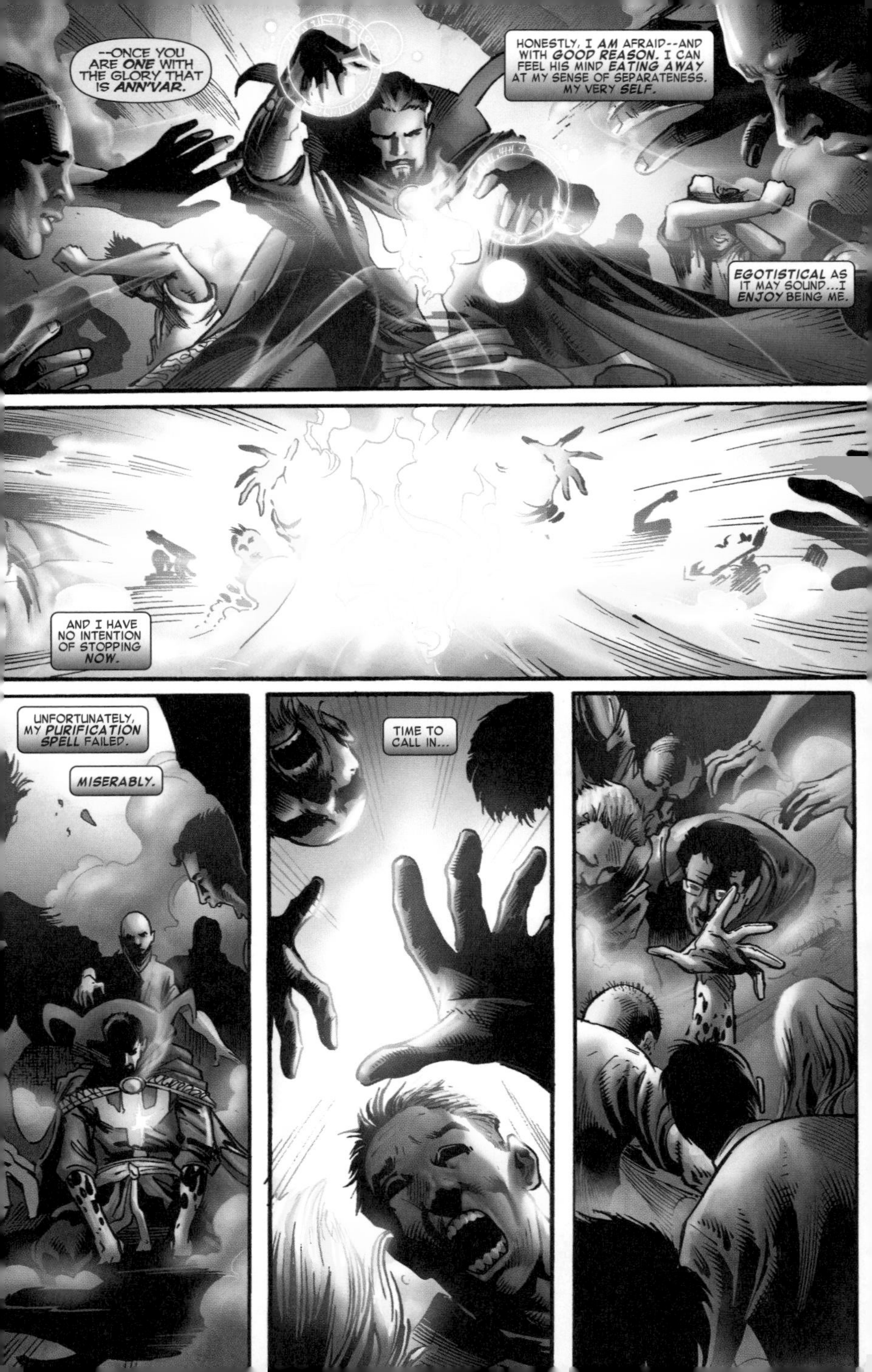
--ONCE YOU ARE ONE WITH THE GLORY THAT IS ANN'VAR.
HONESTLY, I AM AFRAID--AND WITH GOOD REASON. I CAN FEEL HIS MIND EATING AWAY AT MY SENSE OF SEPARATENESS. MY VERY SELF.
EGOTISTICAL AS IT MAY SOUND...I ENJOY BEING ME.
AND I HAVE NO INTENTION OF STOPPING NOW.
UNFORTUNATELY, MY PURIFICATION SPELL FAILED.
MISERABLY.
TIME TO CALL IN...

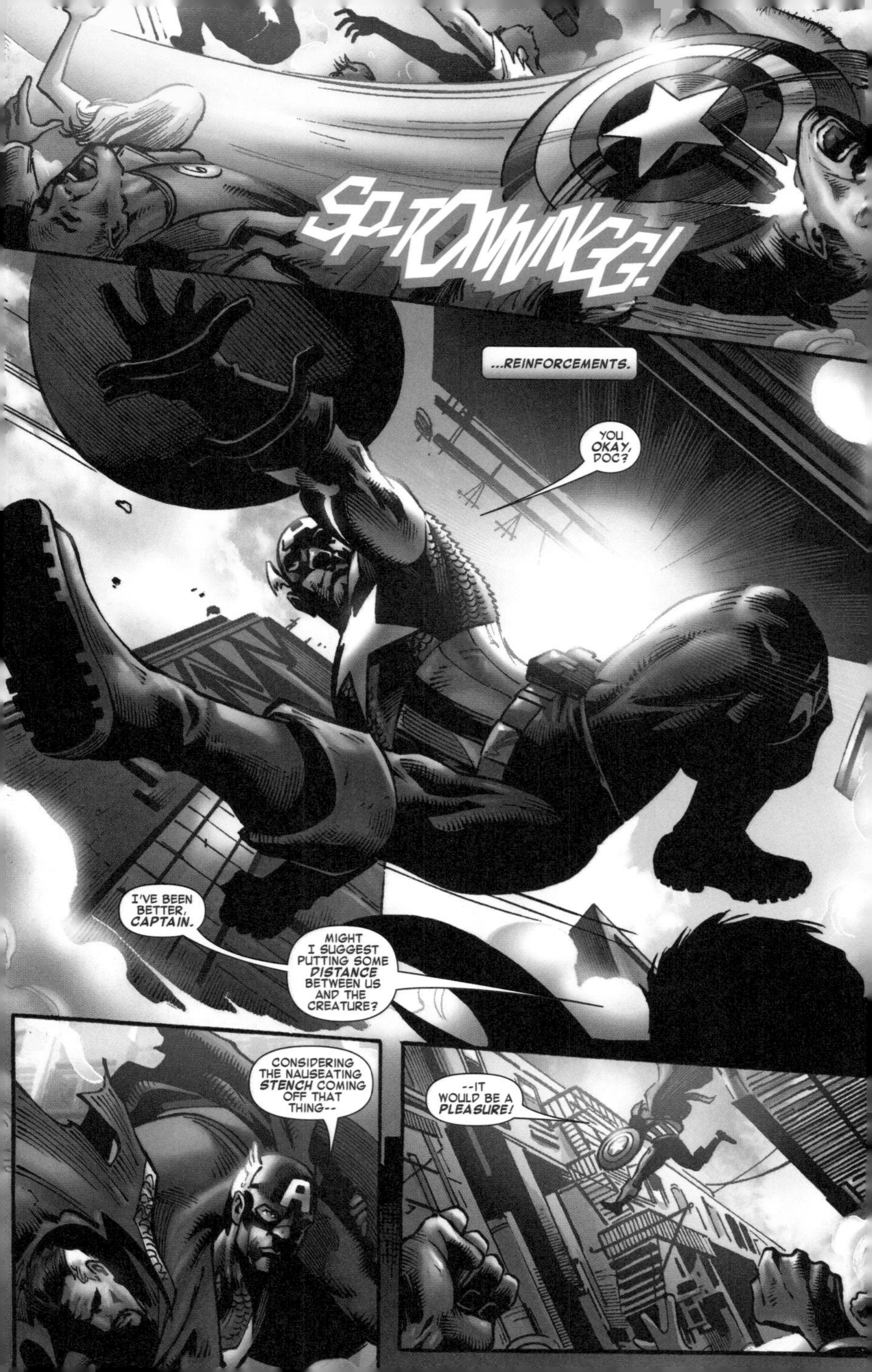
SP-KOWWNGG!
...REINFORCEMENTS.
YOU OKAY, DOC?
I'VE BEEN BETTER, CAPTAIN.
MIGHT I SUGGEST PUTTING SOME DISTANCE BETWEEN US AND THE CREATURE?
CONSIDERING THE NAUSEATING STENCH COMING OFF THAT THING--
--IT WOULD BE A PLEASURE!

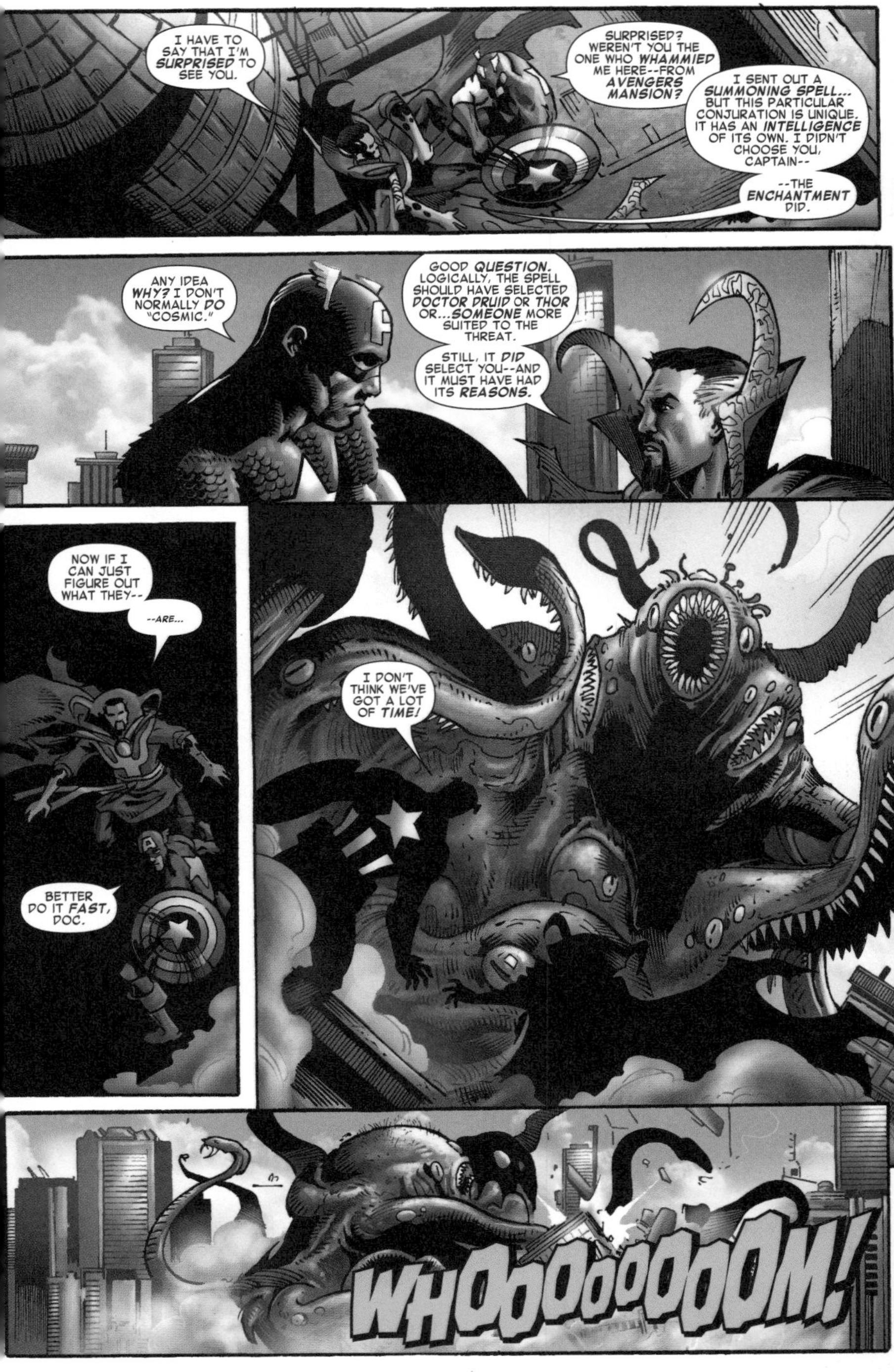
I HAVE TO SAY THAT I'M SURPRISED TO SEE YOU.
SURPRISED? WEREN'T YOU THE ONE WHO WHAMMIED ME HERE--FROM AVENGERS MANSION?
I SENT OUT A SUMMONING SPELL... BUT THIS PARTICULAR CONJURATION IS UNIQUE. IT HAS AN INTELLIGENCE OF ITS OWN. I DIDN'T CHOOSE YOU, CAPTAIN--
--THE ENCHANTMENT DID.
ANY IDEA WHY? I DON'T NORMALLY DO "COSMIC."
GOOD QUESTION. LOGICALLY, THE SPELL SHOULD HAVE SELECTED DOCTOR DRUID OR THOR OR...SOMEONE MORE SUITED TO THE THREAT.
STILL, IT DID SELECT YOU--AND IT MUST HAVE HAD ITS REASONS.
NOW IF I CAN JUST FIGURE OUT WHAT THEY--
--ARE...
I DON'T THINK WE'VE GOT A LOT OF TIME!
BETTER DO IT FAST, DOC.
WHOOOOOOOOOM!

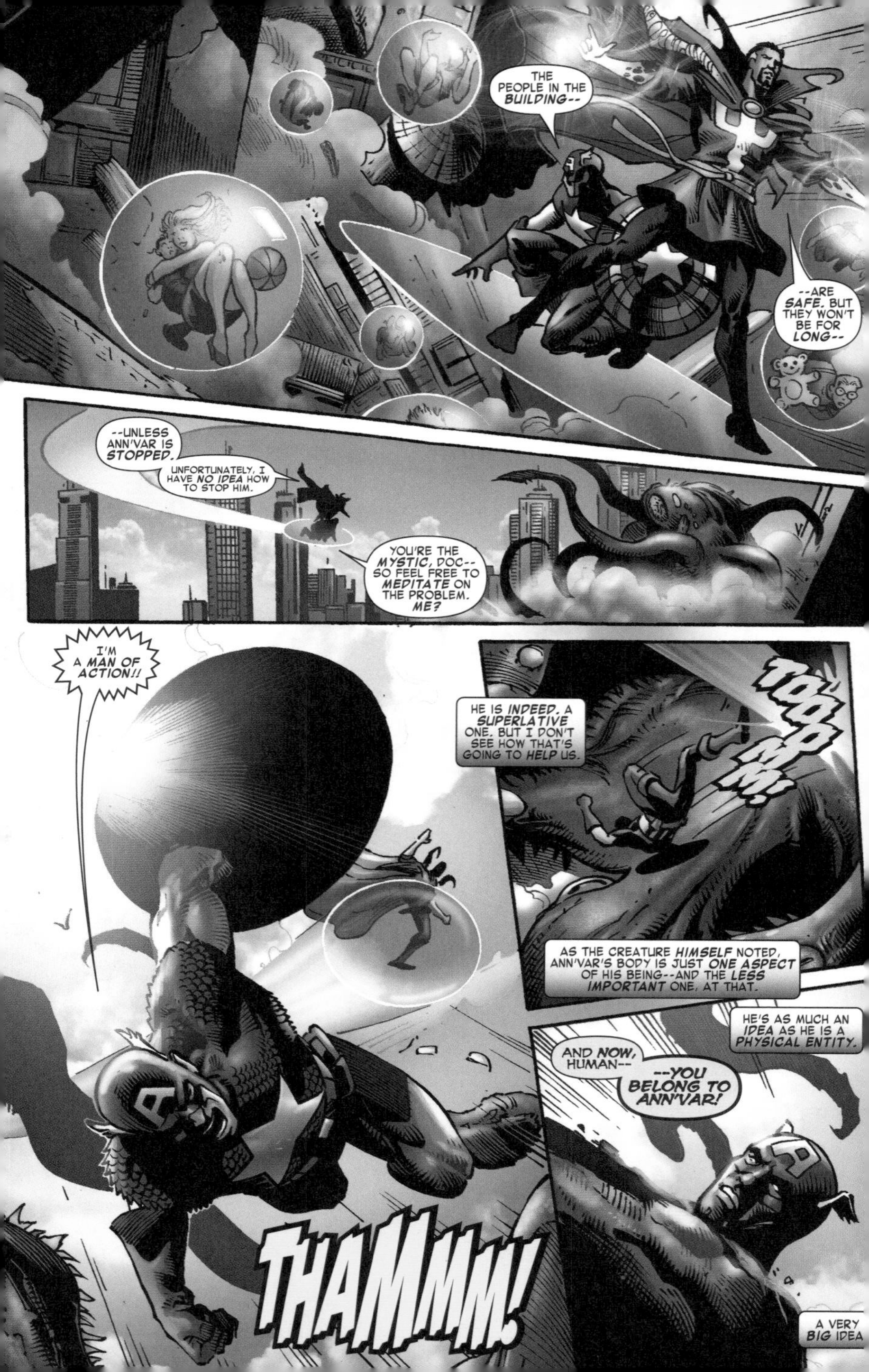
THE PEOPLE IN THE BUILDING--
--ARE SAFE. BUT THEY WON'T BE FOR LONG--
--UNLESS ANN'VAR IS STOPPED.
UNFORTUNATELY, I HAVE NO IDEA HOW TO STOP HIM.
YOU'RE THE MYSTIC, DOC-- SO FEEL FREE TO MEDITATE ON THE PROBLEM. ME?
I'M A MAN OF ACTION!!
HE IS INDEED, A SUPERLATIVE ONE. BUT I DON'T SEE HOW THAT'S GOING TO HELP US.
TOOOMM!
AS THE CREATURE HIMSELF NOTED, ANN'VAR'S BODY IS JUST ONE ASPECT OF HIS BEING--AND THE LESS IMPORTANT ONE, AT THAT.
HE'S AS MUCH AN IDEA AS HE IS A PHYSICAL ENTITY.
AND NOW, HUMAN--
--YOU BELONG TO ANN'VAR!
THAMMMM!
A VERY BIG IDEA

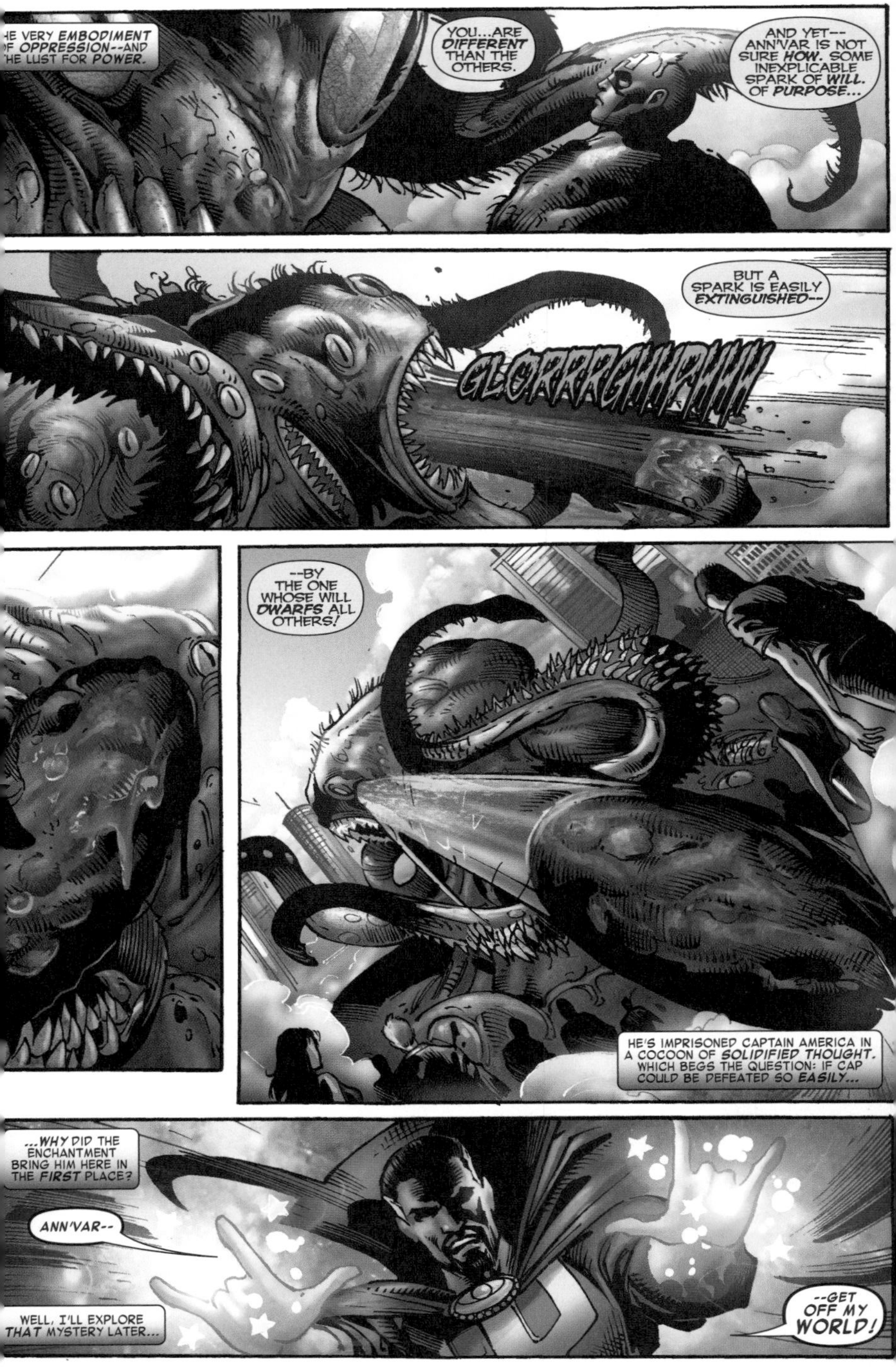

THE VERY EMBODIMENT OF OPPRESSION--AND THE LUST FOR POWER.
YOU...ARE DIFFERENT THAN THE OTHERS.
AND YET--ANN'VAR IS NOT SURE HOW. SOME INEXPLICABLE SPARK OF WILL. OF PURPOSE...
BUT A SPARK IS EASILY EXTINGUISHED--
GLORRRGHHRHHH
--BY THE ONE WHOSE WILL DWARFS ALL OTHERS!
HE'S IMPRISONED CAPTAIN AMERICA IN A COCOON OF SOLIDIFIED THOUGHT. WHICH BEGS THE QUESTION: IF CAP COULD BE DEFEATED SO EASILY...
...WHY DID THE ENCHANTMENT BRING HIM HERE IN THE FIRST PLACE?
ANN'VAR--
WELL, I'LL EXPLORE THAT MYSTERY LATER...
--GET OFF MY WORLD!

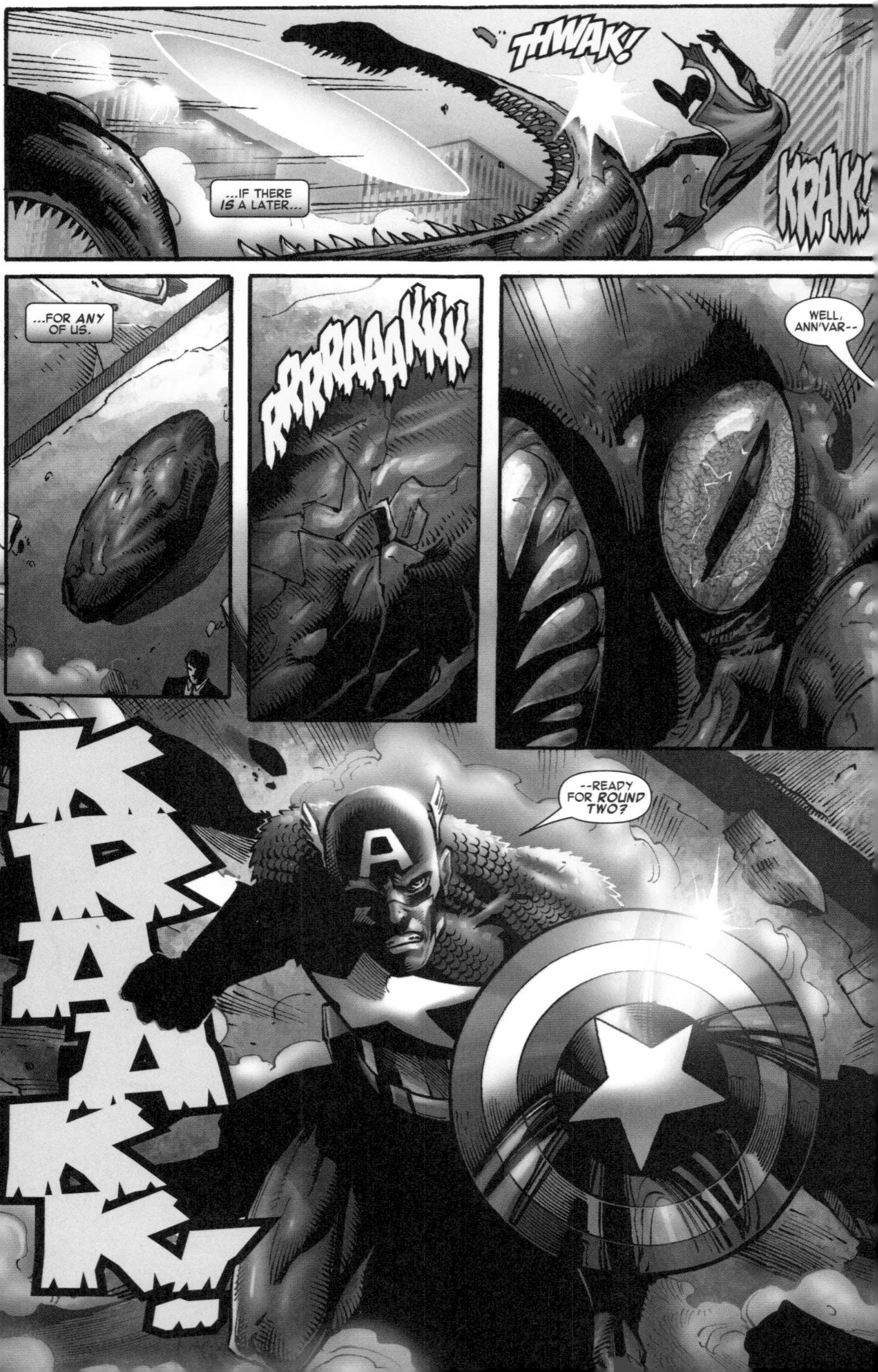
THWAK!
...IF THERE IS A LATER...
KRAK!
...FOR ANY OF US.
RRRRAAAKKK
WELL, ANN'VAR--
--READY FOR ROUND TWO?
KRAAK!

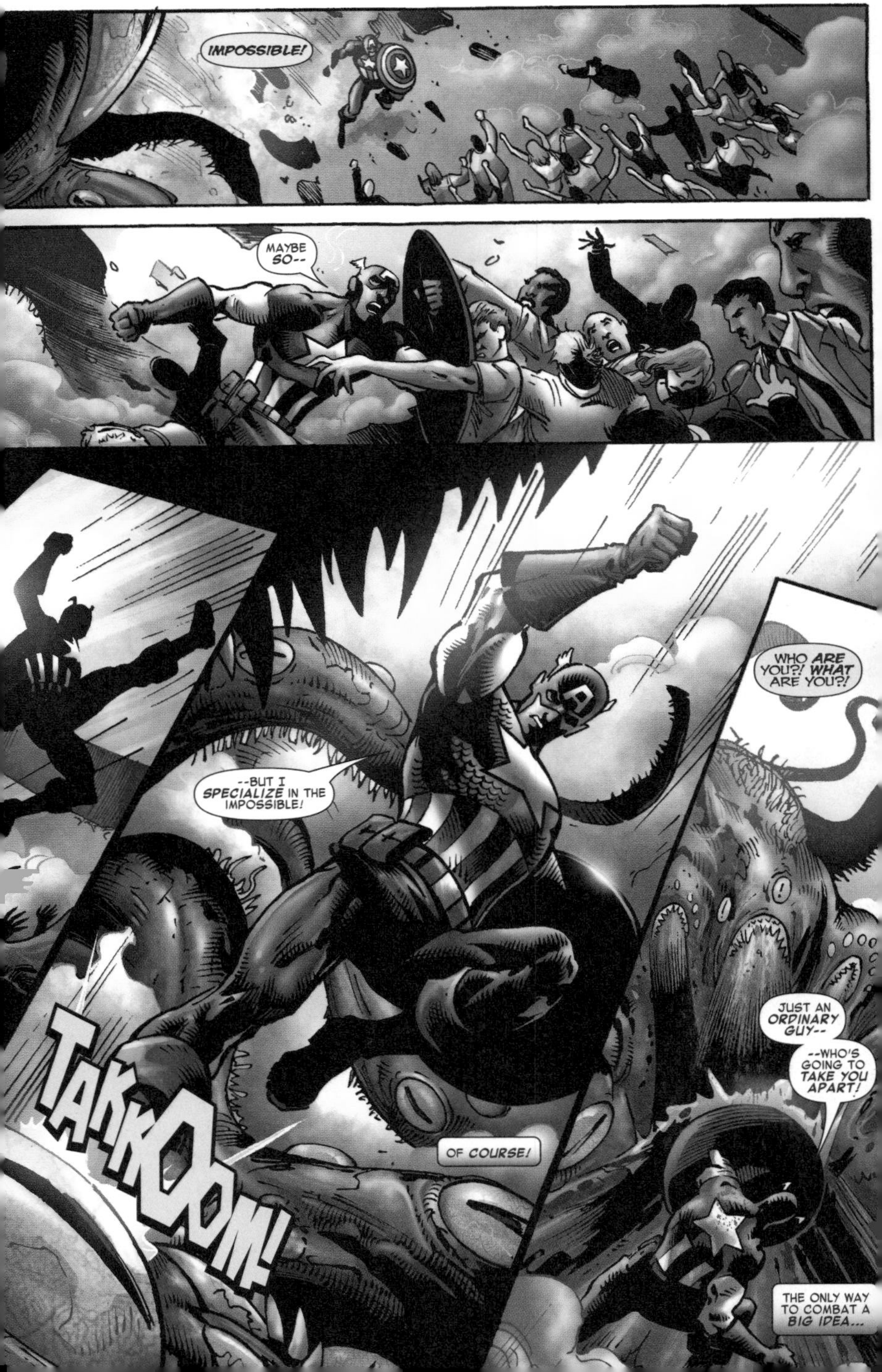
IMPOSSIBLE!
MAYBE SO--
--BUT I SPECIALIZE IN THE IMPOSSIBLE!
WHO ARE YOU?! WHAT ARE YOU?!
TAKKOOM!
OF COURSE!
JUST AN ORDINARY GUY--
--WHO'S GOING TO TAKE YOU APART!
THE ONLY WAY TO COMBAT A BIG IDEA...

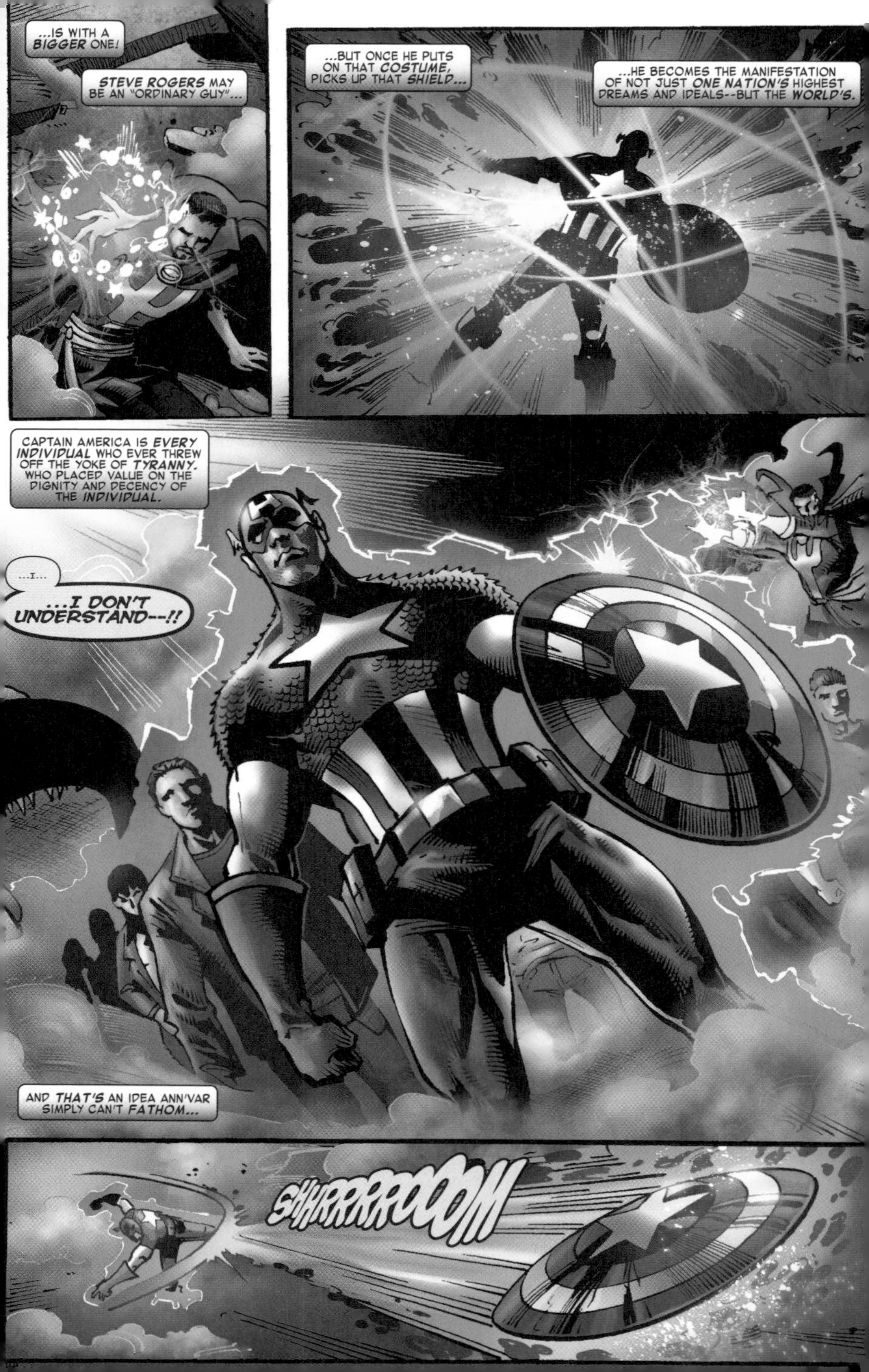
...IS WITH A BIGGER ONE!
STEVE ROGERS MAY BE AN "ORDINARY GUY"...
...BUT ONCE HE PUTS ON THAT COSTUME, PICKS UP THAT SHIELD...
...HE BECOMES THE MANIFESTATION OF NOT JUST ONE NATION'S HIGHEST DREAMS AND IDEALS--BUT THE WORLD'S.
CAPTAIN AMERICA IS EVERY INDIVIDUAL WHO EVER THREW OFF THE YOKE OF TYRANNY. WHO PLACED VALUE ON THE DIGNITY AND DECENCY OF THE INDIVIDUAL.
...I...
...I DON'T UNDERSTAND--!!
AND THAT'S AN IDEA ANN'VAR SIMPLY CAN'T FATHOM...
SHHRRRROOOM

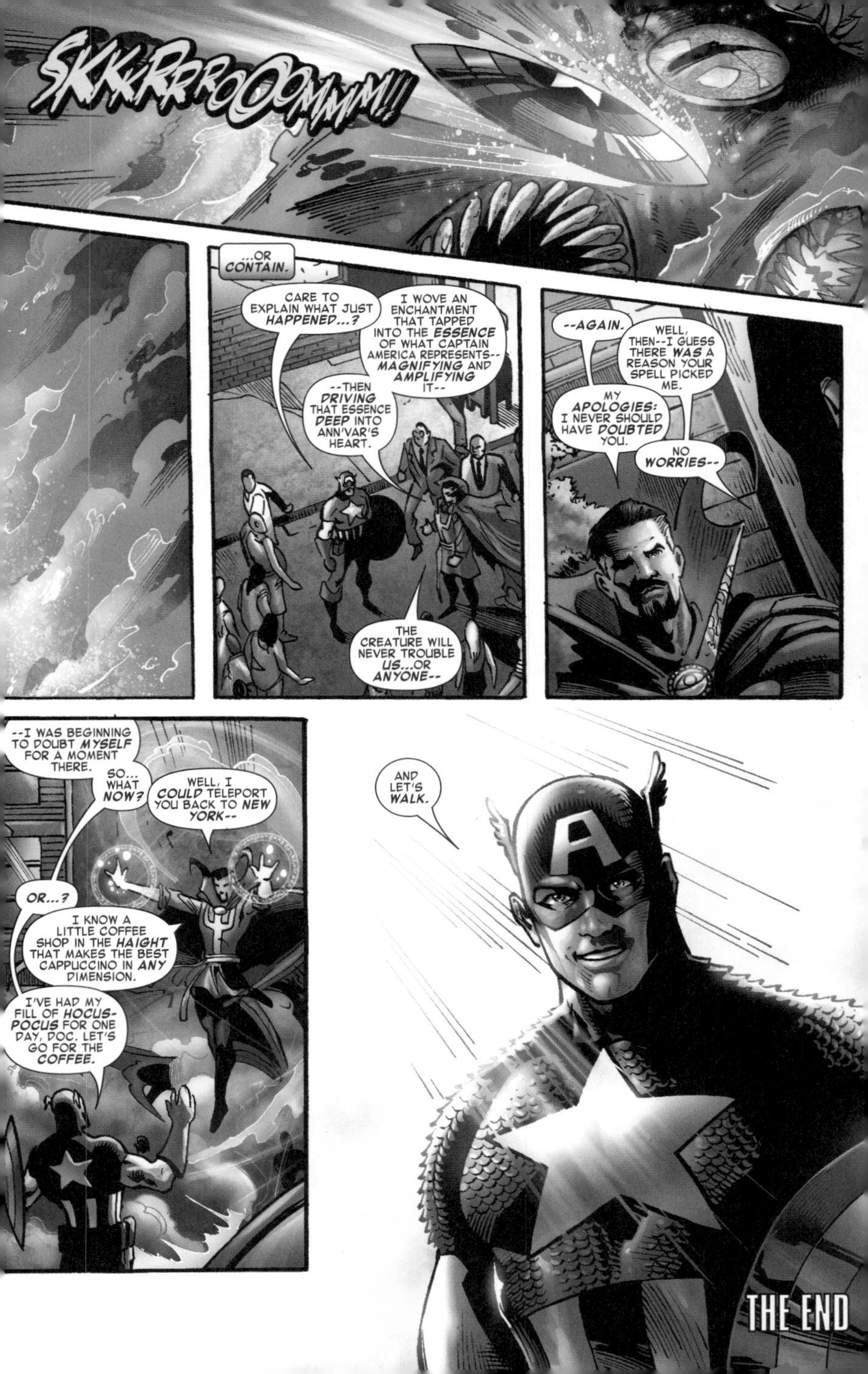
SKKRRROOOMMM!!
...OR CONTAIN.
CARE TO EXPLAIN WHAT JUST HAPPENED...?
I WOVE AN ENCHANTMENT THAT TAPPED INTO THE ESSENCE OF WHAT CAPTAIN AMERICA REPRESENTS-- MAGNIFYING AND AMPLIFYING IT--
--THEN DRIVING THAT ESSENCE DEEP INTO ANN'VAR'S HEART.
THE CREATURE WILL NEVER TROUBLE US...OR ANYONE--
--AGAIN.
WELL, THEN--I GUESS THERE WAS A REASON YOUR SPELL PICKED ME.
MY APOLOGIES: I NEVER SHOULD HAVE DOUBTED YOU.
NO WORRIES--
--I WAS BEGINNING TO DOUBT MYSELF FOR A MOMENT THERE.
SO... WHAT NOW?
WELL, I COULD TELEPORT YOU BACK TO NEW YORK--
OR...?
I KNOW A LITTLE COFFEE SHOP IN THE HAIGHT THAT MAKES THE BEST CAPPUCCINO IN ANY DIMENSION.
I'VE HAD MY FILL OF HOCUS-POCUS FOR ONE DAY, DOC. LET'S GO FOR THE COFFEE.
AND LET'S WALK.
THE END

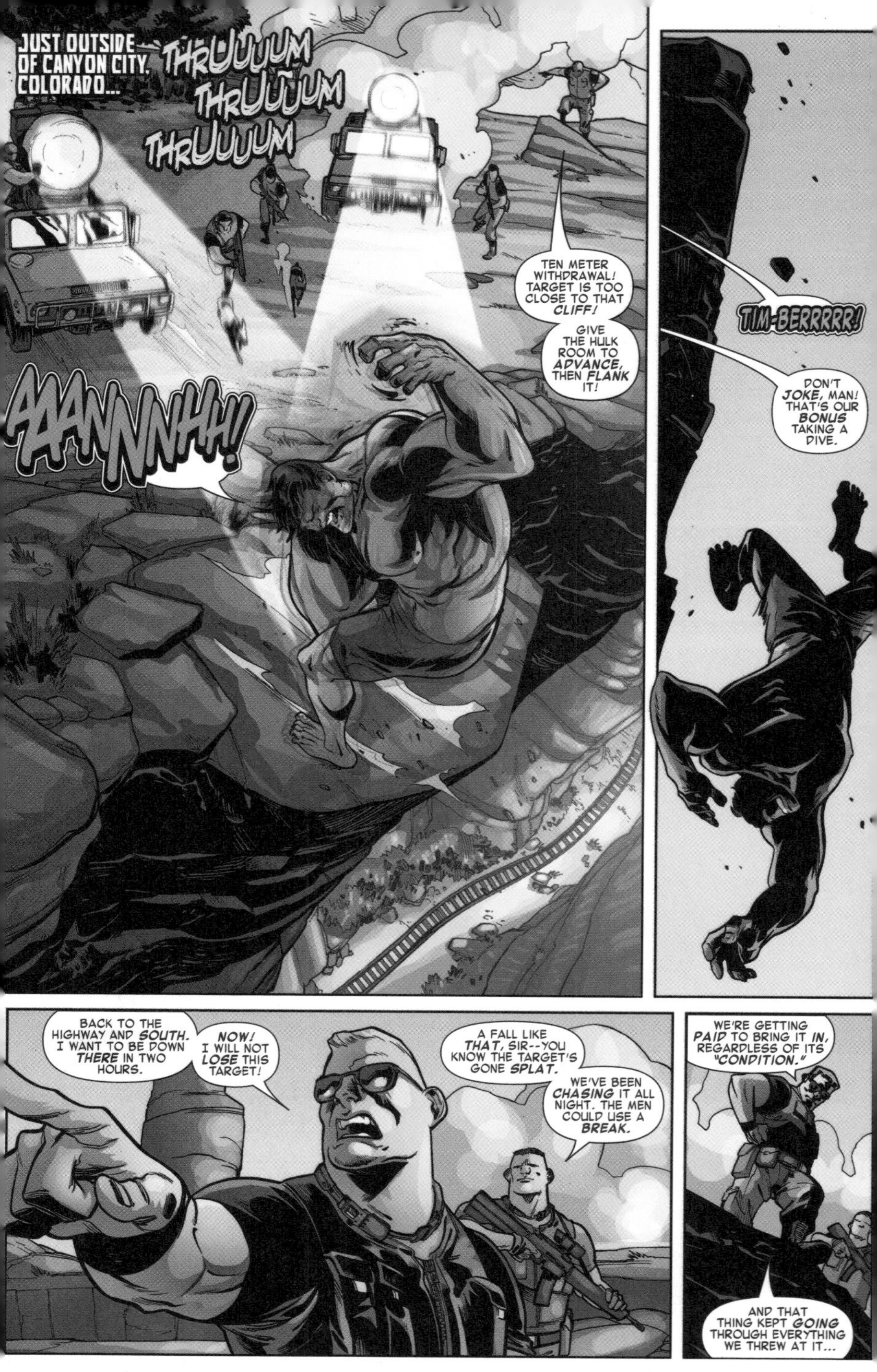
JUST OUTSIDE OF CANYON CITY, COLORADO...
THRUUUUM THRUUUUM THRUUUUM
TEN METER WITHDRAWAL! TARGET IS TOO CLOSE TO THAT CLIFF!
GIVE THE HULK ROOM TO ADVANCE, THEN FLANK IT!
AAANNNHH!
TIM-BERRRRR!
DON'T JOKE, MAN! THAT'S OUR BONUS TAKING A DIVE.
BACK TO THE HIGHWAY AND SOUTH. I WANT TO BE DOWN THERE IN TWO HOURS.
NOW! I WILL NOT LOSE THIS TARGET!
A FALL LIKE THAT, SIR--YOU KNOW THE TARGET'S GONE SPLAT.
WE'VE BEEN CHASING IT ALL NIGHT. THE MEN COULD USE A BREAK.
WE'RE GETTING PAID TO BRING IT IN, REGARDLESS OF ITS "CONDITION."
AND THAT THING KEPT GOING THROUGH EVERYTHING WE THREW AT IT...

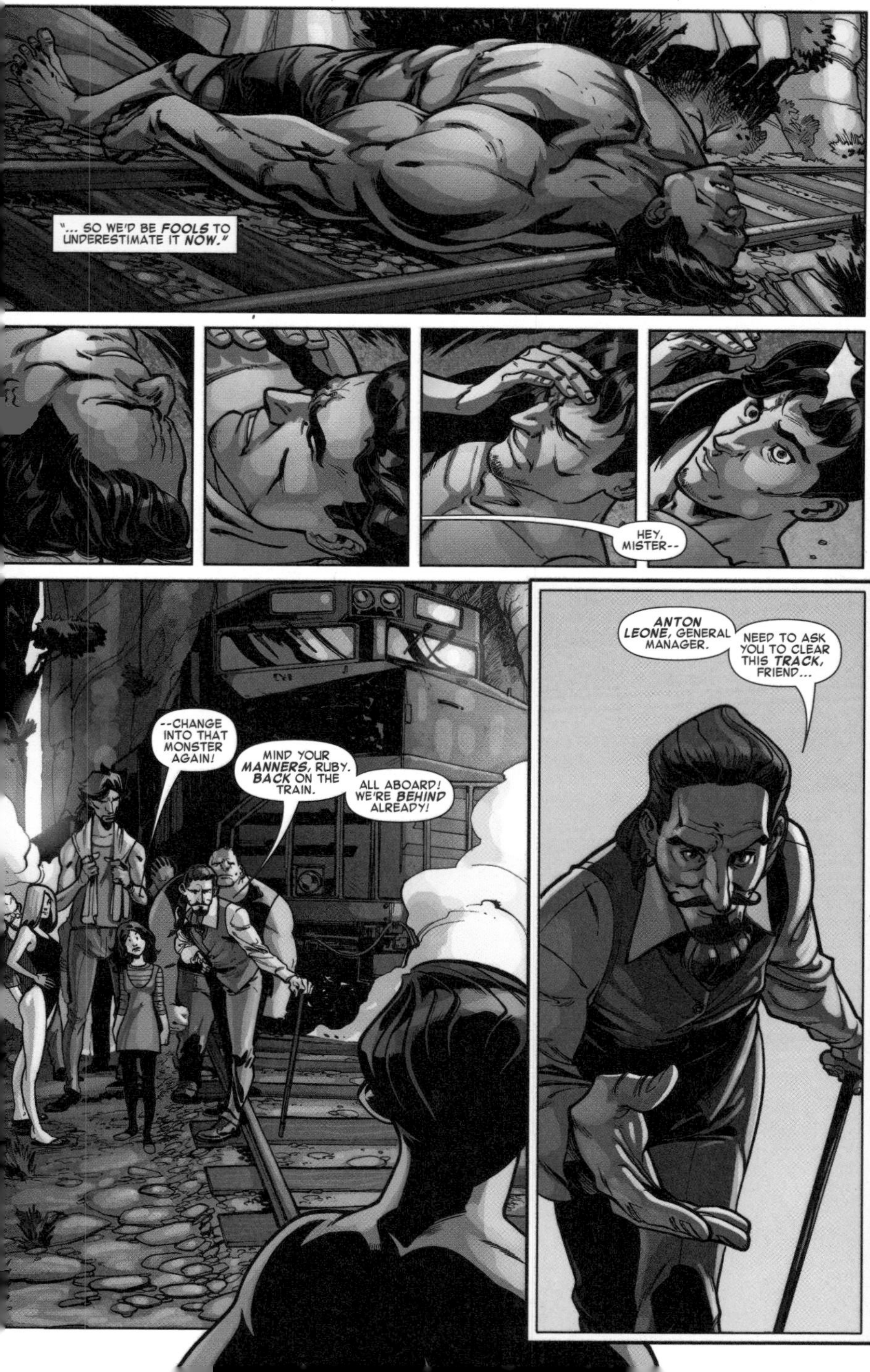
"... SO WE'D BE FOOLS TO UNDERESTIMATE IT NOW."
HEY, MISTER--
--CHANGE INTO THAT MONSTER AGAIN!
MIND YOUR MANNERS, RUBY. BACK ON THE TRAIN.
ALL ABOARD! WE'RE BEHIND ALREADY!
ANTON LEONE, GENERAL MANAGER.
NEED TO ASK YOU TO CLEAR THIS TRACK, FRIEND...

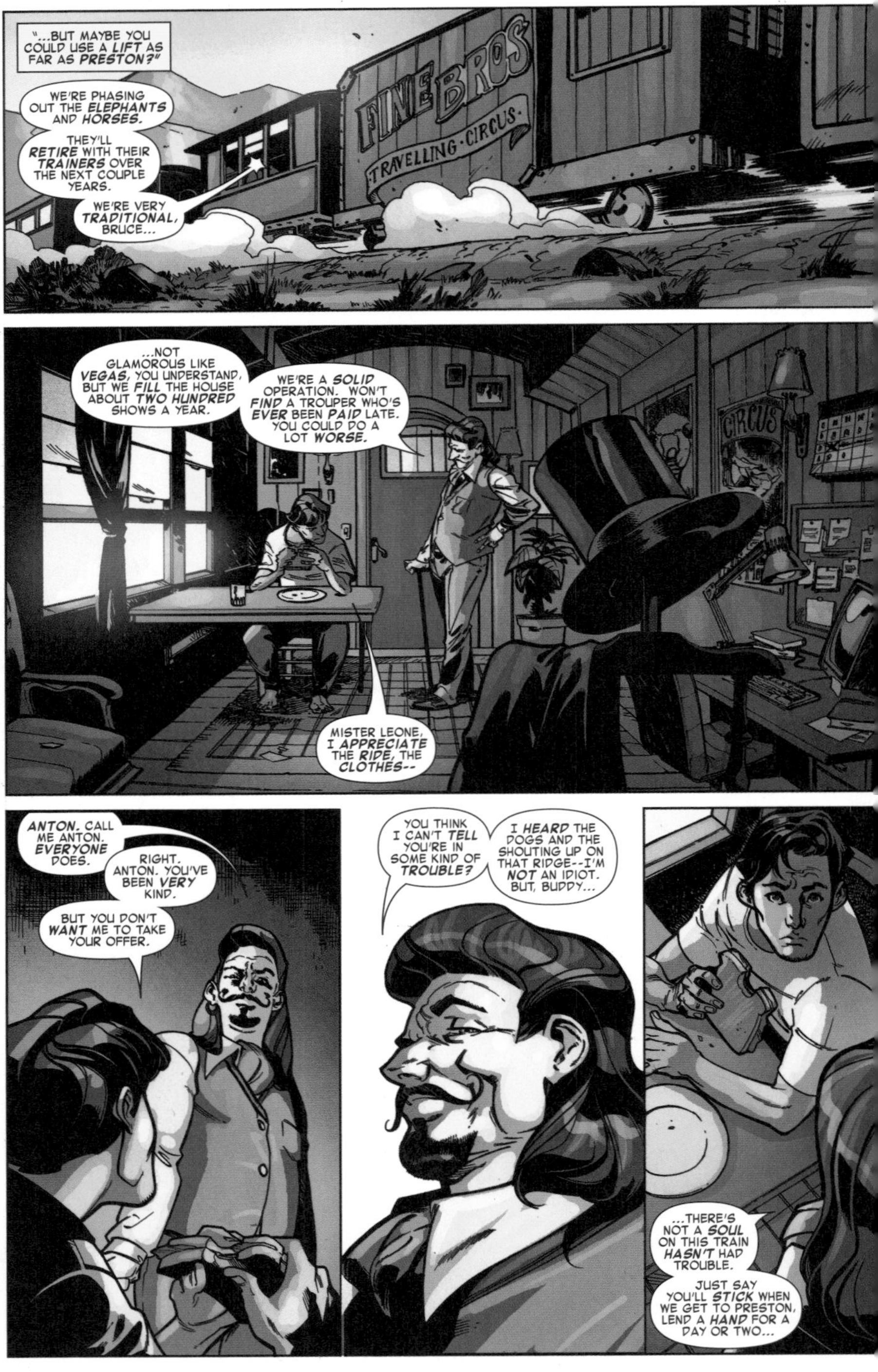

"...BUT MAYBE YOU COULD USE A LIFT AS FAR AS PRESTON?"
FINE BROS TRAVELLING CIRCUS
WE'RE PHASING OUT THE ELEPHANTS AND HORSES.
THEY'LL RETIRE WITH THEIR TRAINERS OVER THE NEXT COUPLE YEARS.
WE'RE VERY TRADITIONAL, BRUCE...
...NOT GLAMOROUS LIKE VEGAS, YOU UNDERSTAND, BUT WE FILL THE HOUSE ABOUT TWO HUNDRED SHOWS A YEAR.
WE'RE A SOLID OPERATION. WON'T FIND A TROUPER WHO'S EVER BEEN PAID LATE. YOU COULD DO A LOT WORSE.
CIRCUS
MISTER LEONE, I APPRECIATE THE RIDE, THE CLOTHES--
ANTON. CALL ME ANTON. EVERYONE DOES.
RIGHT. ANTON. YOU'VE BEEN VERY KIND.
BUT YOU DON'T WANT ME TO TAKE YOUR OFFER.
YOU THINK I CAN'T TELL YOU'RE IN SOME KIND OF TROUBLE?
I HEARD THE DOGS AND THE SHOUTING UP ON THAT RIDGE--I'M NOT AN IDIOT. BUT, BUDDY...
...THERE'S NOT A SOUL ON THIS TRAIN HASN'T HAD TROUBLE.
JUST SAY YOU'LL STICK WHEN WE GET TO PRESTON, LEND A HAND FOR A DAY OR TWO...

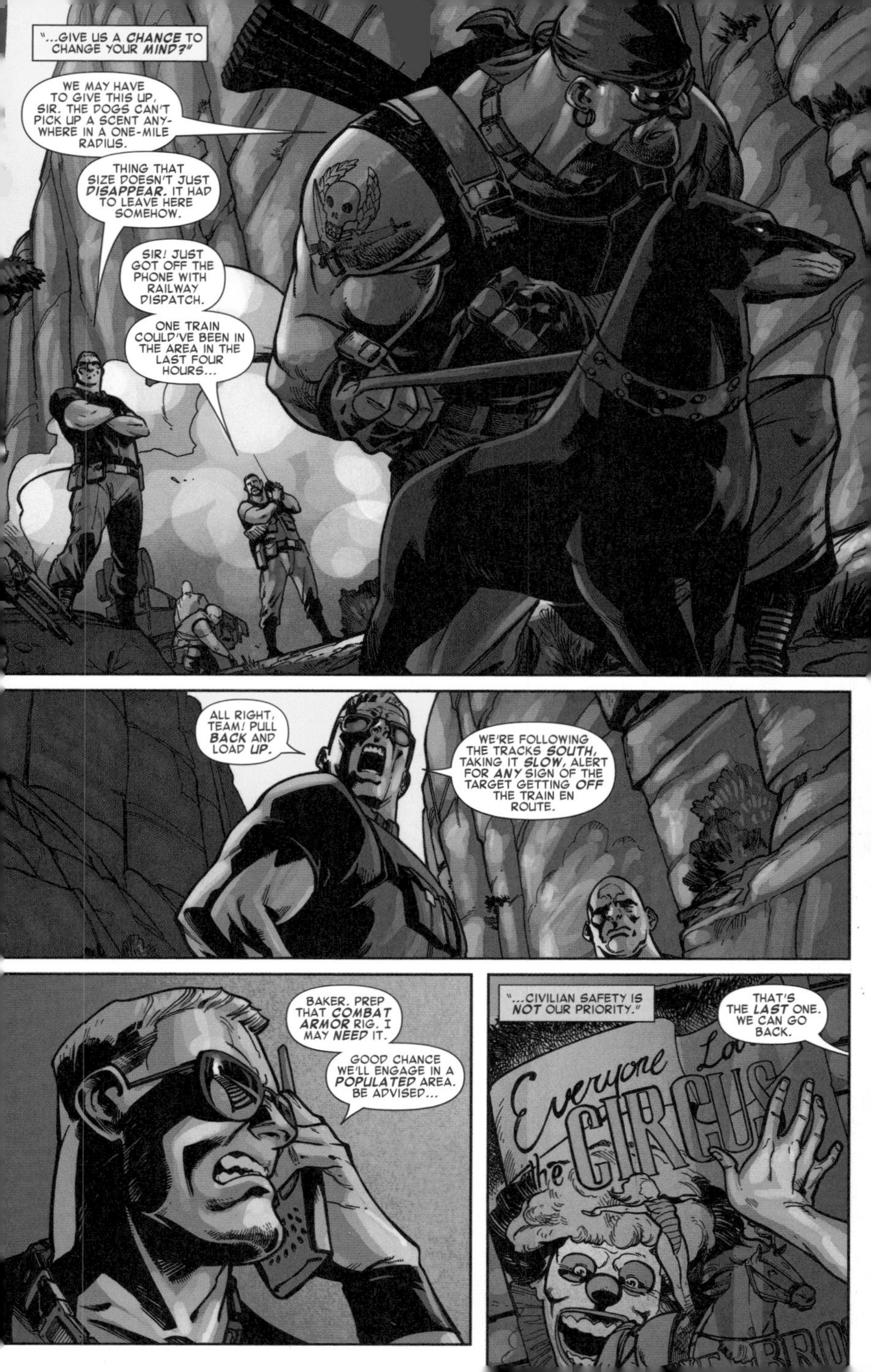

"...GIVE US A CHANCE TO CHANGE YOUR MIND?"
WE MAY HAVE TO GIVE THIS UP, SIR. THE DOGS CAN'T PICK UP A SCENT ANYWHERE IN A ONE-MILE RADIUS.
THING THAT SIZE DOESN'T JUST DISAPPEAR. IT HAD TO LEAVE HERE SOMEHOW.
SIR! JUST GOT OFF THE PHONE WITH RAILWAY DISPATCH.
ONE TRAIN COULD'VE BEEN IN THE AREA IN THE LAST FOUR HOURS...
ALL RIGHT, TEAM! PULL BACK AND LOAD UP.
WE'RE FOLLOWING THE TRACKS SOUTH, TAKING IT SLOW, ALERT FOR ANY SIGN OF THE TARGET GETTING OFF THE TRAIN EN ROUTE.
BAKER. PREP THAT COMBAT ARMOR RIG. I MAY NEED IT.
GOOD CHANCE WE'LL ENGAGE IN A POPULATED AREA. BE ADVISED...
"...CIVILIAN SAFETY IS NOT OUR PRIORITY."
THAT'S THE LAST ONE. WE CAN GO BACK.
Everyone
the CIRCUS

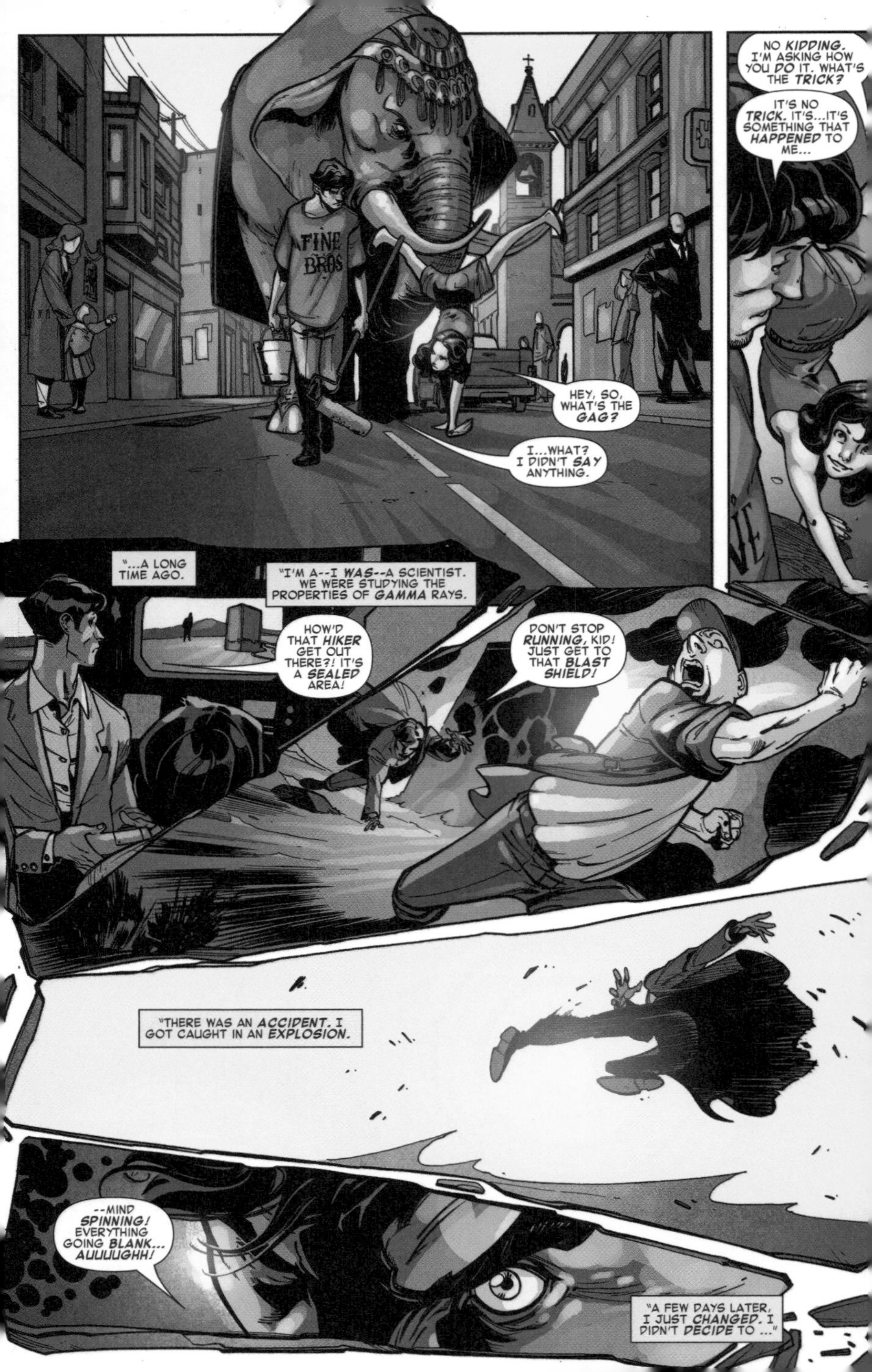
FINE BROS
HEY, SO, WHAT'S THE GAG?
I...WHAT? I DIDN'T SAY ANYTHING.
NO KIDDING. I'M ASKING HOW YOU DO IT. WHAT'S THE TRICK?
IT'S NO TRICK. IT'S...IT'S SOMETHING THAT HAPPENED TO ME...
"...A LONG TIME AGO.
"I'M A--I WAS--A SCIENTIST. WE WERE STUDYING THE PROPERTIES OF GAMMA RAYS.
HOW'D THAT HIKER GET OUT THERE?! IT'S A SEALED AREA!
DON'T STOP RUNNING, KID! JUST GET TO THAT BLAST SHIELD!
"THERE WAS AN ACCIDENT. I GOT CAUGHT IN AN EXPLOSION.
--MIND SPINNING! EVERYTHING GOING BLANK... AUUUUGHH!
"A FEW DAYS LATER, I JUST CHANGED. I DIDN'T DECIDE TO ..."

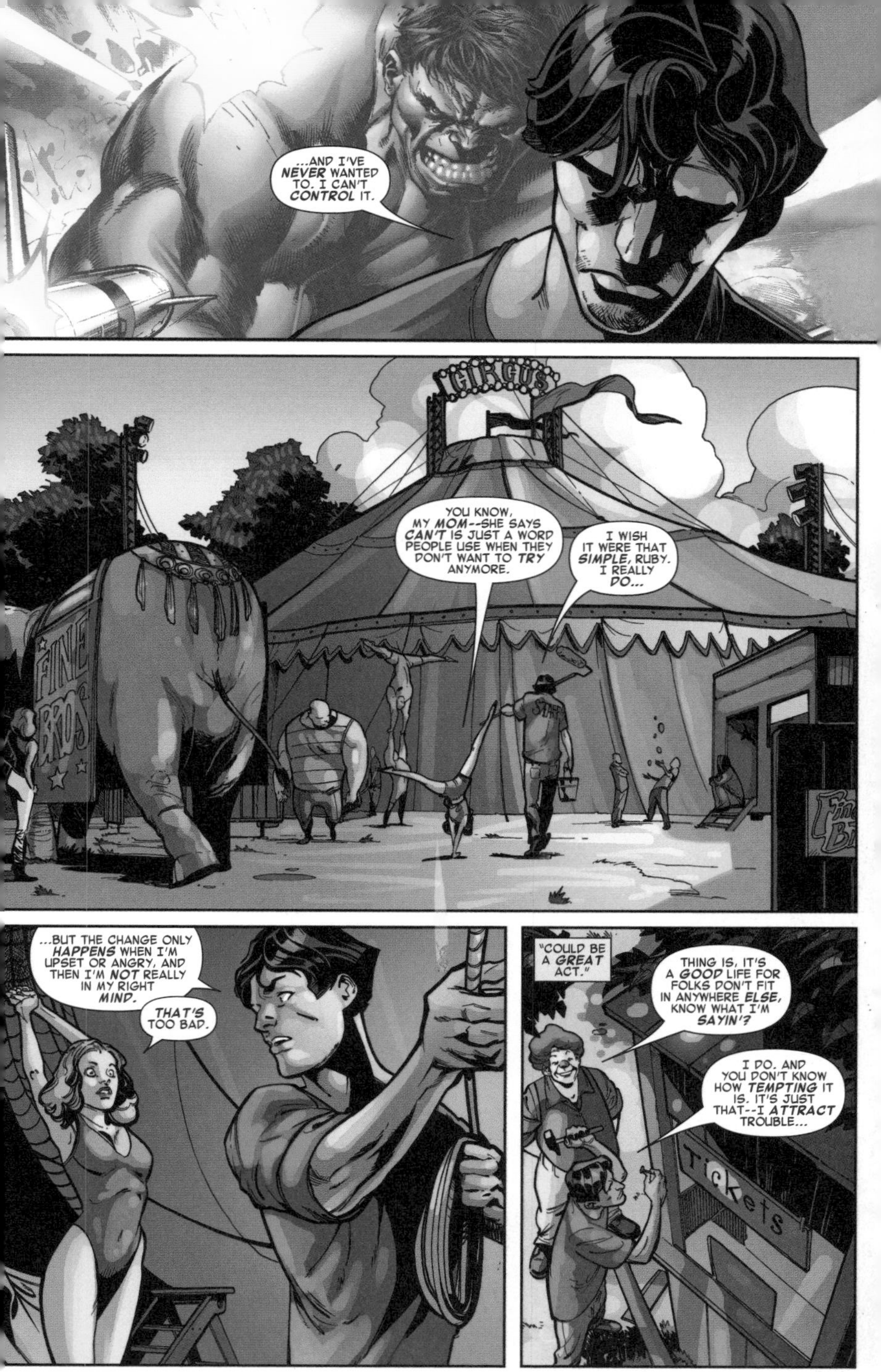
...AND I'VE NEVER WANTED TO. I CAN'T CONTROL IT.
CIRCUS
YOU KNOW, MY MOM--SHE SAYS CAN'T IS JUST A WORD PEOPLE USE WHEN THEY DON'T WANT TO TRY ANYMORE.
I WISH IT WERE THAT SIMPLE, RUBY. I REALLY DO...
FINE BROS
...BUT THE CHANGE ONLY HAPPENS WHEN I'M UPSET OR ANGRY, AND THEN I'M NOT REALLY IN MY RIGHT MIND.
THAT'S TOO BAD.
"COULD BE A GREAT ACT."
THING IS, IT'S A GOOD LIFE FOR FOLKS DON'T FIT IN ANYWHERE ELSE, KNOW WHAT I'M SAYIN'?
I DO. AND YOU DON'T KNOW HOW TEMPTING IT IS. IT'S JUST THAT--I ATTRACT TROUBLE...
Tickets

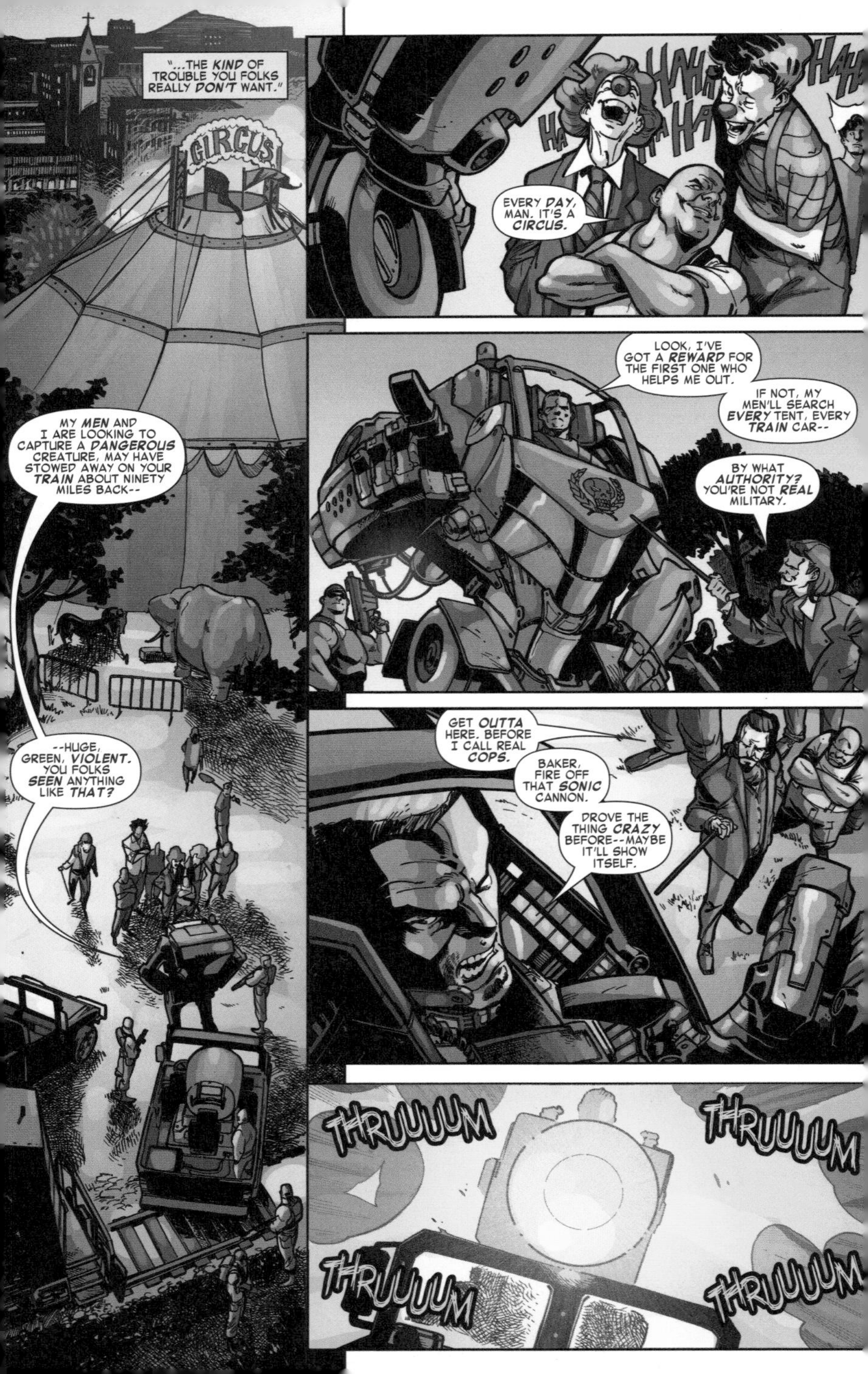
"...THE KIND OF TROUBLE YOU FOLKS REALLY DON'T WANT."
CIRCUS
HAHAHA
EVERY DAY, MAN. IT'S A CIRCUS.
MY MEN AND I ARE LOOKING TO CAPTURE A DANGEROUS CREATURE, MAY HAVE STOWED AWAY ON YOUR TRAIN ABOUT NINETY MILES BACK--
--HUGE, GREEN, VIOLENT. YOU FOLKS SEEN ANYTHING LIKE THAT?
LOOK, I'VE GOT A REWARD FOR THE FIRST ONE WHO HELPS ME OUT.
IF NOT, MY MEN'LL SEARCH EVERY TENT, EVERY TRAIN CAR--
BY WHAT AUTHORITY? YOU'RE NOT REAL MILITARY.
GET OUTTA HERE. BEFORE I CALL REAL COPS.
BAKER, FIRE OFF THAT SONIC CANNON.
DROVE THE THING CRAZY BEFORE--MAYBE IT'LL SHOW ITSELF.
THRUUUM
THRUUUUM
THRUUUM
THRUUUUM

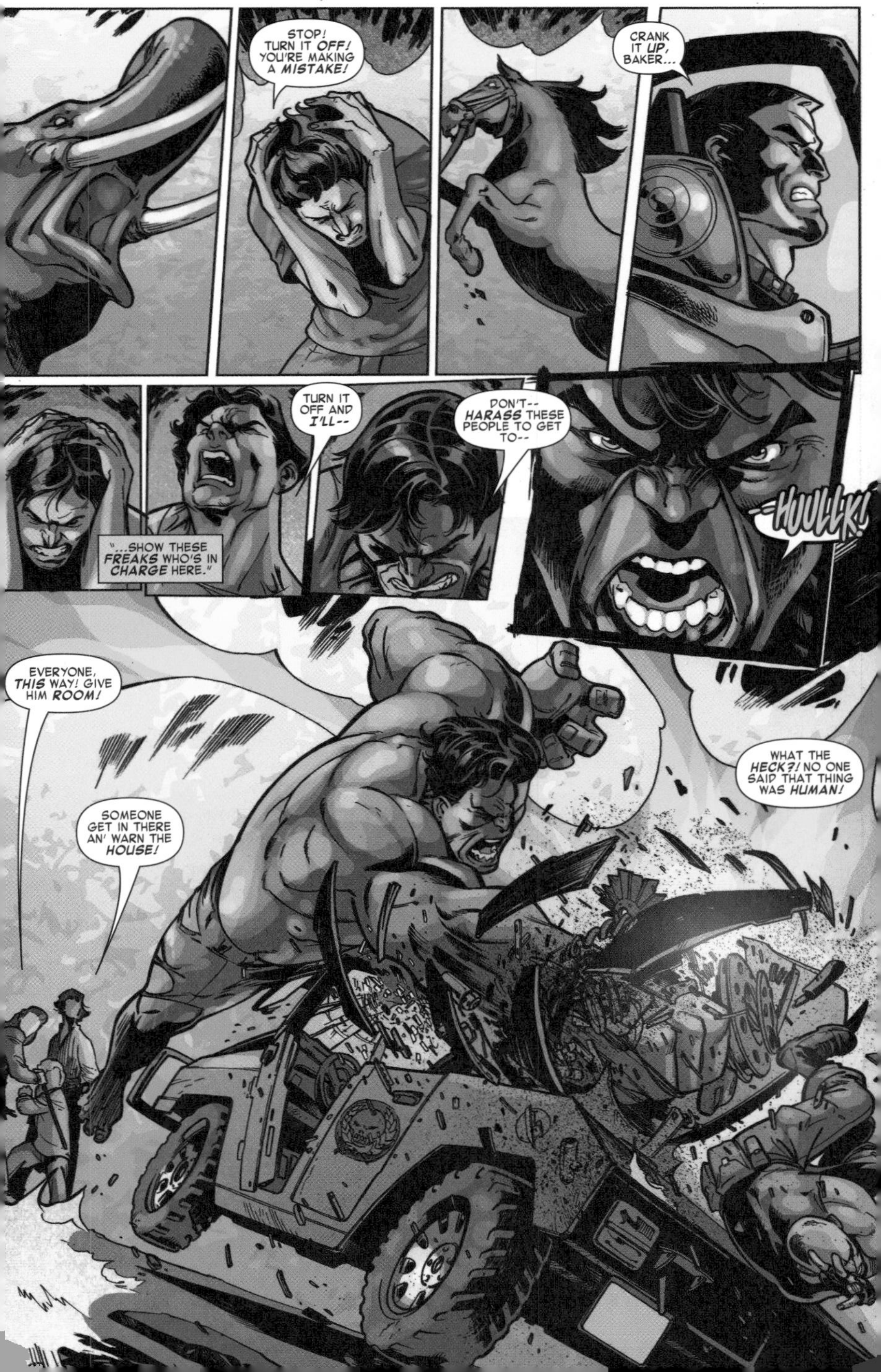

STOP! TURN IT OFF! YOU'RE MAKING A MISTAKE!
CRANK IT UP, BAKER...
"...SHOW THESE FREAKS WHO'S IN CHARGE HERE."
TURN IT OFF AND I'LL--
DON'T-- HARASS THESE PEOPLE TO GET TO--
HUULLK!
EVERYONE, THIS WAY! GIVE HIM ROOM!
SOMEONE GET IN THERE AN' WARN THE HOUSE!
WHAT THE HECK?! NO ONE SAID THAT THING WAS HUMAN!

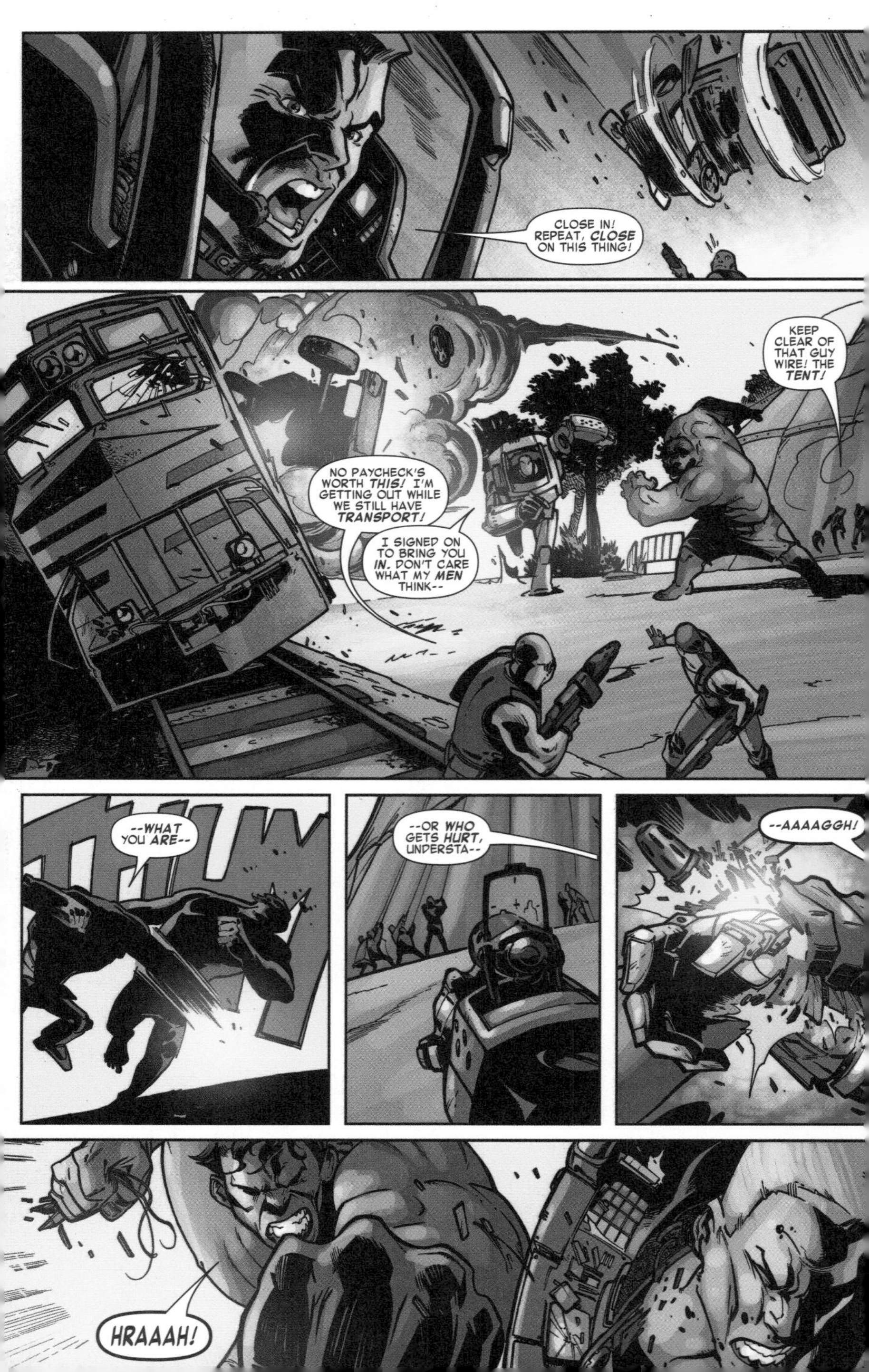
CLOSE IN! REPEAT, CLOSE ON THIS THING!
KEEP CLEAR OF THAT GUY WIRE! THE TENT!
NO PAYCHECK'S WORTH THIS! I'M GETTING OUT WHILE WE STILL HAVE TRANSPORT!
I SIGNED ON TO BRING YOU IN. DON'T CARE WHAT MY MEN THINK--
--WHAT YOU ARE--
--OR WHO GETS HURT, UNDERSTA--
--AAAAGGH!
HRAAAH!

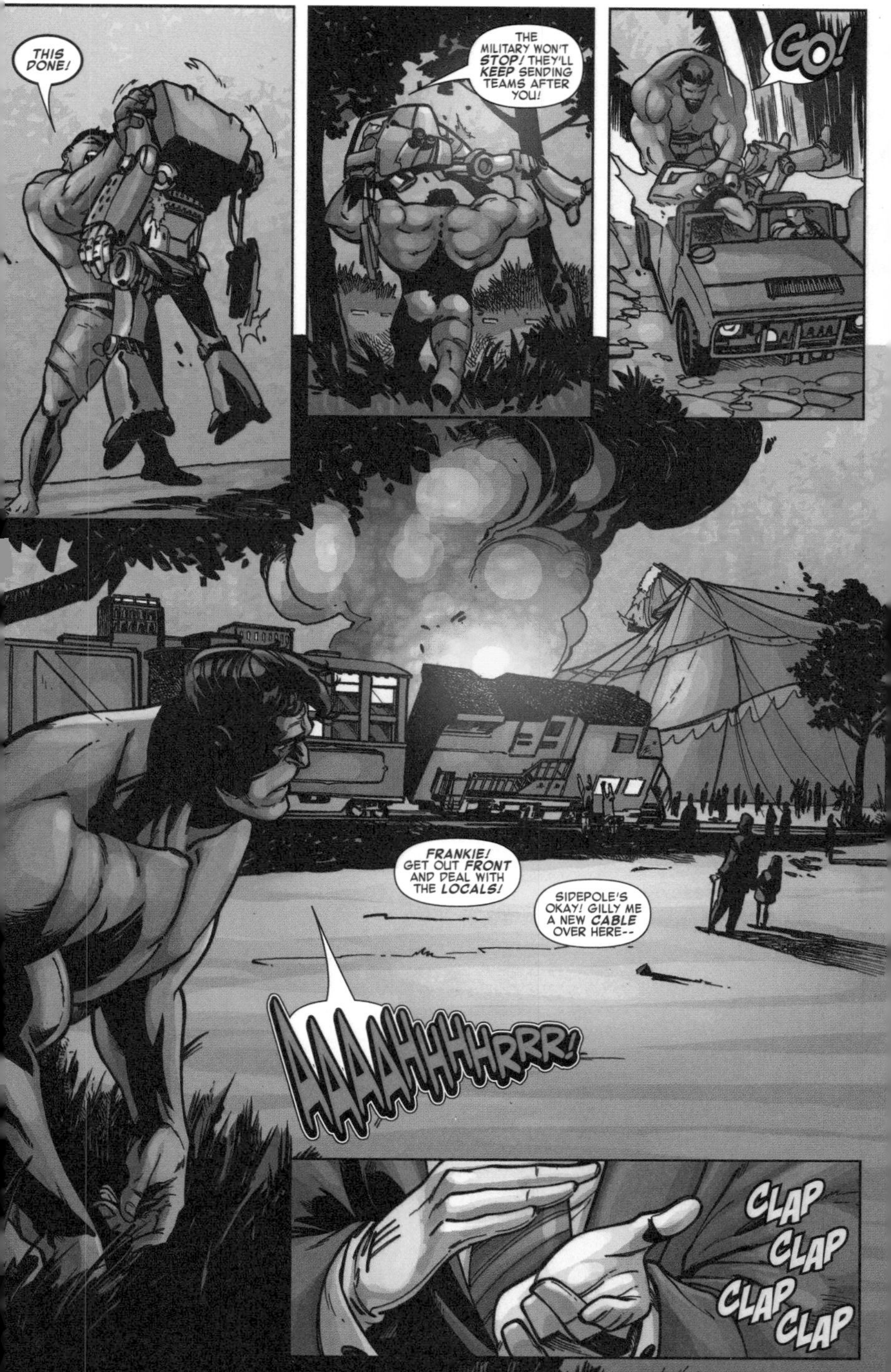
THIS DONE!
THE MILITARY WON'T STOP! THEY'LL KEEP SENDING TEAMS AFTER YOU!
GO!
FRANKIE! GET OUT FRONT AND DEAL WITH THE LOCALS!
SIDEPOLE'S OKAY! GILLY ME A NEW CABLE OVER HERE--
AAAAHHHHRRR!
CLAP
CLAP
CLAP
CLAP

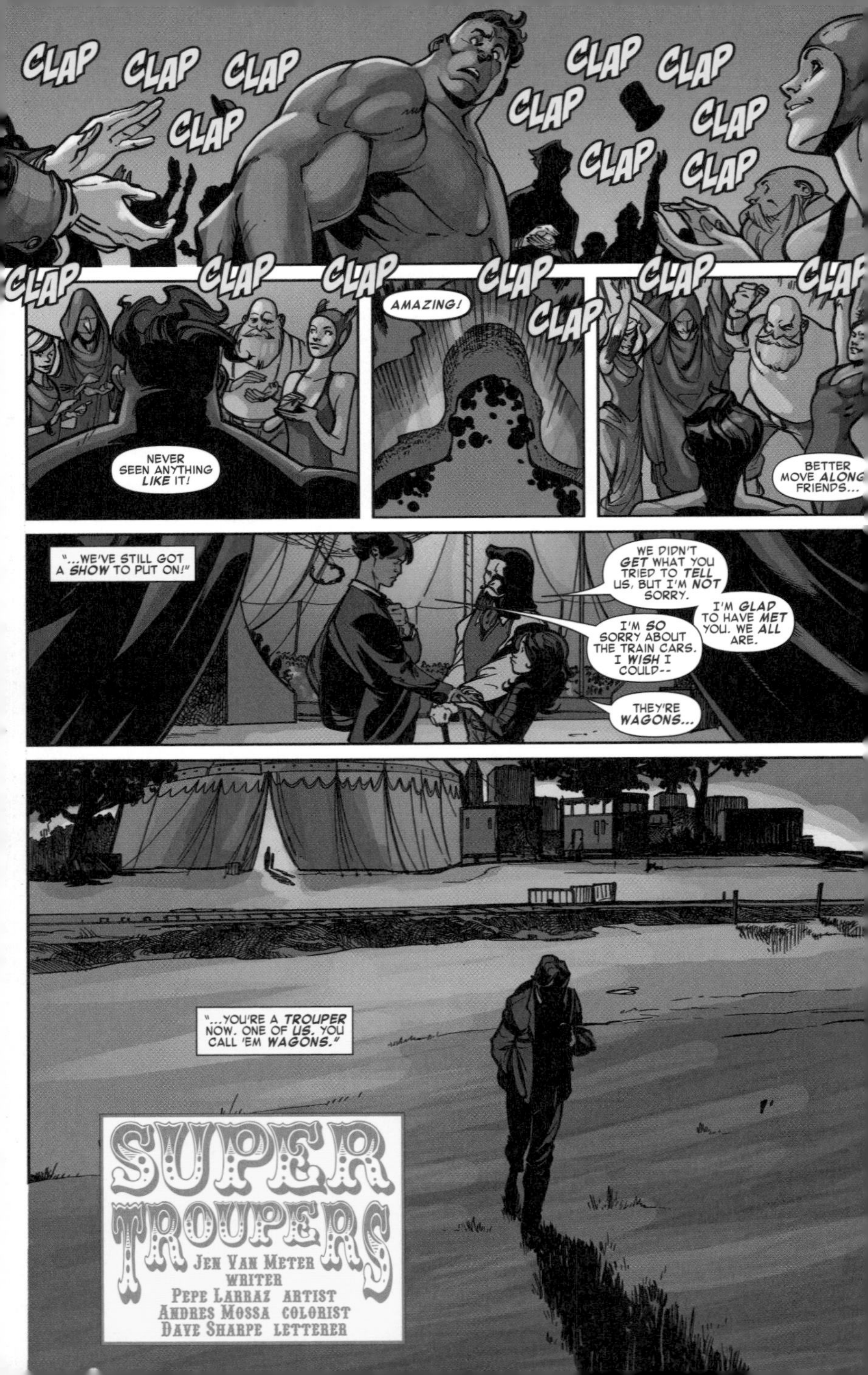
CLAP CLAP CLAP
CLAP
CLAP CLAP
CLAP CLAP
CLAP CLAP
CLAP CLAP CLAP CLAP CLAP CLAP CLAP
NEVER SEEN ANYTHING LIKE IT!
AMAZING!
BETTER MOVE ALONG FRIENDS...
"...WE'VE STILL GOT A SHOW TO PUT ON!"
WE DIDN'T GET WHAT YOU TRIED TO TELL US, BUT I'M NOT SORRY.
I'M GLAD TO HAVE MET YOU. WE ALL ARE.
I'M SO SORRY ABOUT THE TRAIN CARS. I WISH I COULD--
THEY'RE WAGONS...
"...YOU'RE A TROUPER NOW. ONE OF US. YOU CALL 'EM WAGONS."
SUPER TROUPERS
JEN VAN METER WRITER
PEPE LARRAZ ARTIST
ANDRES MOSSA COLORIST
DAVE SHARPE LETTERER

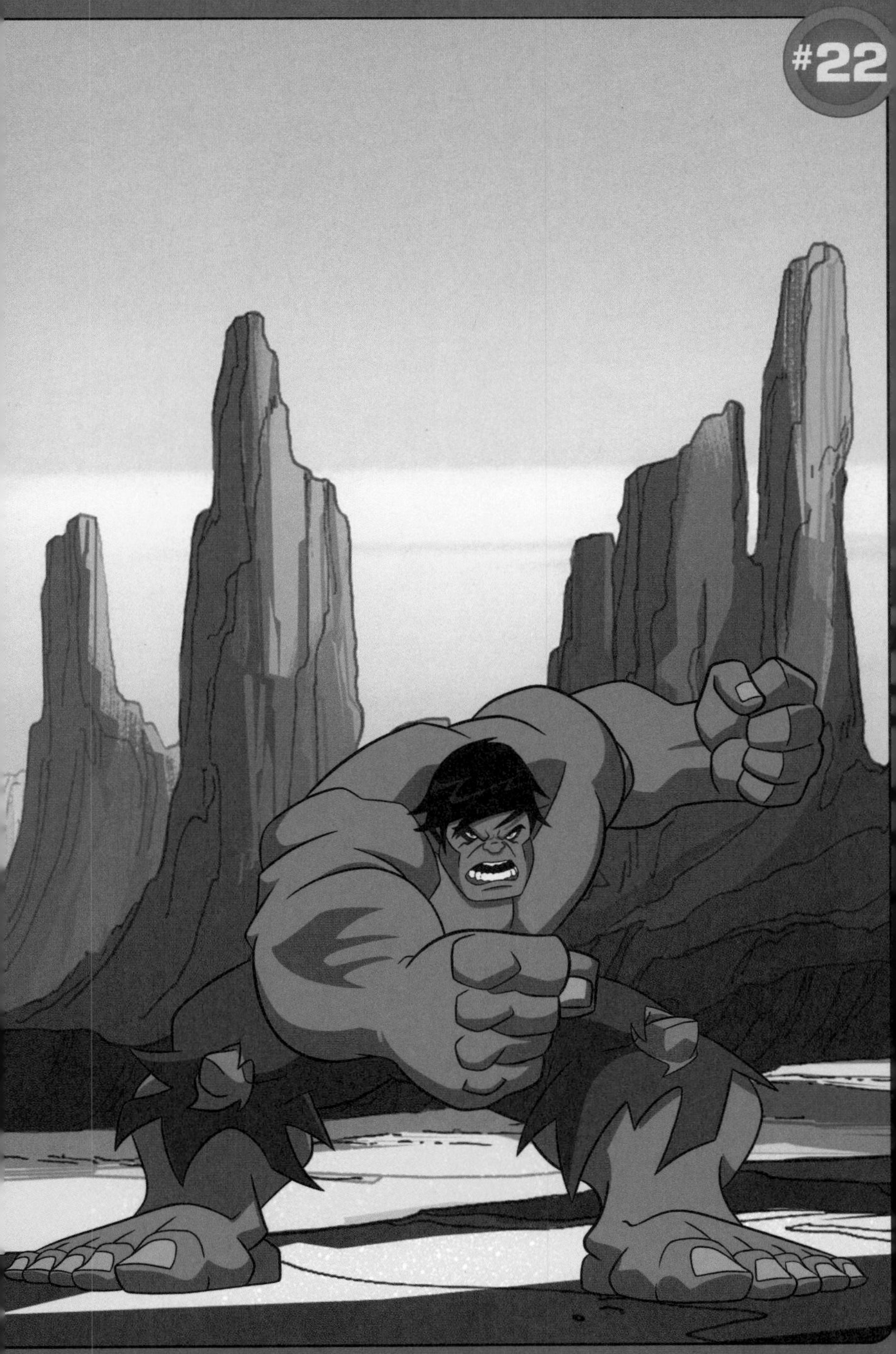
#22

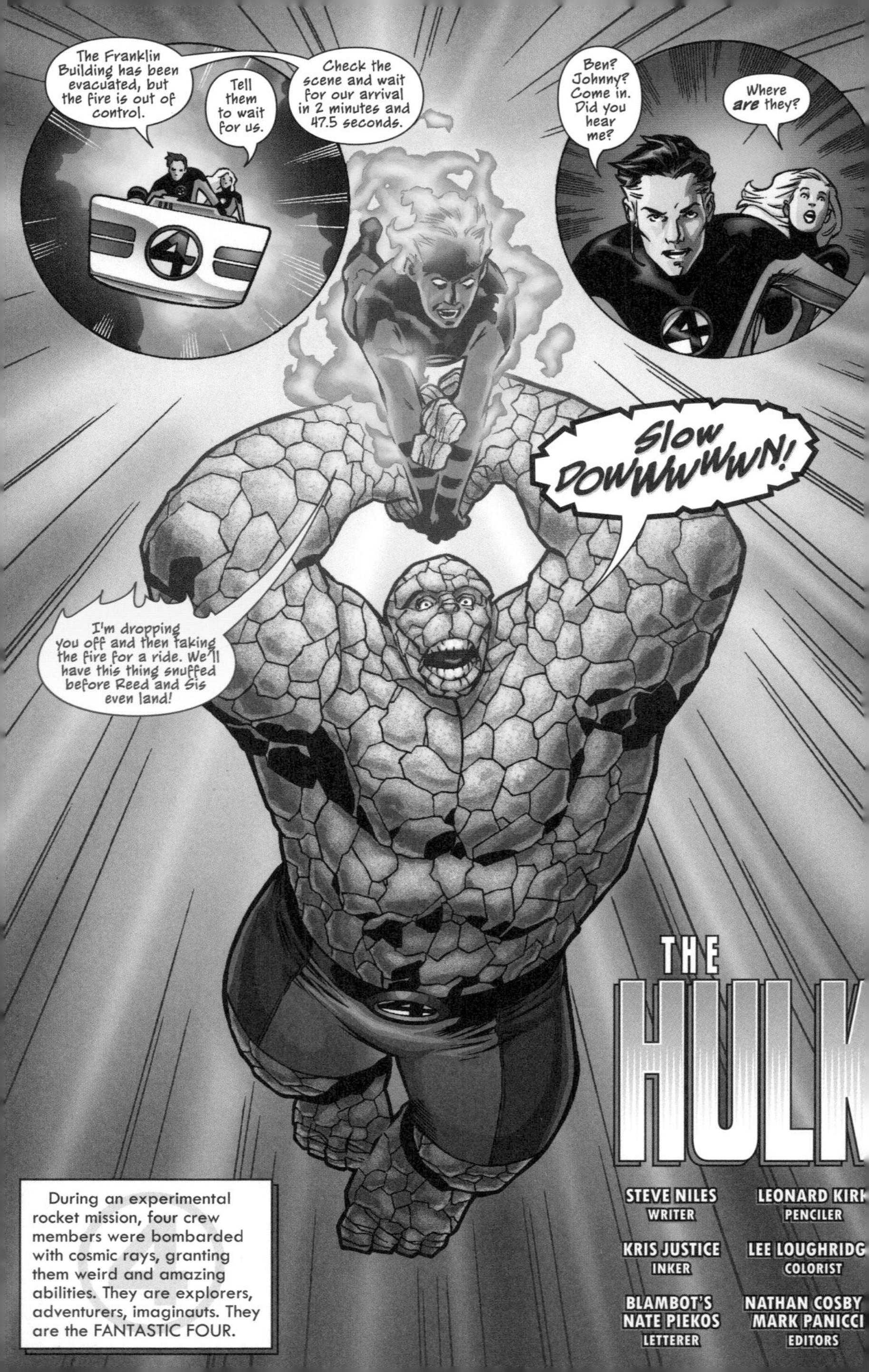

The Franklin Building has been evacuated, but the fire is out of control.
Tell them to wait for us.
Check the scene and wait for our arrival in 2 minutes and 47.5 seconds.
Ben? Johnny? Come in. Did you hear me?
Where *are* they?
I'm dropping you off and then taking the fire for a ride. We'll have this thing snuffed before Reed and Sis even land!
Slow DOWWWWWN!
THE HULK
During an experimental rocket mission, four crew members were bombarded with cosmic rays, granting them weird and amazing abilities. They are explorers, adventurers, imaginauts. They are the FANTASTIC FOUR.
STEVE NILES WRITER
LEONARD KIRI PENCILER
KRIS JUSTICE INKER
LEE LOUGHRIDG COLORIST
BLAMBOT'S NATE PIEKOS LETTERER
NATHAN COSBY MARK PANICCI EDITORS

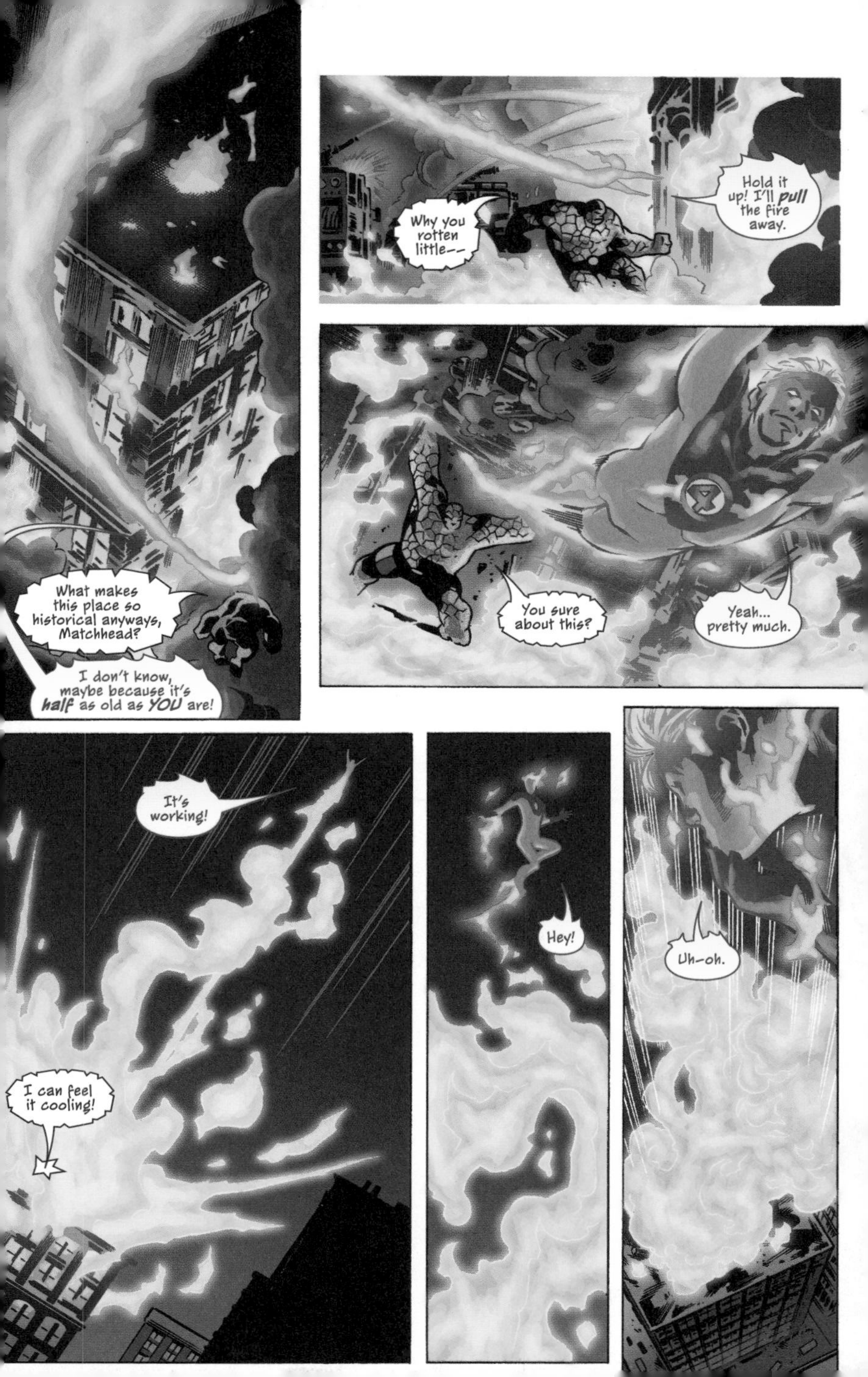
What makes this place so historical anyways, Matchhead?
I don't know, maybe because it's half as old as YOU are!
Why you rotten little--
Hold it up! I'll pull the fire away.
You sure about this?
Yeah... pretty much.
It's working!
I can feel it cooling!
Hey!
Uh-oh.

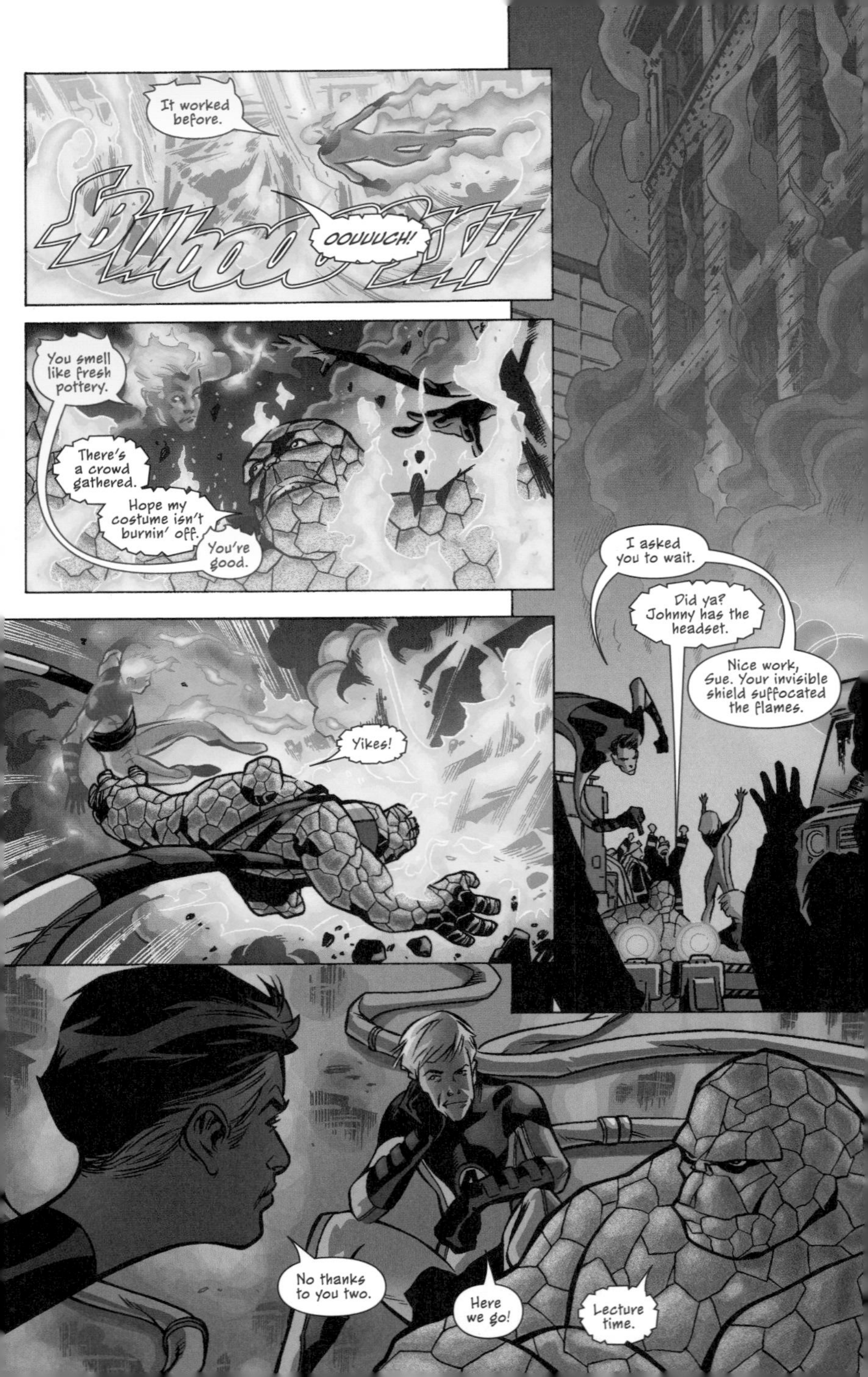
It worked before.
OOUUUCH!
You smell like fresh pottery.
There's a crowd gathered.
Hope my costume isn't burnin' off.
You're good.
Yikes!
I asked you to wait.
Did ya? Johnny has the headset.
Nice work, Sue. Your invisible shield suffocated the flames.
No thanks to you two.
Here we go!
Lecture time.

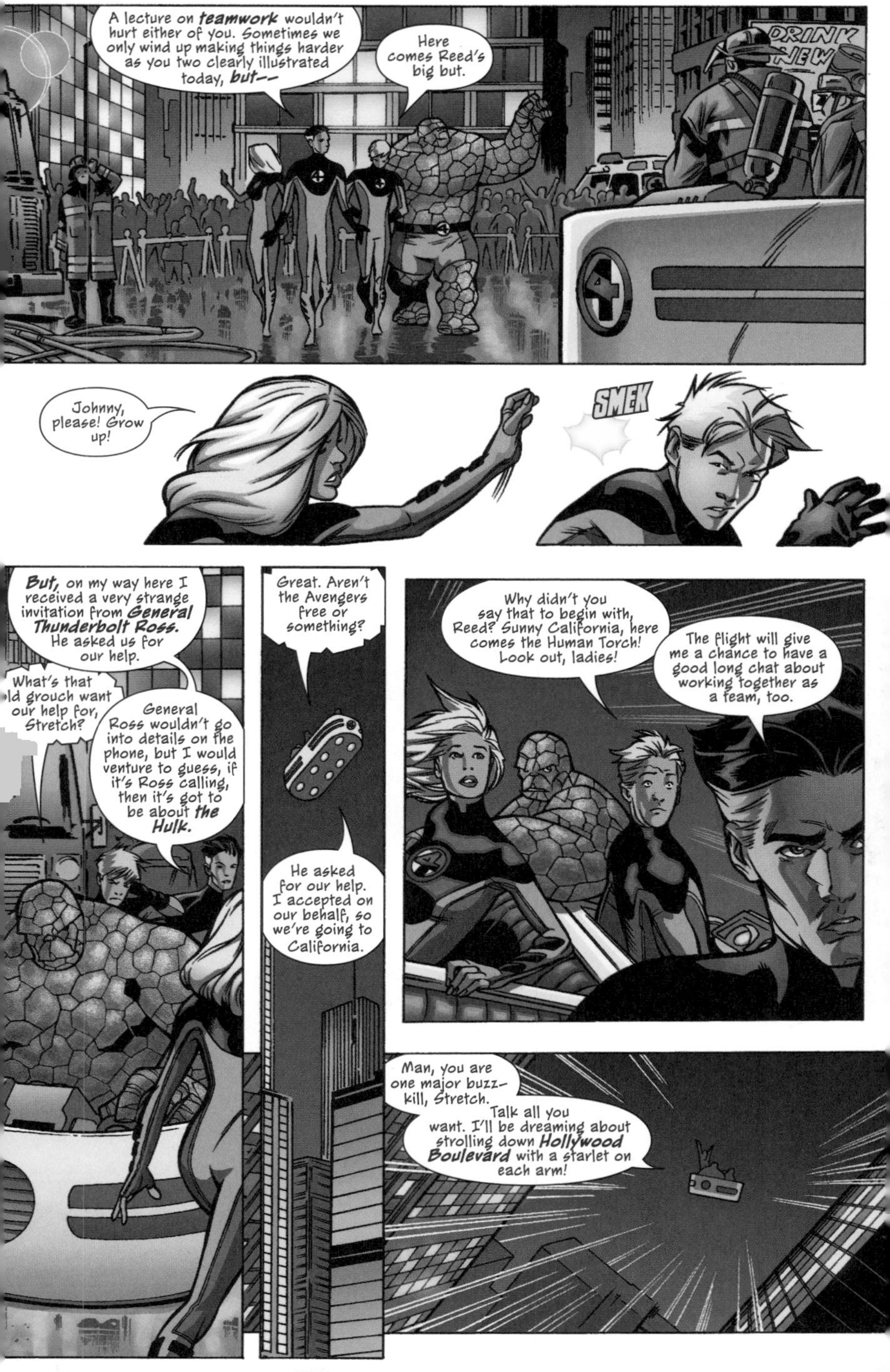
A lecture on teamwork wouldn't hurt either of you. Sometimes we only wind up making things harder as you two clearly illustrated today, but--
Here comes Reed's big but.
DRINK NEW
Johnny, please! Grow up!
SMEK
But, on my way here I received a very strange invitation from General Thunderbolt Ross. He asked us for our help.
What's that ld grouch want our help for, Stretch?
General Ross wouldn't go into details on the phone, but I would venture to guess, if it's Ross calling, then it's got to be about the Hulk.
Great. Aren't the Avengers free or something?
He asked for our help. I accepted on our behalf, so we're going to California.
Why didn't you say that to begin with, Reed? Sunny California, here comes the Human Torch! Look out, ladies!
The flight will give me a chance to have a good long chat about working together as a team, too.
Man, you are one major buzz-kill, Stretch.
Talk all you want. I'll be dreaming about strolling down Hollywood Boulevard with a starlet on each arm!

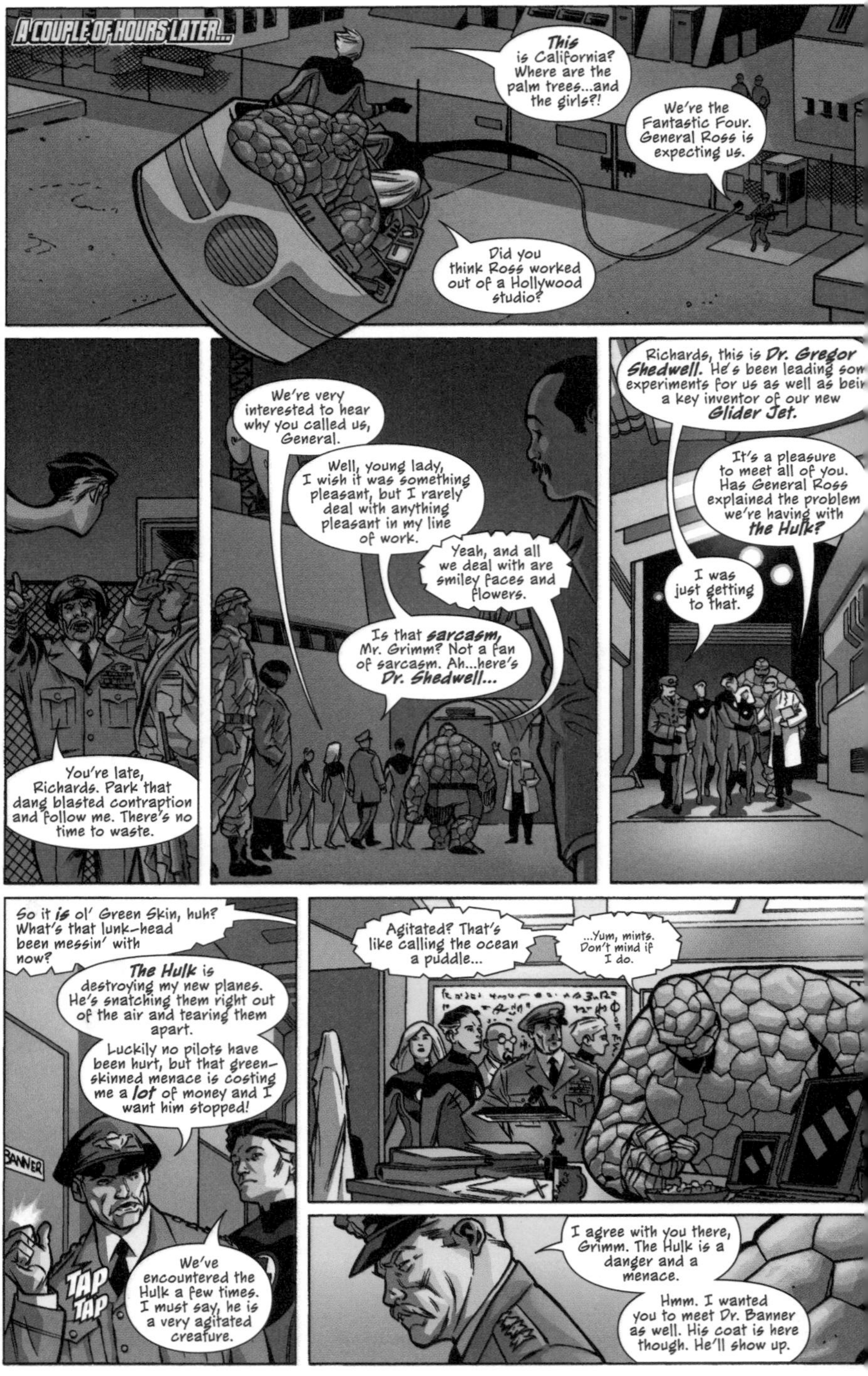
A COUPLE OF HOURS LATER...
This is California? Where are the palm trees...and the girls?!
We're the Fantastic Four. General Ross is expecting us.
Did you think Ross worked out of a Hollywood studio?
You're late, Richards. Park that dang blasted contraption and follow me. There's no time to waste.
We're very interested to hear why you called us, General.
Well, young lady, I wish it was something pleasant, but I rarely deal with anything pleasant in my line of work.
Yeah, and all we deal with are smiley faces and flowers.
Is that sarcasm, Mr. Grimm? Not a fan of sarcasm. Ah...here's Dr. Shedwell...
Richards, this is Dr. Gregor Shedwell. He's been leading som experiments for us as well as bein a key inventor of our new Glider Jet.
It's a pleasure to meet all of you. Has General Ross explained the problem we're having with the Hulk?
I was just getting to that.
So it is ol' Green Skin, huh? What's that lunk-head been messin' with now?
The Hulk is destroying my new planes. He's snatching them right out of the air and tearing them apart.
Luckily no pilots have been hurt, but that green-skinned menace is costing me a lot of money and I want him stopped!
BANNER
TAP TAP
We've encountered the Hulk a few times. I must say, he is a very agitated creature.
Agitated? That's like calling the ocean a puddle...
...Yum, mints. Don't mind if I do.
I agree with you there, Grimm. The Hulk is a danger and a menace.
Hmm. I wanted you to meet Dr. Banner as well. His coat is here though. He'll show up.

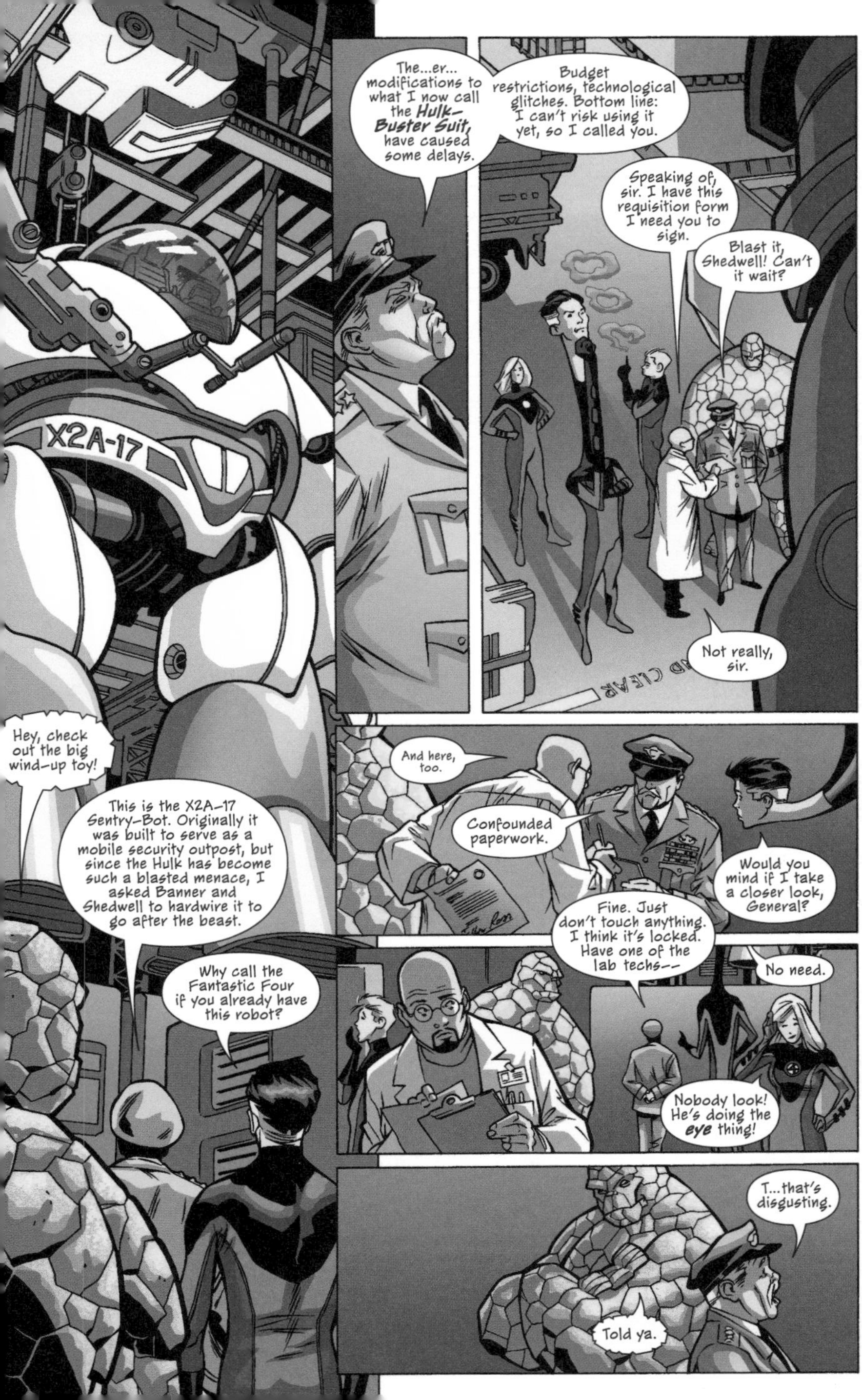
X2A-17
The...er... modifications to what I now call the Hulk-Buster Suit, have caused some delays.
Budget restrictions, technological glitches. Bottom line: I can't risk using it yet, so I called you.
Speaking of, sir. I have this requisition form I need you to sign.
Blast it, Shedwell! Can't it wait?
Not really, sir.
Hey, check out the big wind-up toy!
This is the X2A-17 Sentry-Bot. Originally it was built to serve as a mobile security outpost, but since the Hulk has become such a blasted menace, I asked Banner and Shedwell to hardwire it to go after the beast.
Why call the Fantastic Four if you already have this robot?
And here, too.
Confounded paperwork.
Would you mind if I take a closer look, General?
Fine. Just don't touch anything. I think it's locked. Have one of the lab techs--
No need.
Nobody look! He's doing the eye thing!
T...that's disgusting.
Told ya.

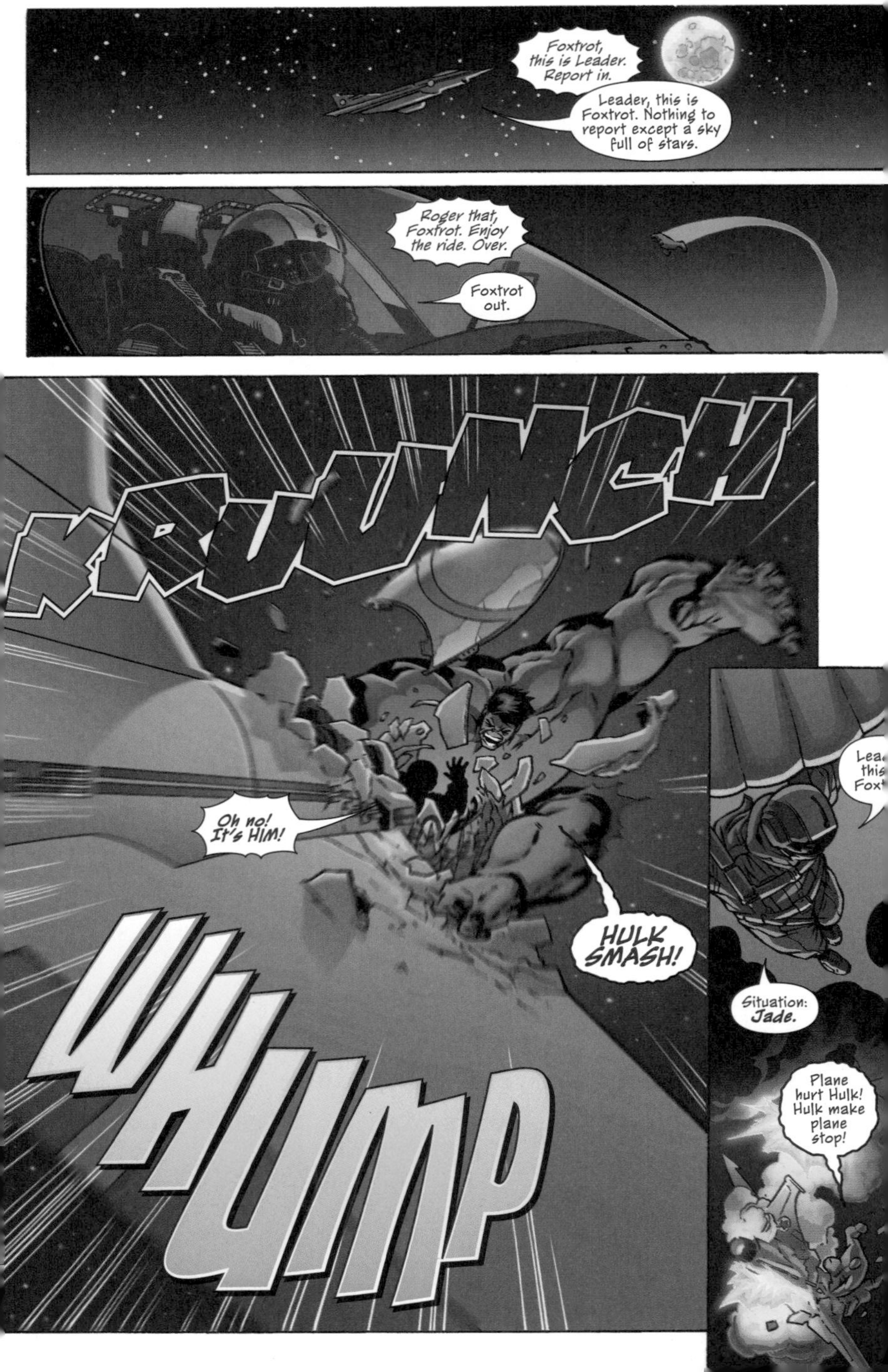

Foxtrot, this is Leader. Report in.
Leader, this is Foxtrot. Nothing to report except a sky full of stars.
Roger that, Foxtrot. Enjoy the ride. Over.
Foxtrot out.
KRUUNCH
Oh no! It's HIM!
HULK SMASH!
WHUMP
Situation: Jade.
Plane hurt Hulk! Hulk make plane stop!

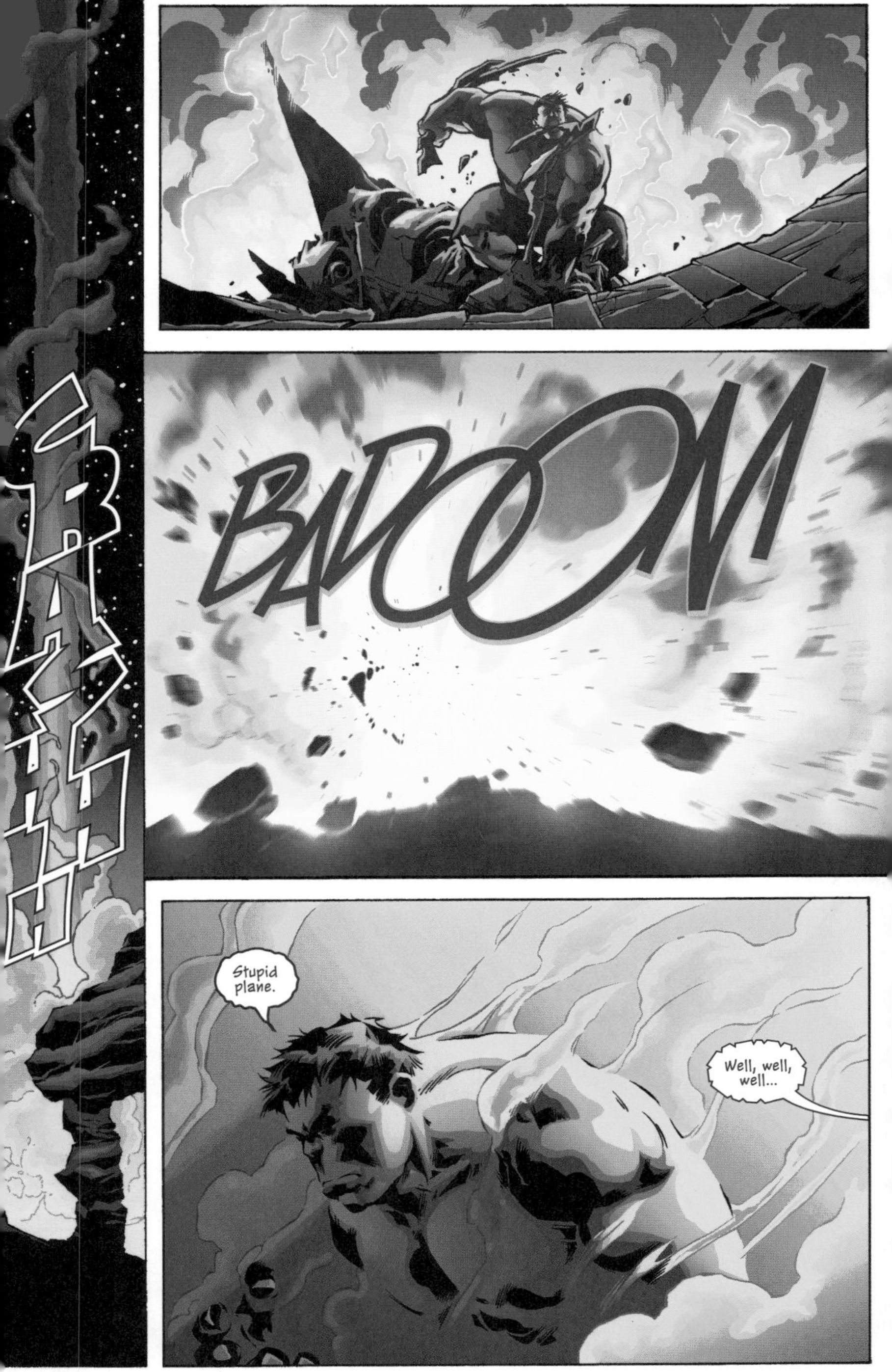
BADOOM
Stupid plane.
Well, well, well...

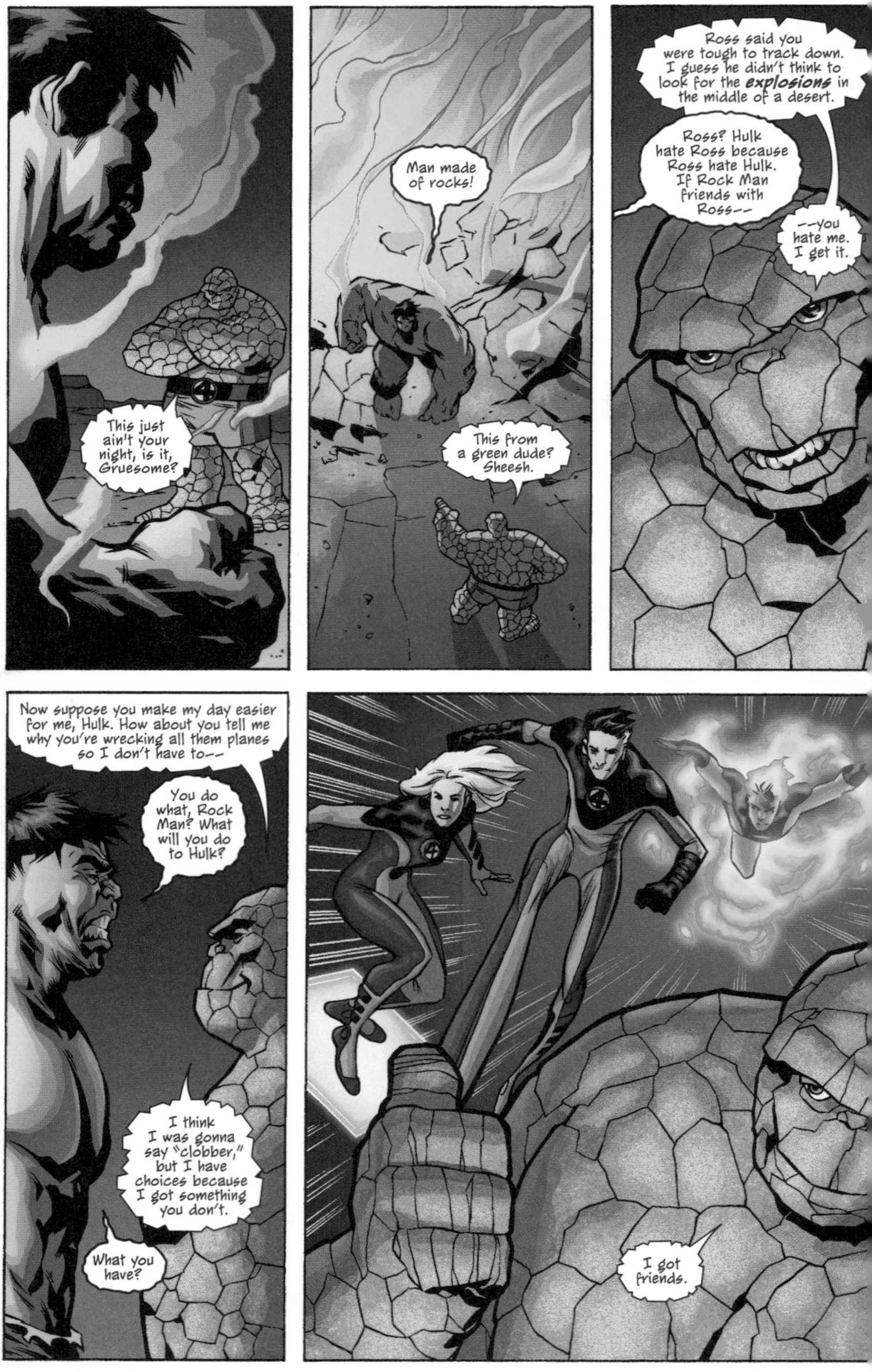
This just ain't your night, is it, Gruesome?
Man made of rocks!
This from a green dude? Sheesh.
Ross said you were tough to track down. I guess he didn't think to look for the *explosions* in the middle of a desert.
Ross? Hulk hate Ross because Ross hate Hulk. If Rock Man friends with Ross--
--you hate me. I get it.
Now suppose you make my day easier for me, Hulk. How about you tell me why you're wrecking all them planes so I don't have to--
You do what, Rock Man? What will you do to Hulk?
I think I was gonna say "clobber," but I have choices because I got something you don't.
What you have?
I got friends.

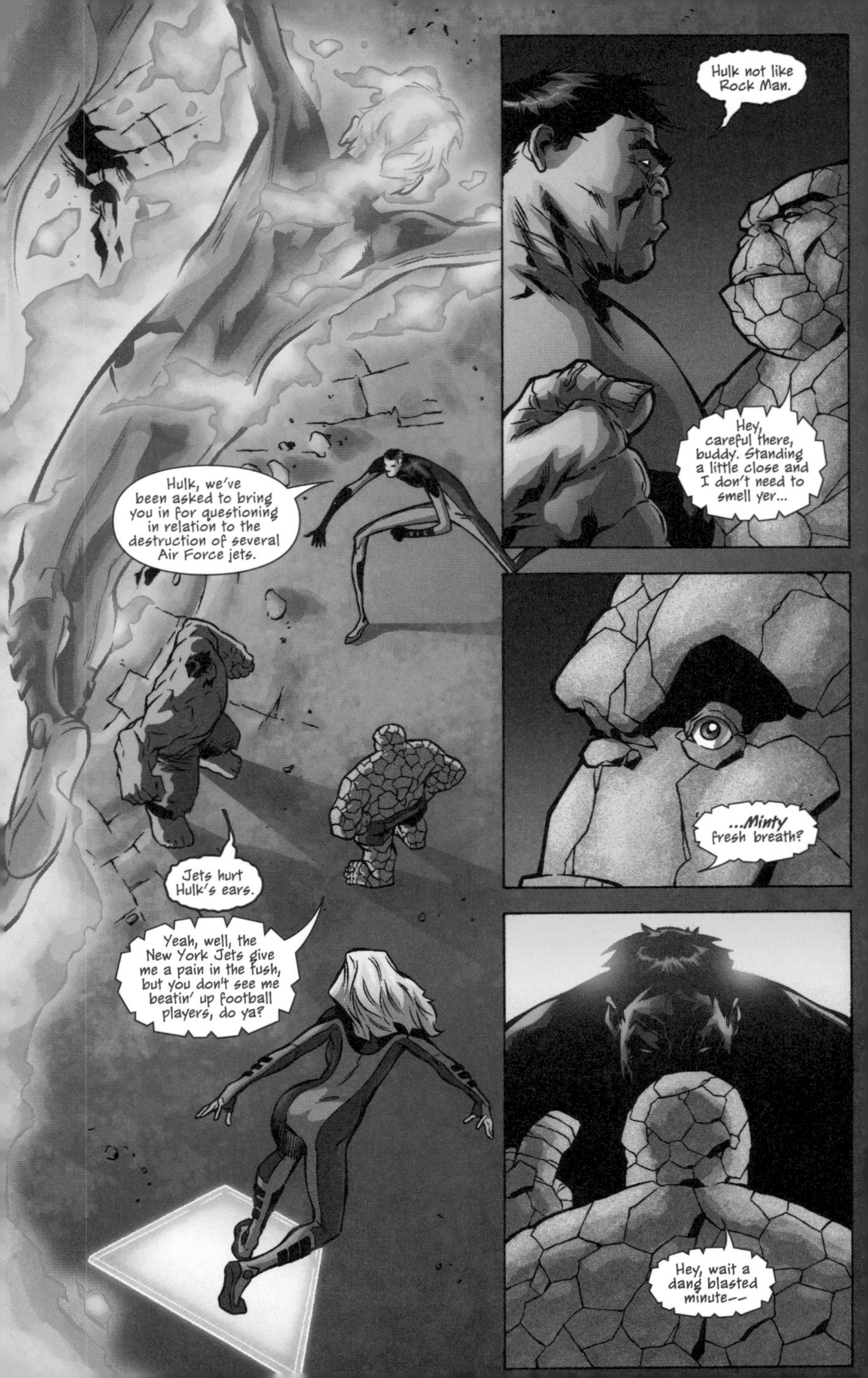
Hulk, we've been asked to bring you in for questioning in relation to the destruction of several Air Force jets.
Jets hurt Hulk's ears.
Yeah, well, the New York Jets give me a pain in the tush, but you don't see me beatin' up football players, do ya?
Hulk not like Rock Man.
Hey, careful there, buddy. Standing a little close and I don't need to smell yer...
...Minty fresh breath?
Hey, wait a dang blasted minute--

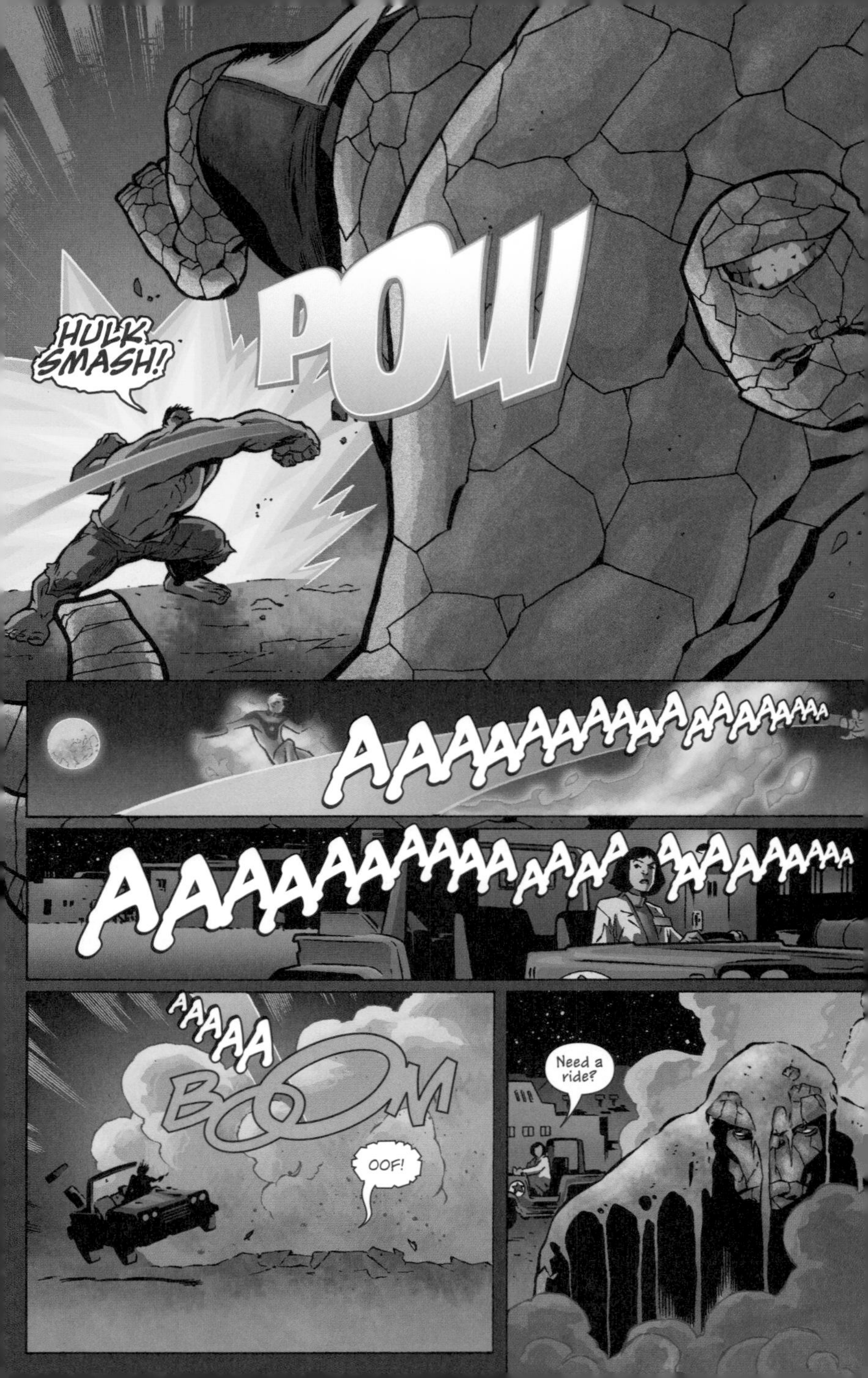
HULK SMASH!
POW
AAAAAAAAAAAAAAAAAAA
AAAAAAAAAAAAAAAAAAAAAAA
AAAAA
BOOM
OOF!
Need a ride?

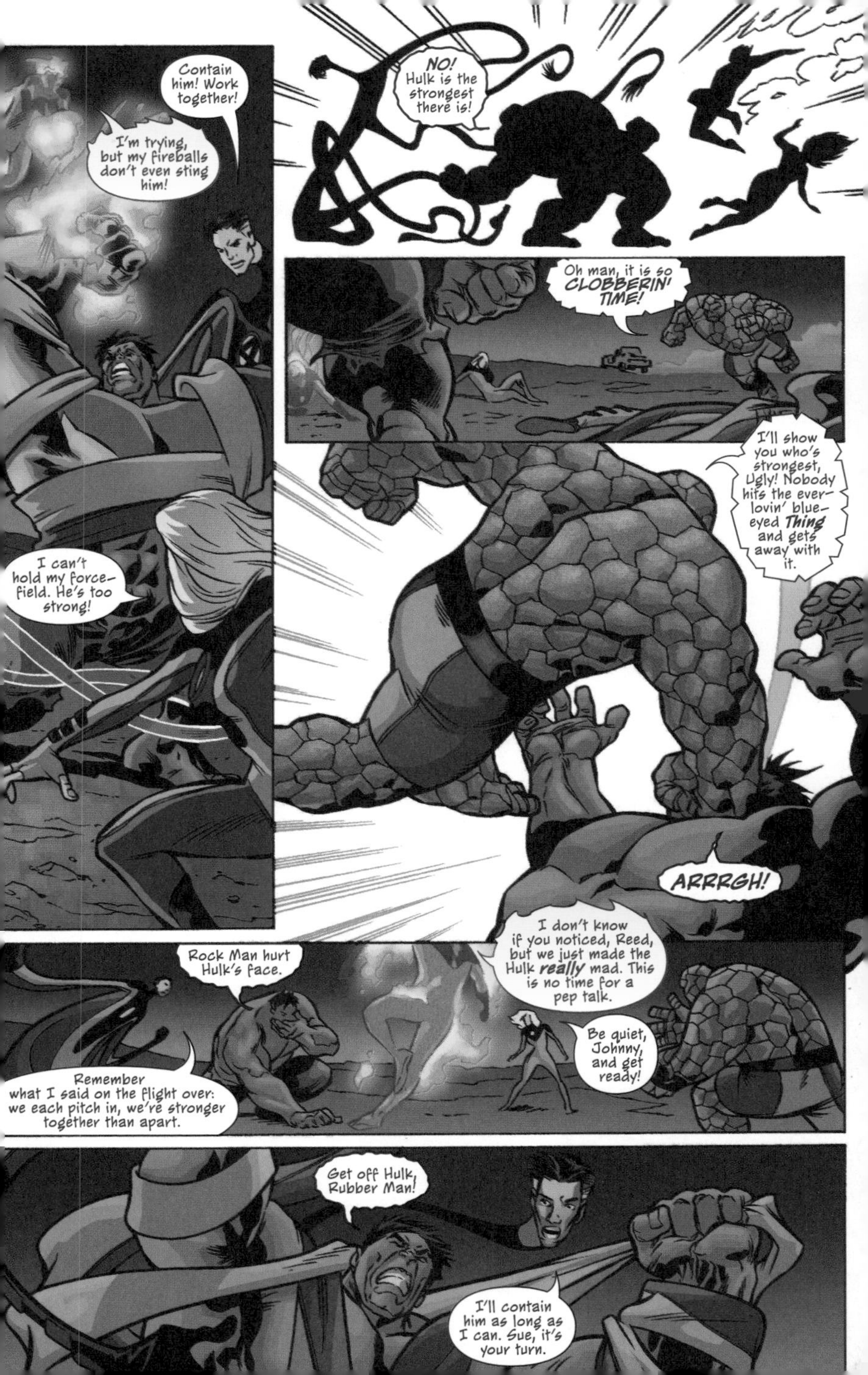
Contain him! Work together!
I'm trying, but my fireballs don't even sting him!
NO! Hulk is the strongest there is!
Oh man, it is so CLOBBERIN' TIME!
I'll show you who's strongest, Ugly! Nobody hits the ever-lovin' blue-eyed Thing and gets away with it.
I can't hold my force-field. He's too strong!
ARRRGH!
Rock Man hurt Hulk's face.
I don't know if you noticed, Reed, but we just made the Hulk really mad. This is no time for a pep talk.
Be quiet, Johnny, and get ready!
Remember what I said on the flight over: we each pitch in, we're stronger together than apart.
Get off Hulk, Rubber Man!
I'll contain him as long as I can. Sue, it's your turn.

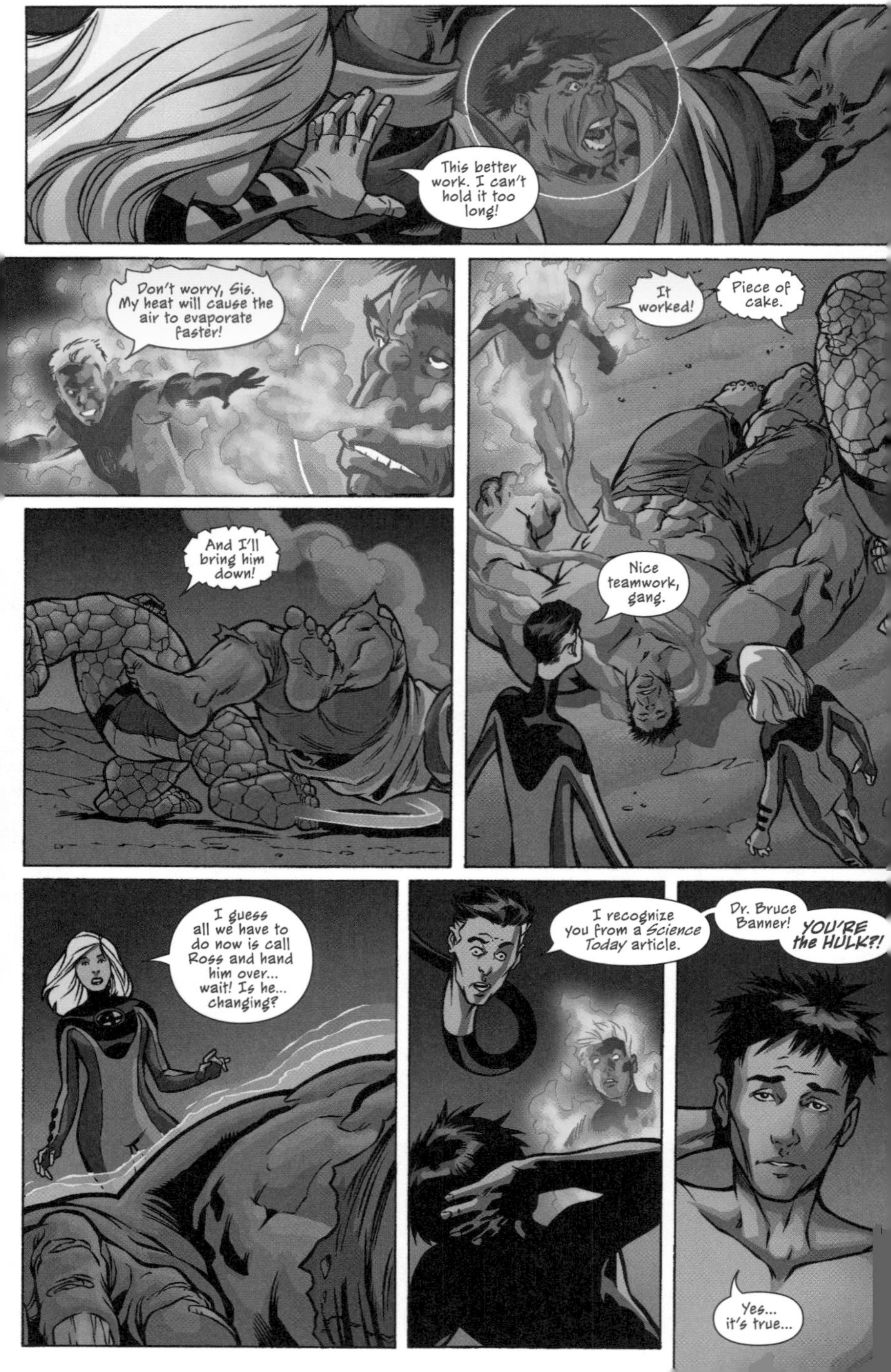
This better work. I can't hold it too long!
Don't worry, Sis. My heat will cause the air to evaporate faster!
It worked!
Piece of cake.
And I'll bring him down!
Nice teamwork, gang.
I guess all we have to do now is call Ross and hand him over... wait! Is he... changing?
I recognize you from a *Science Today* article.
Dr. Bruce Banner!
YOU'RE the HULK?!
Yes... it's true...

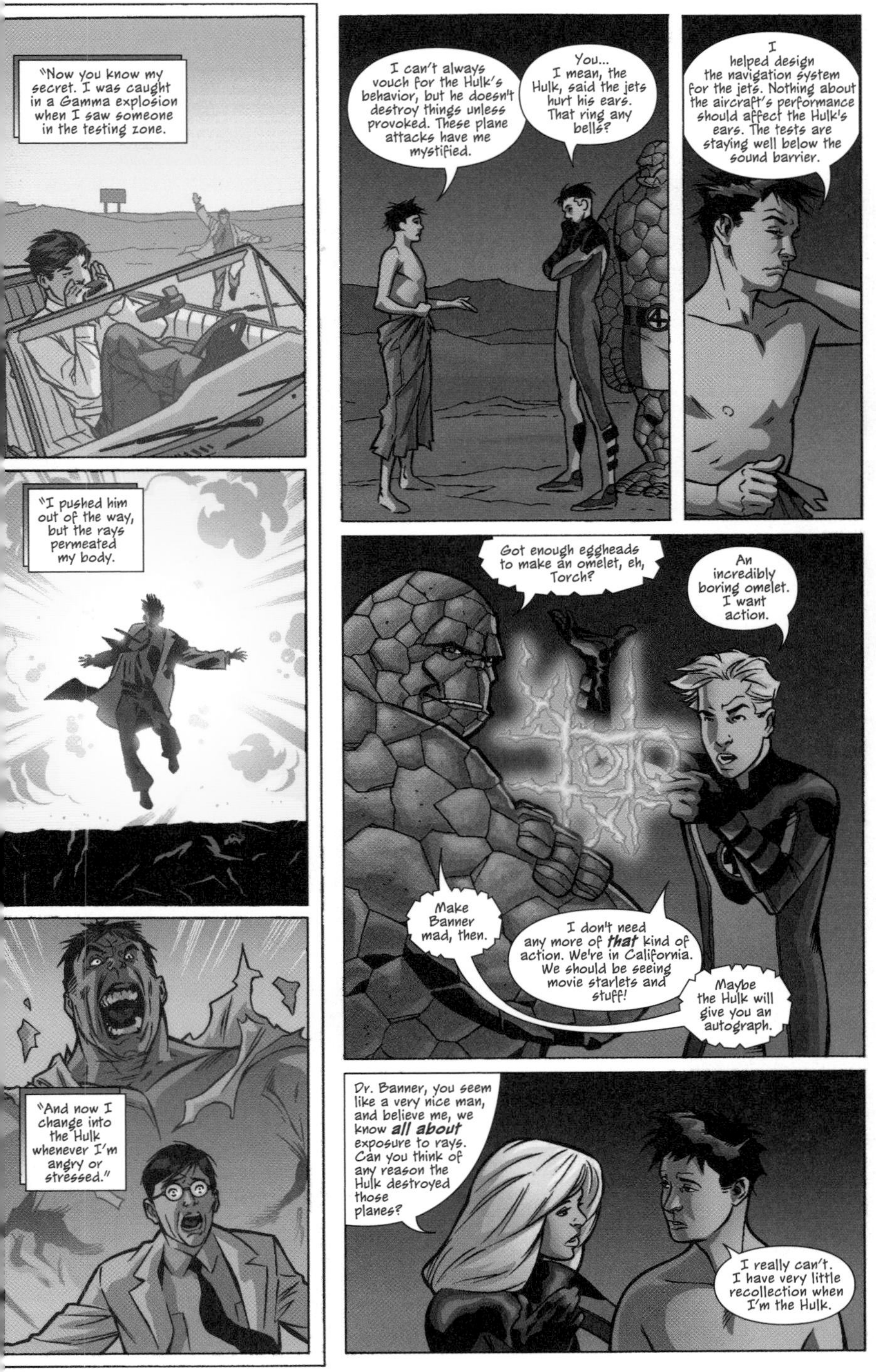
"Now you know my secret. I was caught in a Gamma explosion when I saw someone in the testing zone.
"I pushed him out of the way, but the rays permeated my body.
"And now I change into the Hulk whenever I'm angry or stressed."
I can't always vouch for the Hulk's behavior, but he doesn't destroy things unless provoked. These plane attacks have me mystified.
You... I mean, the Hulk, said the jets hurt his ears. That ring any bells?
I helped design the navigation system for the jets. Nothing about the aircraft's performance should affect the Hulk's ears. The tests are staying well below the sound barrier.
Got enough eggheads to make an omelet, eh, Torch?
An incredibly boring omelet. I want action.
Make Banner mad, then.
I don't need any more of *that* kind of action. We're in California. We should be seeing movie starlets and stuff!
Maybe the Hulk will give you an autograph.
Dr. Banner, you seem like a very nice man, and believe me, we know **all about** exposure to rays. Can you think of any reason the Hulk destroyed those planes?
I really can't. I have very little recollection when I'm the Hulk.

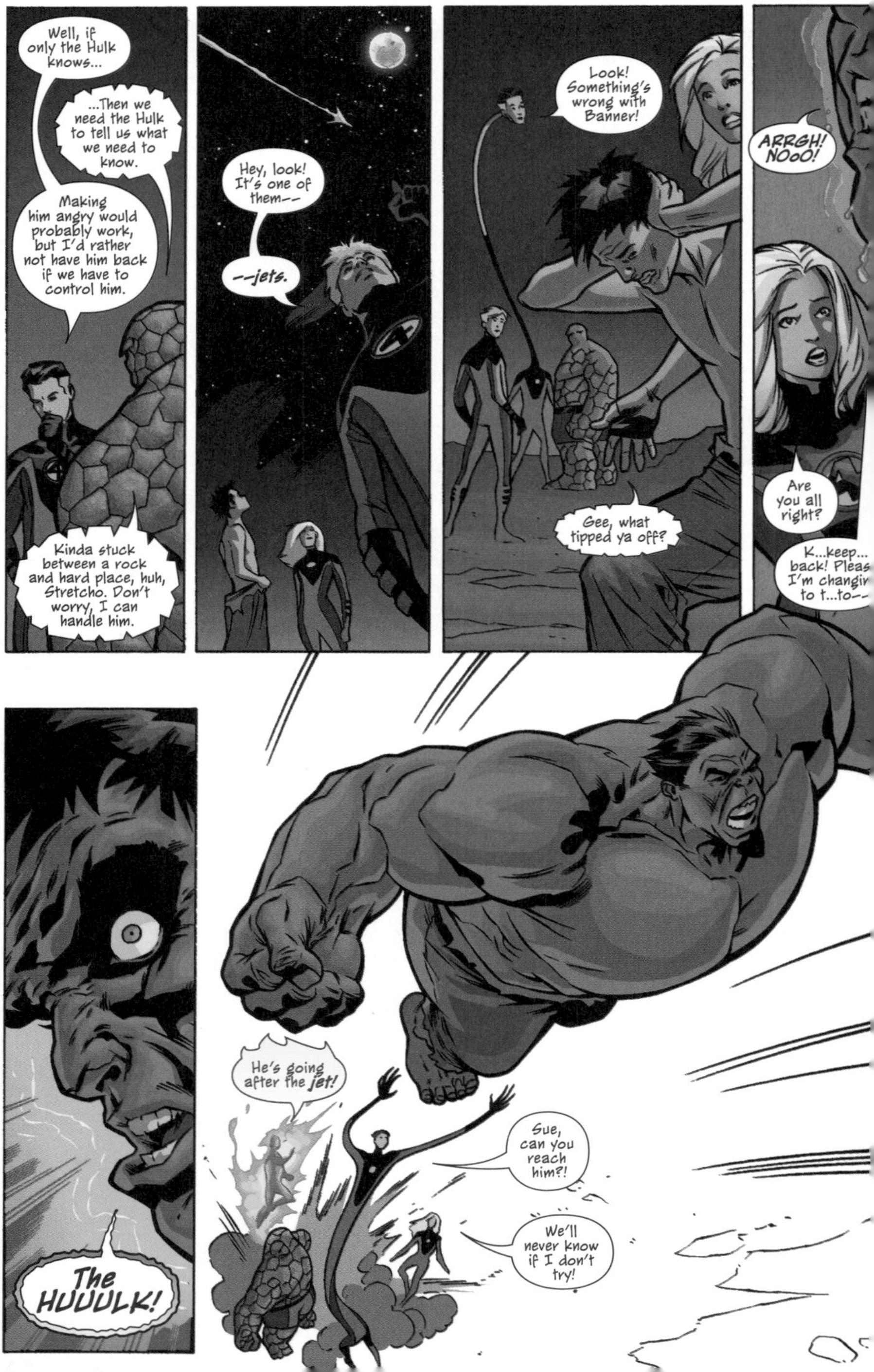
Well, if only the Hulk knows...
...Then we need the Hulk to tell us what we need to know.
Making him angry would probably work, but I'd rather not have him back if we have to control him.
Kinda stuck between a rock and hard place, huh, Stretcho. Don't worry, I can handle him.
Hey, look! It's one of them--
--jets.
Look! Something's wrong with Banner!
Gee, what tipped ya off?
ARRGH! NOoO!
Are you all right?
K...keep... back! Pleas
I'm changin
to t...to--
The HUUULK!
He's going after the jet!
Sue, can you reach him?!
We'll never know if I don't try!

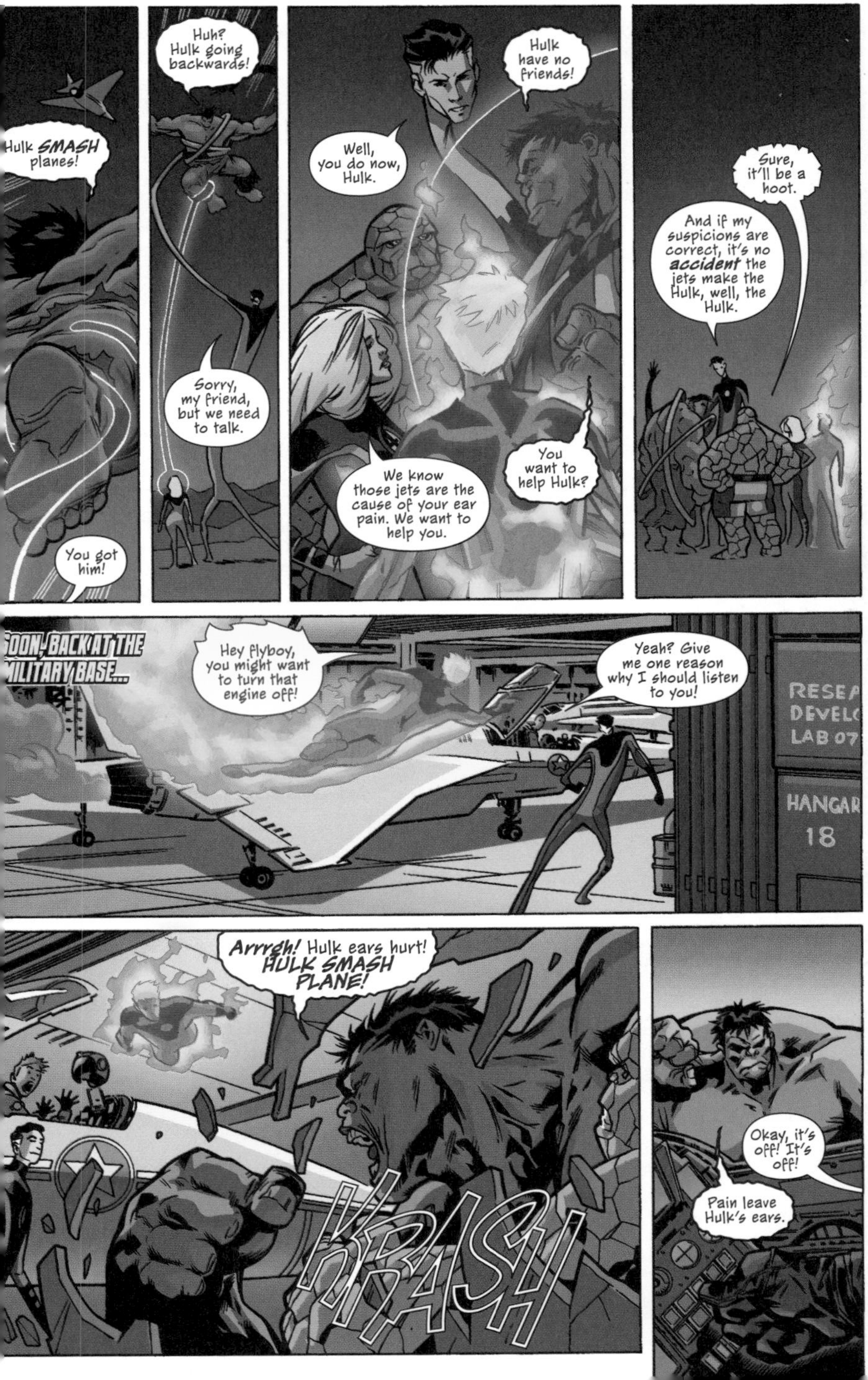

Hulk SMASH planes!
You got him!
Huh? Hulk going backwards!
Sorry, my friend, but we need to talk.
Hulk have no friends!
Well, you do now, Hulk.
We know those jets are the cause of your ear pain. We want to help you.
You want to help Hulk?
Sure, it'll be a hoot.
And if my suspicions are correct, it's no accident the jets make the Hulk, well, the Hulk.
SOON, BACK AT THE MILITARY BASE...
Hey flyboy, you might want to turn that engine off!
Yeah? Give me one reason why I should listen to you!
RESEA DEVELC LAB 07
HANGAR 18
Arrrgh! Hulk ears hurt! HULK SMASH PLANE!
KRASH
Okay, it's off! It's off!
Pain leave Hulk's ears.

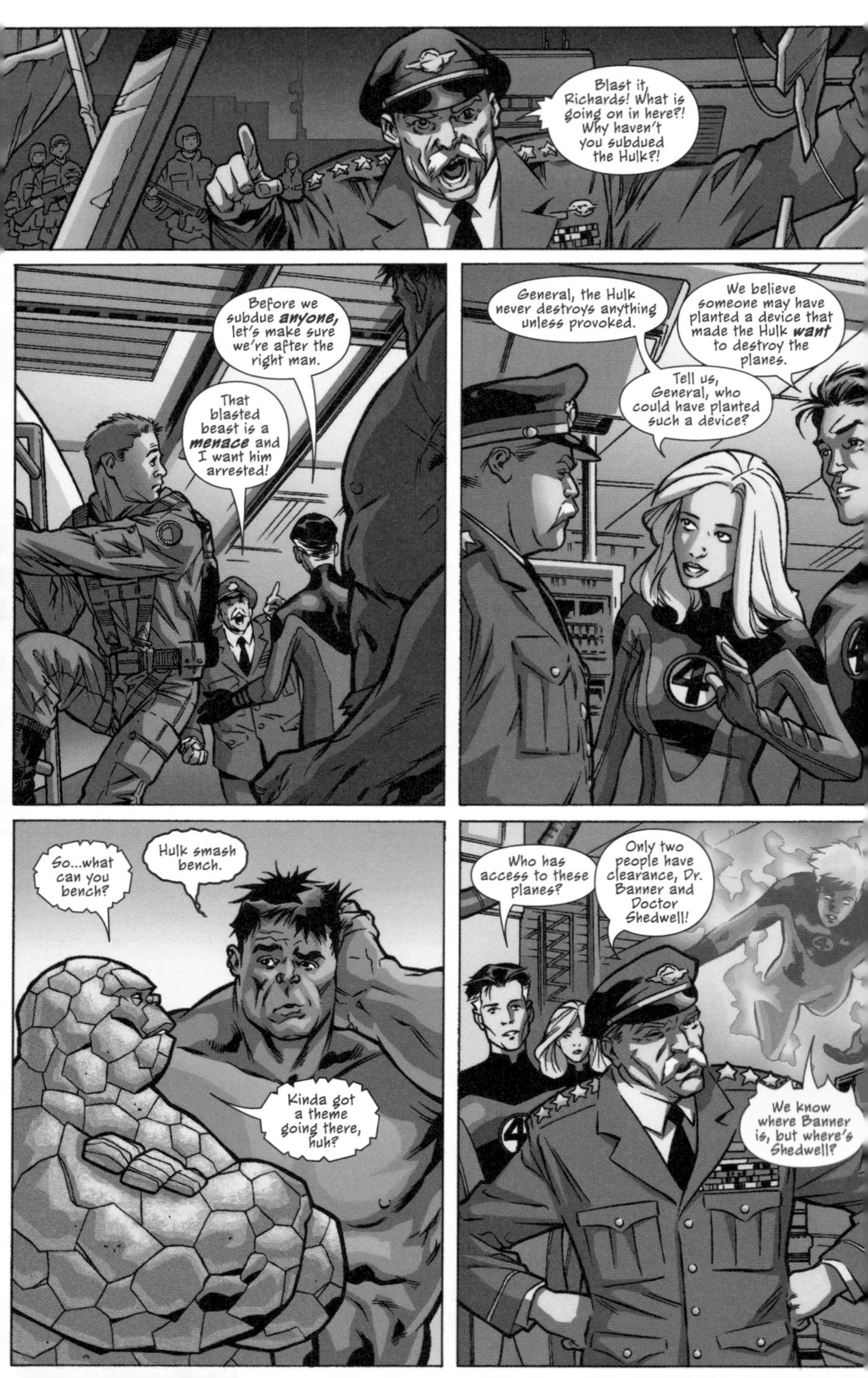
Blast it, Richards! What is going on in here?! Why haven't you subdued the Hulk?!
Before we subdue **anyone,** let's make sure we're after the right man.
That blasted beast is a **menace** and I want him arrested!
General, the Hulk never destroys anything unless provoked.
We believe someone may have planted a device that made the Hulk **want** to destroy the planes.
Tell us, General, who could have planted such a device?
So...what can you bench?
Hulk smash bench.
Kinda got a theme going there, huh?
Who has access to these planes?
Only two people have clearance, Dr. Banner and Doctor Shedwell!
We know where Banner is, but where's Shedwell?

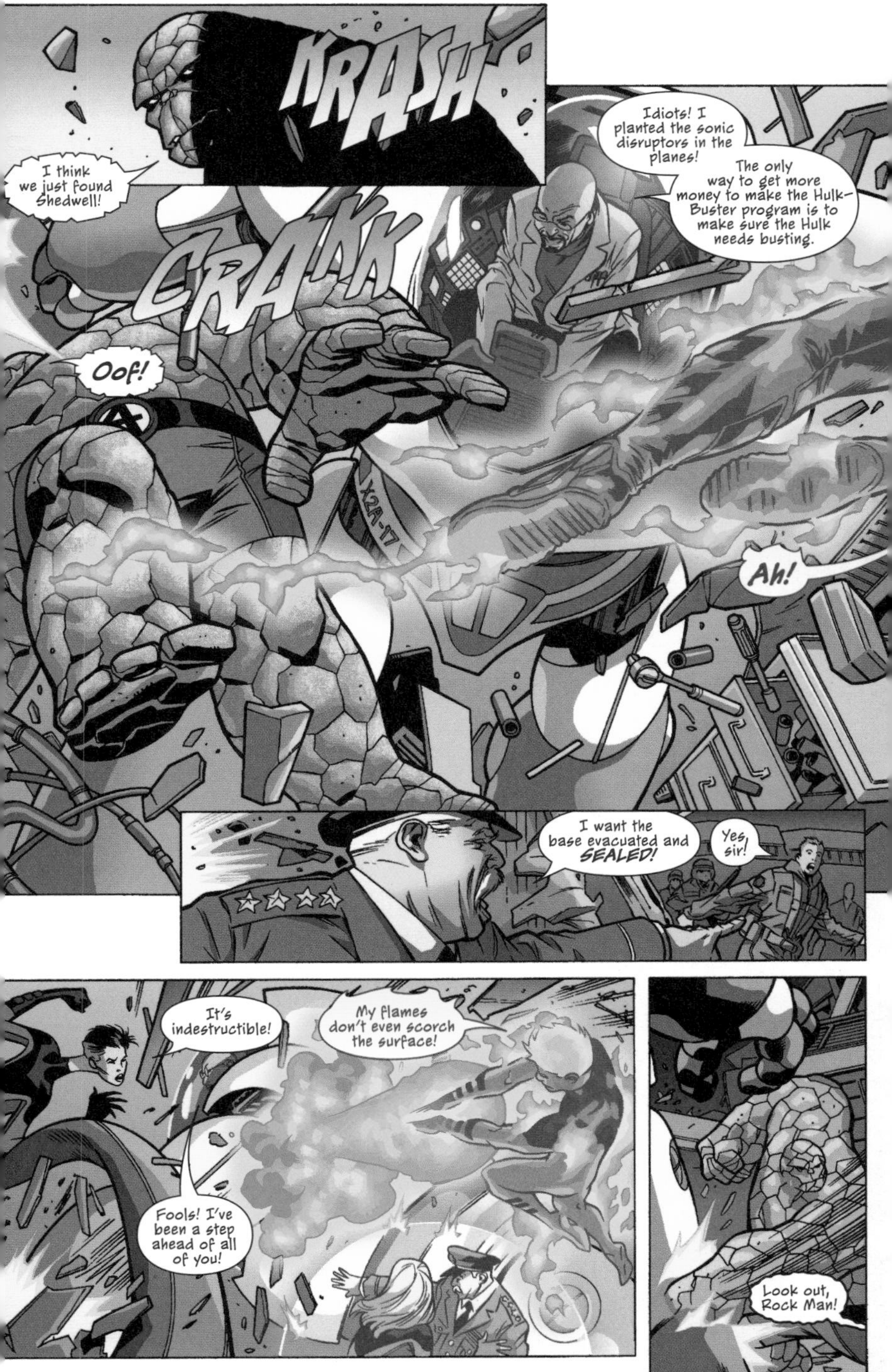
KRASH
I think we just found Shedwell!
CRAKK
Idiots! I planted the sonic disruptors in the planes!
The only way to get more money to make the Hulk-Buster program is to make sure the Hulk needs busting.
Oof!
X2A-17
Ah!
I want the base evacuated and SEALED!
Yes, sir!
It's indestructible!
My flames don't even scorch the surface!
Fools! I've been a step ahead of all of you!
Look out, Rock Man!

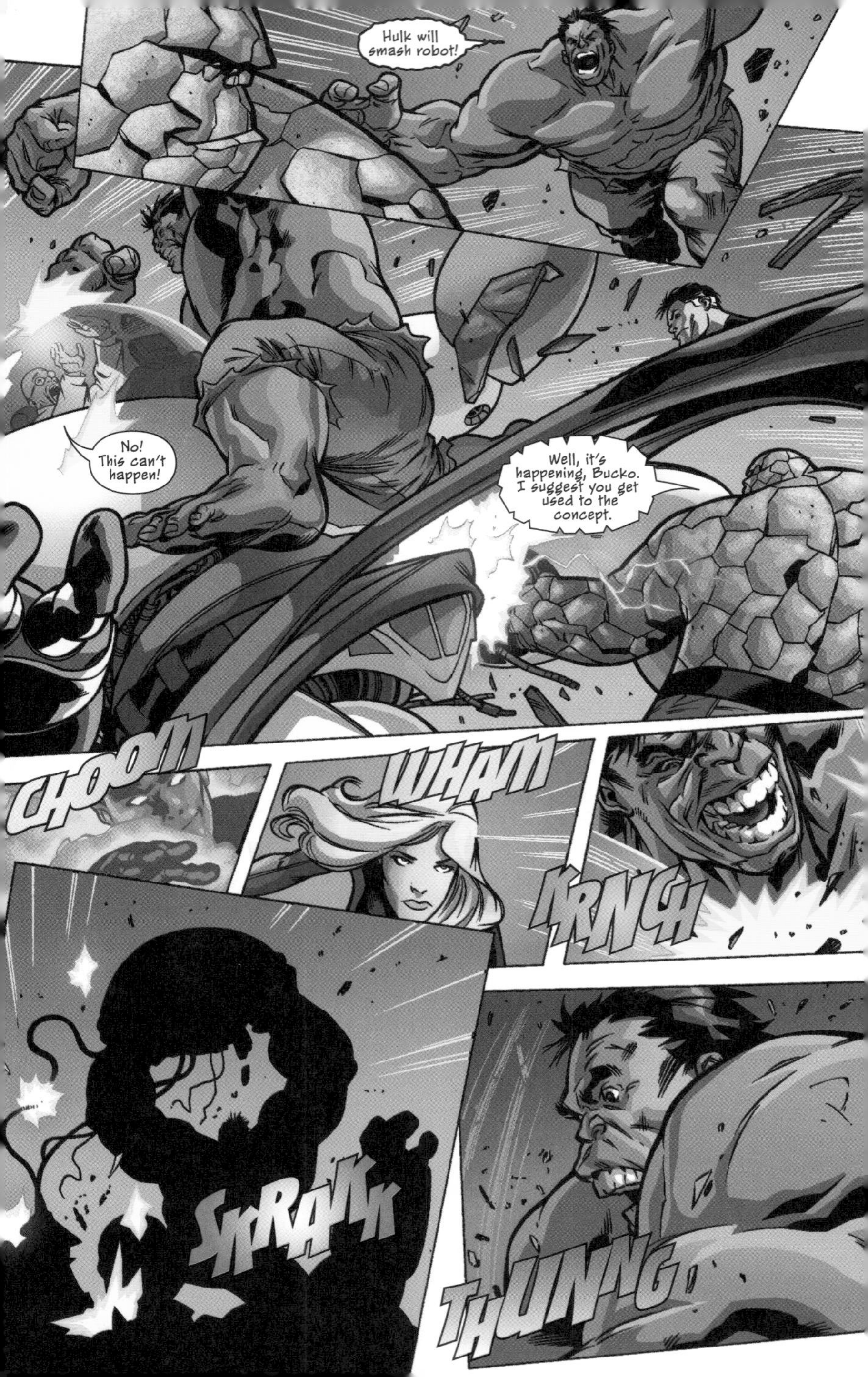
Hulk will smash robot!
No! This can't happen!
Well, it's happening, Bucko. I suggest you get used to the concept.
CHOOM
WHAM
KRNCH
SKRAKK
THUNNG

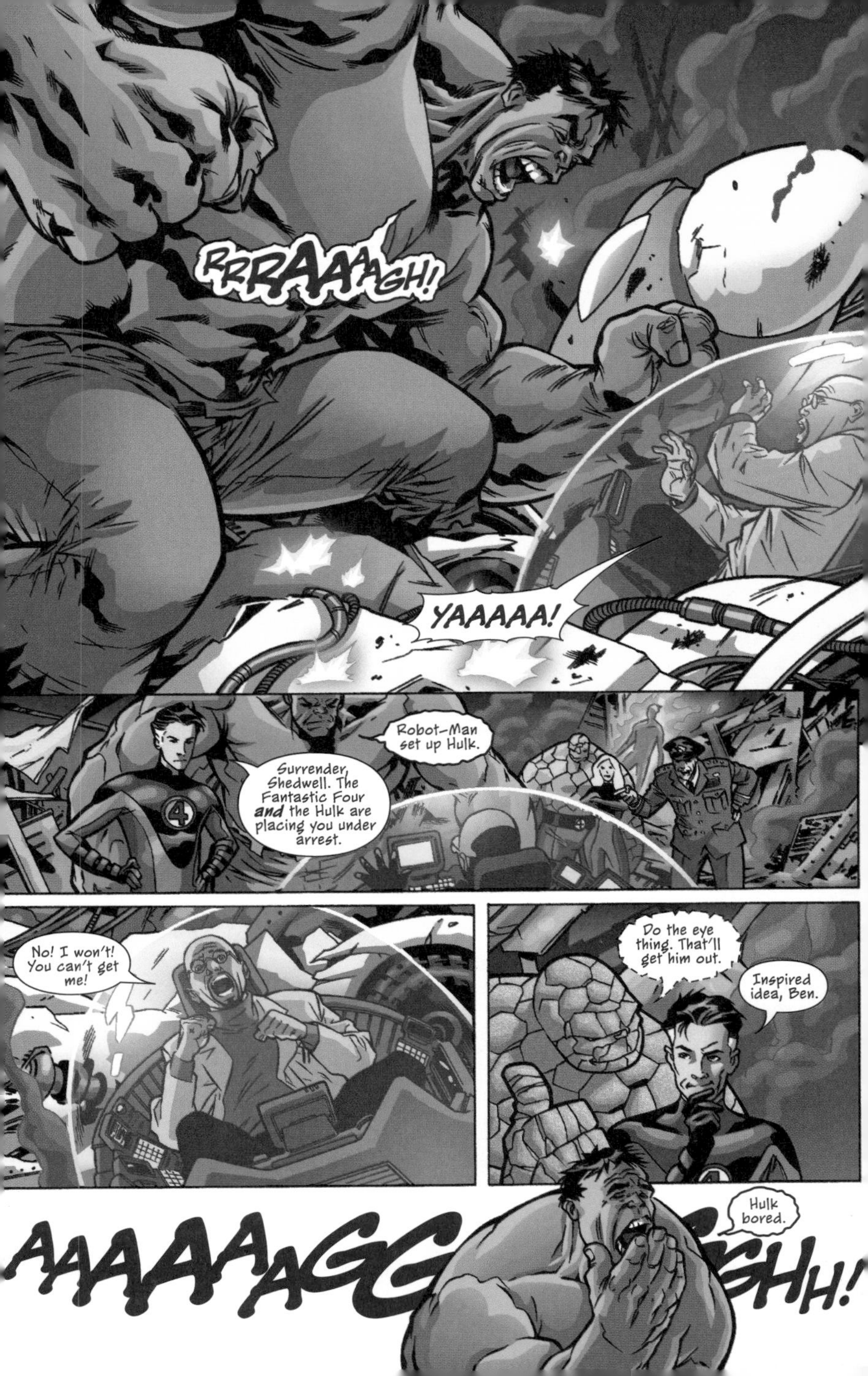
RRRRAAAAAGH!
YAAAAA!
Robot-Man set up Hulk.
Surrender, Shedwell. The Fantastic Four **and** the Hulk are placing you under arrest.
No! I won't! You can't get me!
Do the eye thing. That'll get him out.
Inspired idea, Ben.
AAAAAAGG
GHH!
Hulk bored.

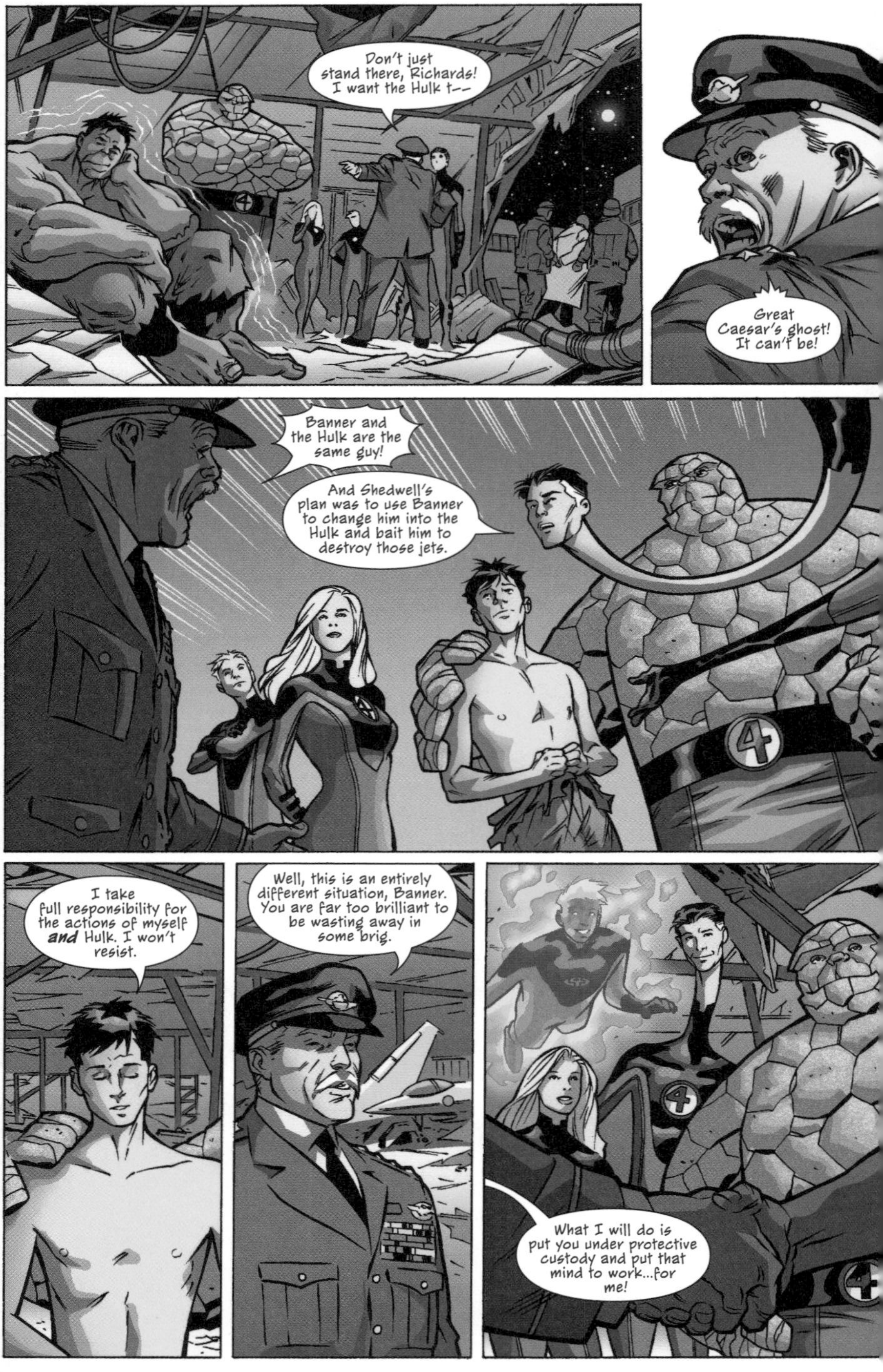
Don't just stand there, Richards! I want the Hulk t--
Great Caesar's ghost! It can't be!
Banner and the Hulk are the same guy!
And Shedwell's plan was to use Banner to change him into the Hulk and bait him to destroy those jets.
I take full responsibility for the actions of myself **and** Hulk. I won't resist.
Well, this is an entirely different situation, Banner. You are far too brilliant to be wasting away in some brig.
What I will do is put you under protective custody and put that mind to work...for me!

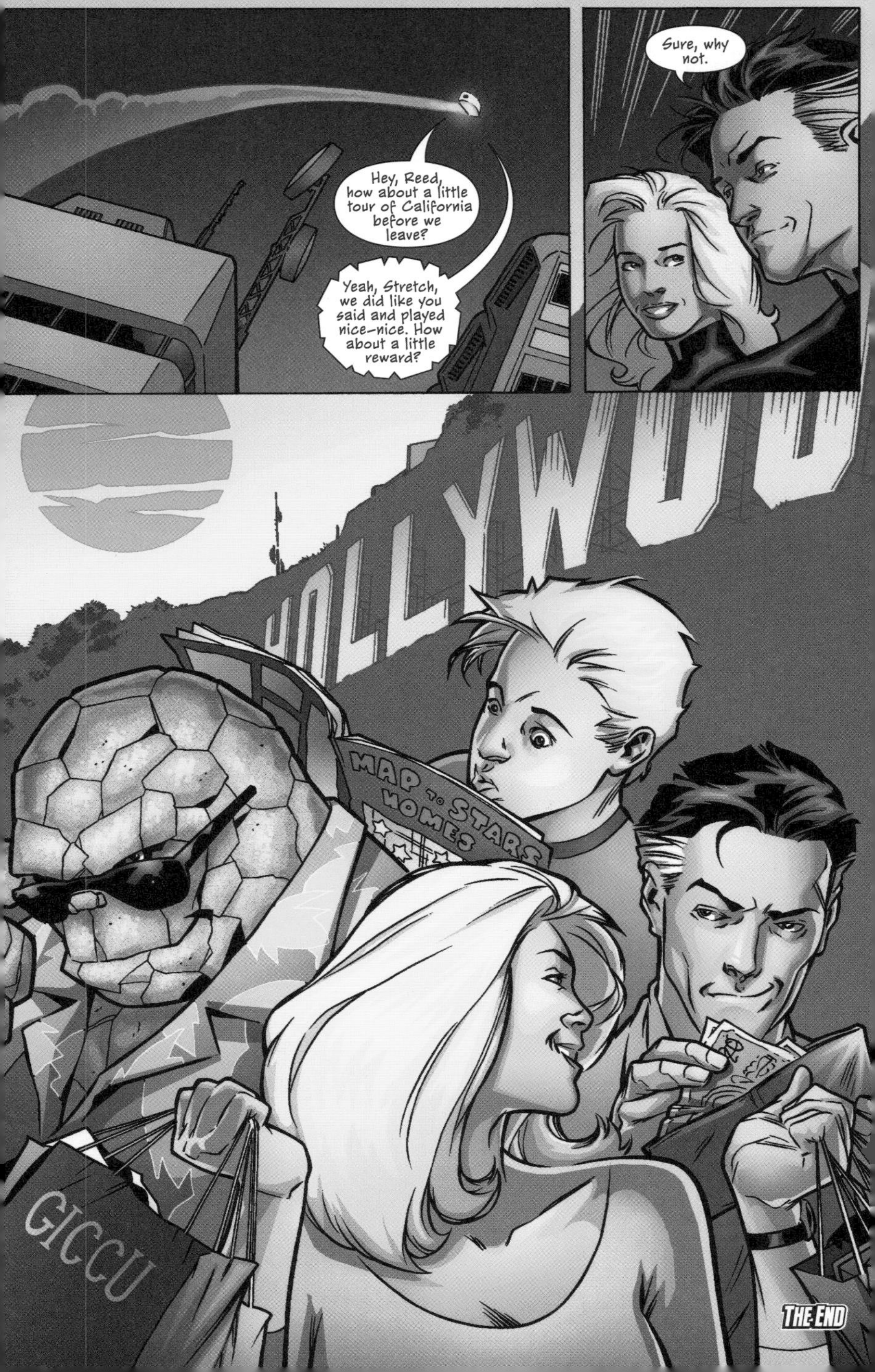
Hey, Reed, how about a little tour of California before we leave?
Yeah, Stretch, we did like you said and played nice-nice. How about a little reward?
Sure, why not.
HOLLYWOO
MAP TO STARS HOMES
GICCU
THE END

#23

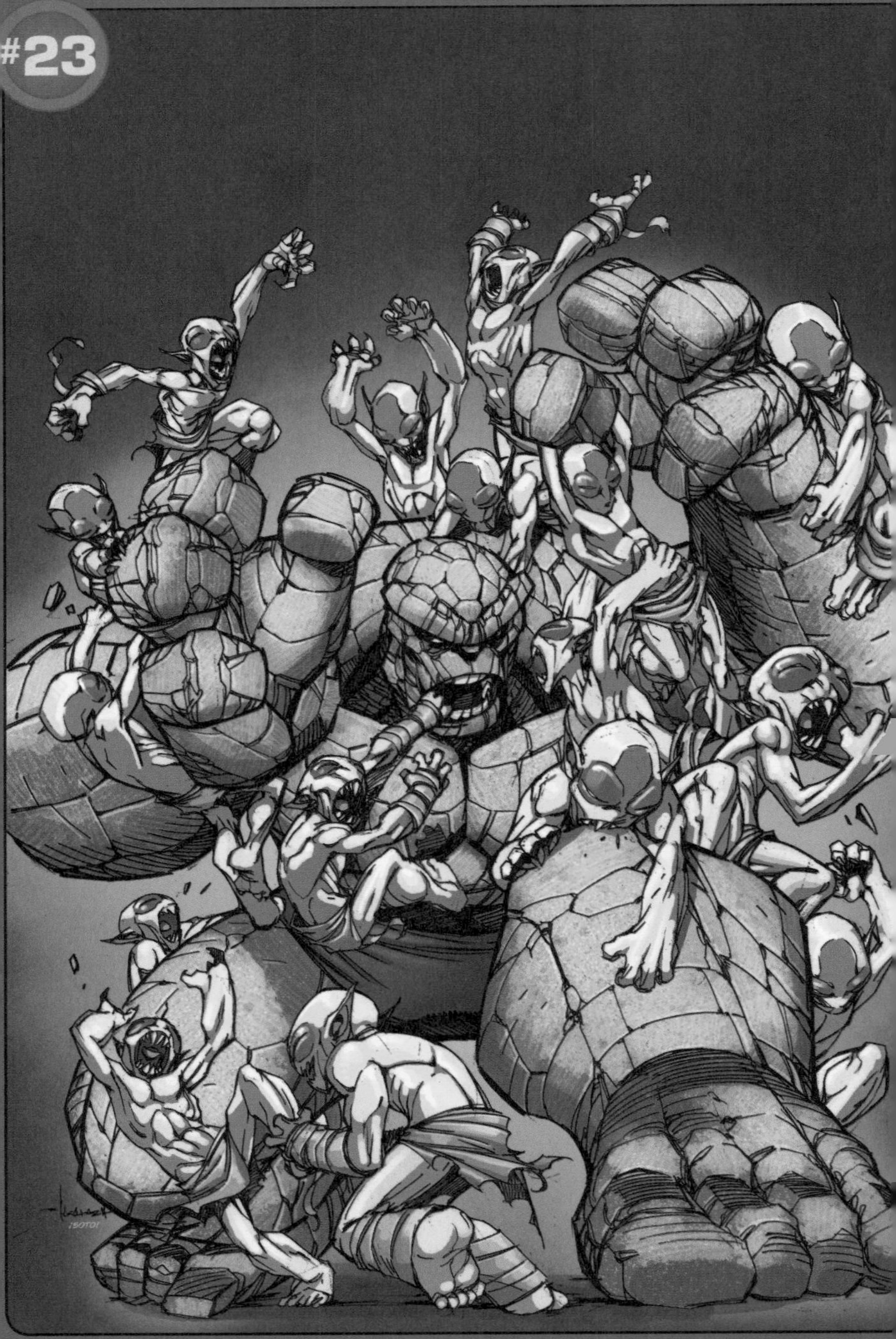

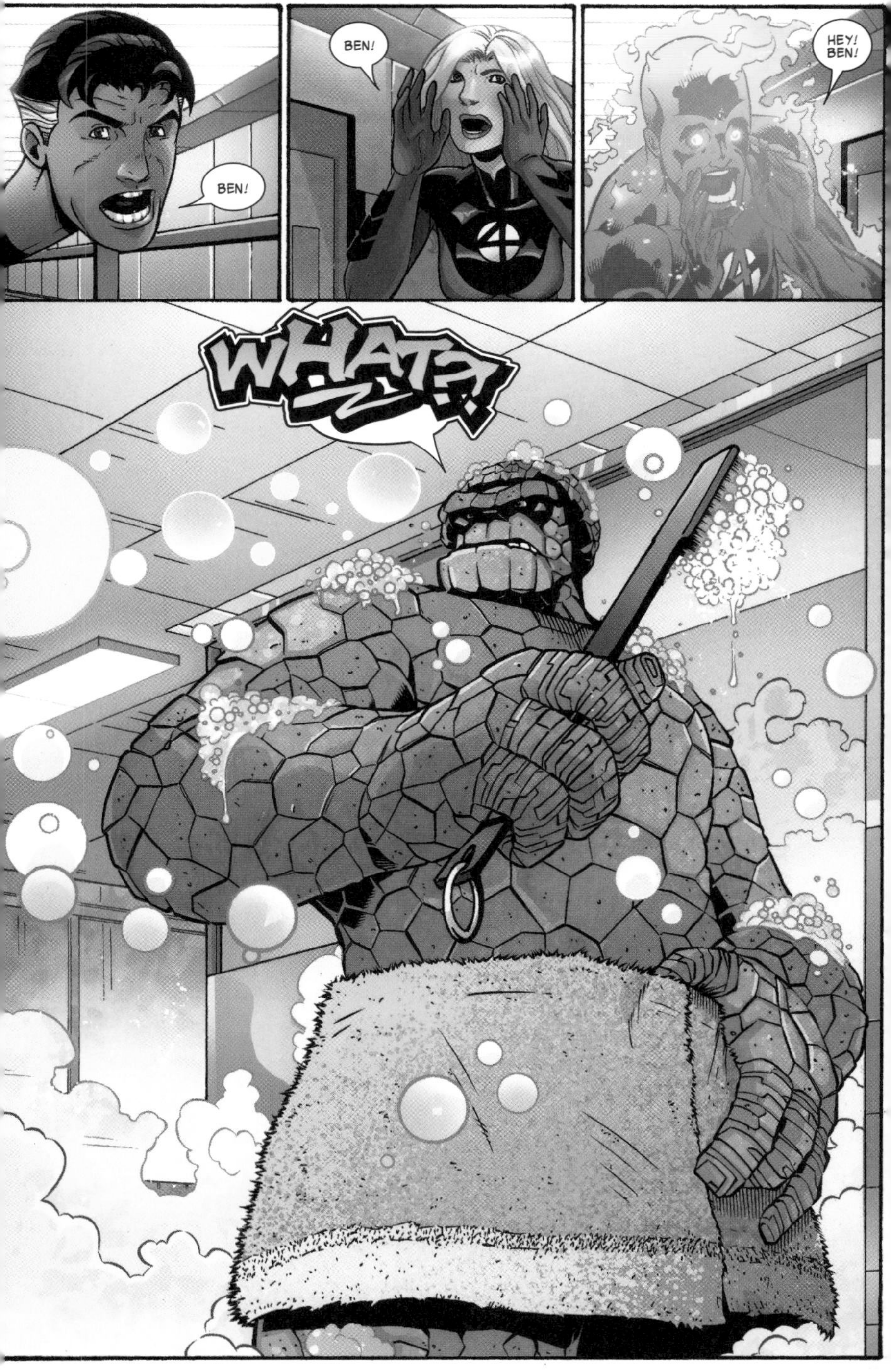
BEN!
BEN!
HEY! BEN!
WHAT?!

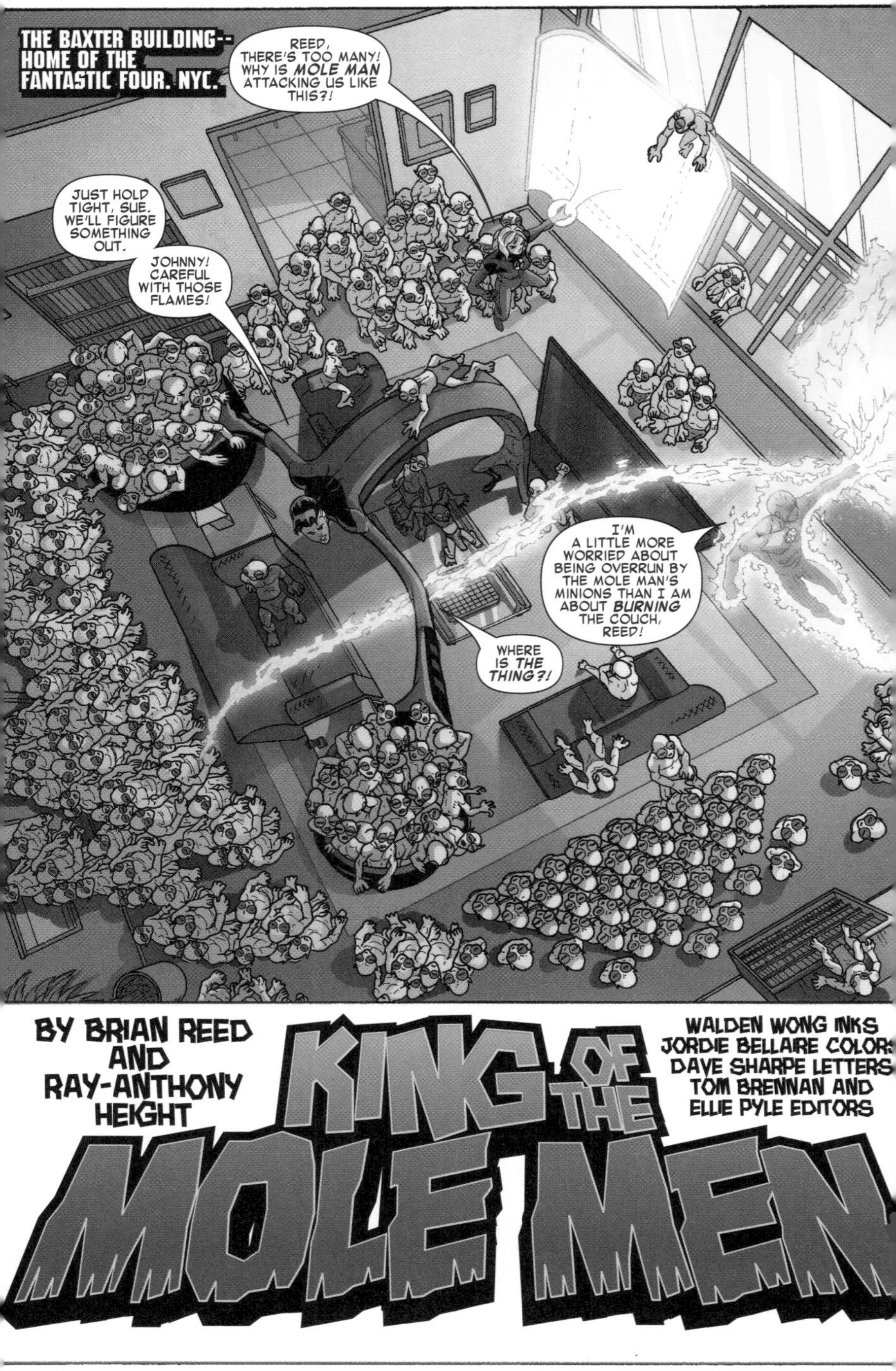
THE BAXTER BUILDING--HOME OF THE FANTASTIC FOUR. NYC.
REED, THERE'S TOO MANY! WHY IS *MOLE MAN* ATTACKING US LIKE THIS?!
JUST HOLD TIGHT, SUE. WE'LL FIGURE SOMETHING OUT.
JOHNNY! CAREFUL WITH THOSE FLAMES!
I'M A LITTLE MORE WORRIED ABOUT BEING OVERRUN BY THE MOLE MAN'S MINIONS THAN I AM ABOUT *BURNING* THE COUCH, REED!
WHERE IS *THE THING?!*

BY BRIAN REED AND RAY-ANTHONY HEIGHT

KING OF THE MOLE MEN

WALDEN WONG INKS
JORDIE BELLAIRE COLORS
DAVE SHARPE LETTERS
TOM BRENNAN AND ELLIE PYLE EDITORS

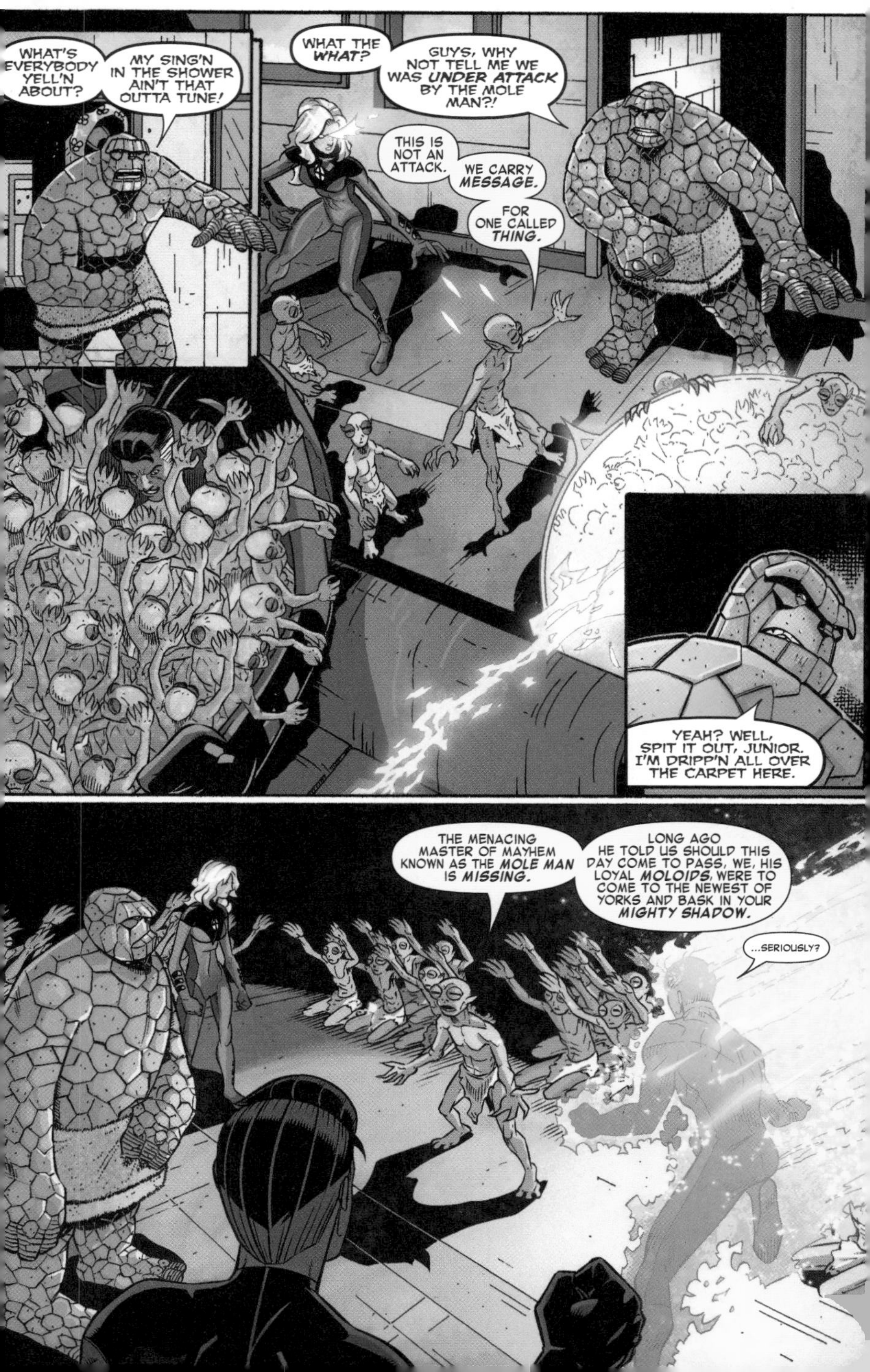
WHAT'S EVERYBODY YELL'N ABOUT?
MY SING'N IN THE SHOWER AIN'T THAT OUTTA TUNE!
WHAT THE *WHAT?*
GUYS, WHY NOT TELL ME WE WAS *UNDER ATTACK* BY THE MOLE MAN?!
THIS IS NOT AN ATTACK.
WE CARRY *MESSAGE.*
FOR ONE CALLED *THING.*
YEAH? WELL, SPIT IT OUT, JUNIOR. I'M DRIPP'N ALL OVER THE CARPET HERE.
THE MENACING MASTER OF MAYHEM KNOWN AS THE *MOLE MAN* IS *MISSING.*
LONG AGO HE TOLD US SHOULD THIS DAY COME TO PASS, WE, HIS LOYAL *MOLOIDS,* WERE TO COME TO THE NEWEST OF YORKS AND BASK IN YOUR *MIGHTY SHADOW.*
...SERIOUSLY?

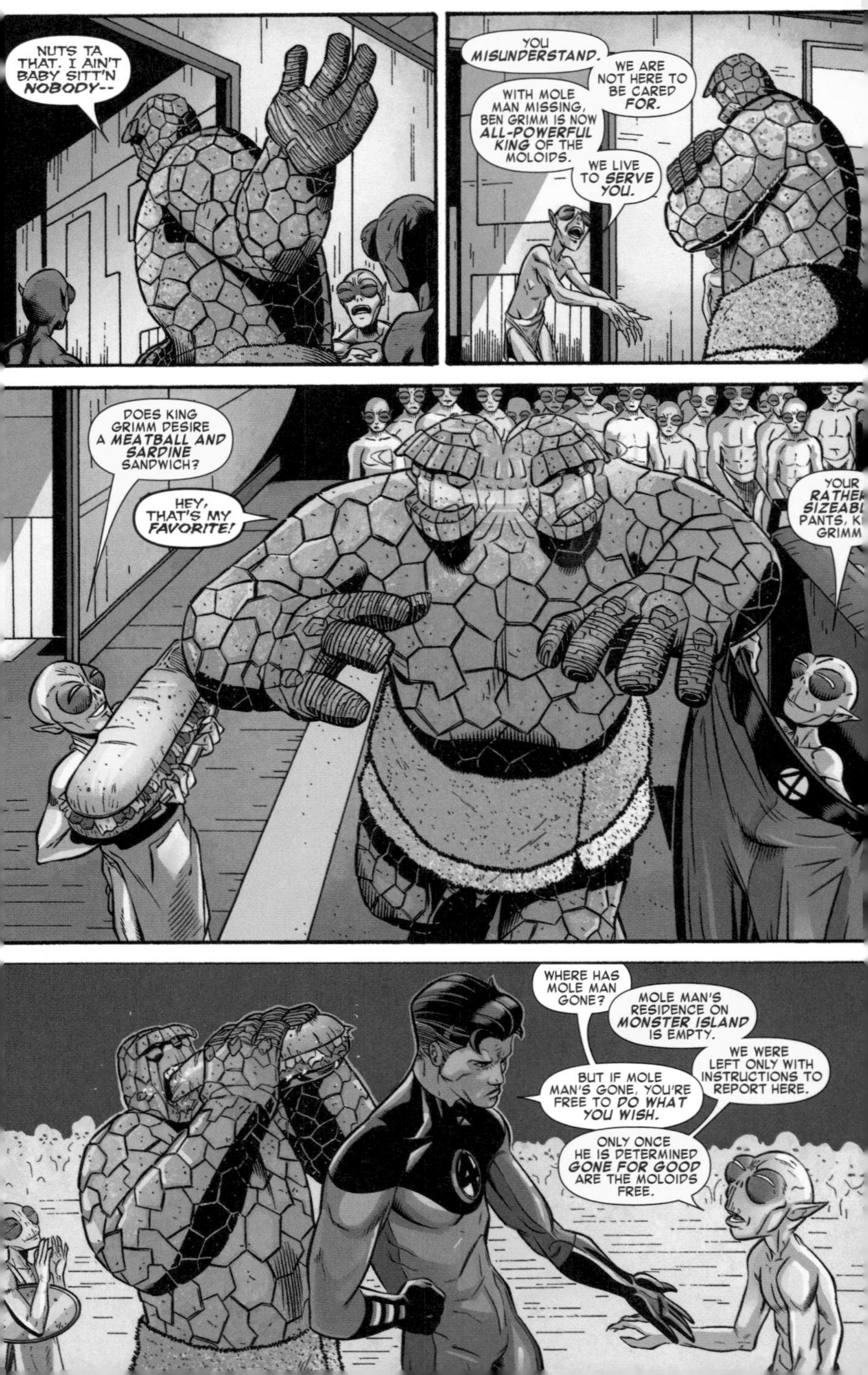
NUTS TA THAT. I AIN'T BABY SITT'N ***NOBODY***--
YOU ***MISUNDERSTAND.***
WE ARE NOT HERE TO BE CARED ***FOR.***
WITH MOLE MAN MISSING, BEN GRIMM IS NOW ***ALL-POWERFUL KING*** OF THE MOLOIDS.
WE LIVE TO ***SERVE YOU.***
DOES KING GRIMM DESIRE A ***MEATBALL AND SARDINE*** SANDWICH?
HEY, THAT'S MY ***FAVORITE!***
WHERE HAS MOLE MAN GONE?
MOLE MAN'S RESIDENCE ON ***MONSTER ISLAND*** IS EMPTY.
WE WERE LEFT ONLY WITH INSTRUCTIONS TO REPORT HERE.
BUT IF MOLE MAN'S GONE, YOU'RE FREE TO ***DO WHAT YOU WISH.***
ONLY ONCE HE IS DETERMINED ***GONE FOR GOOD*** ARE THE MOLOIDS FREE.

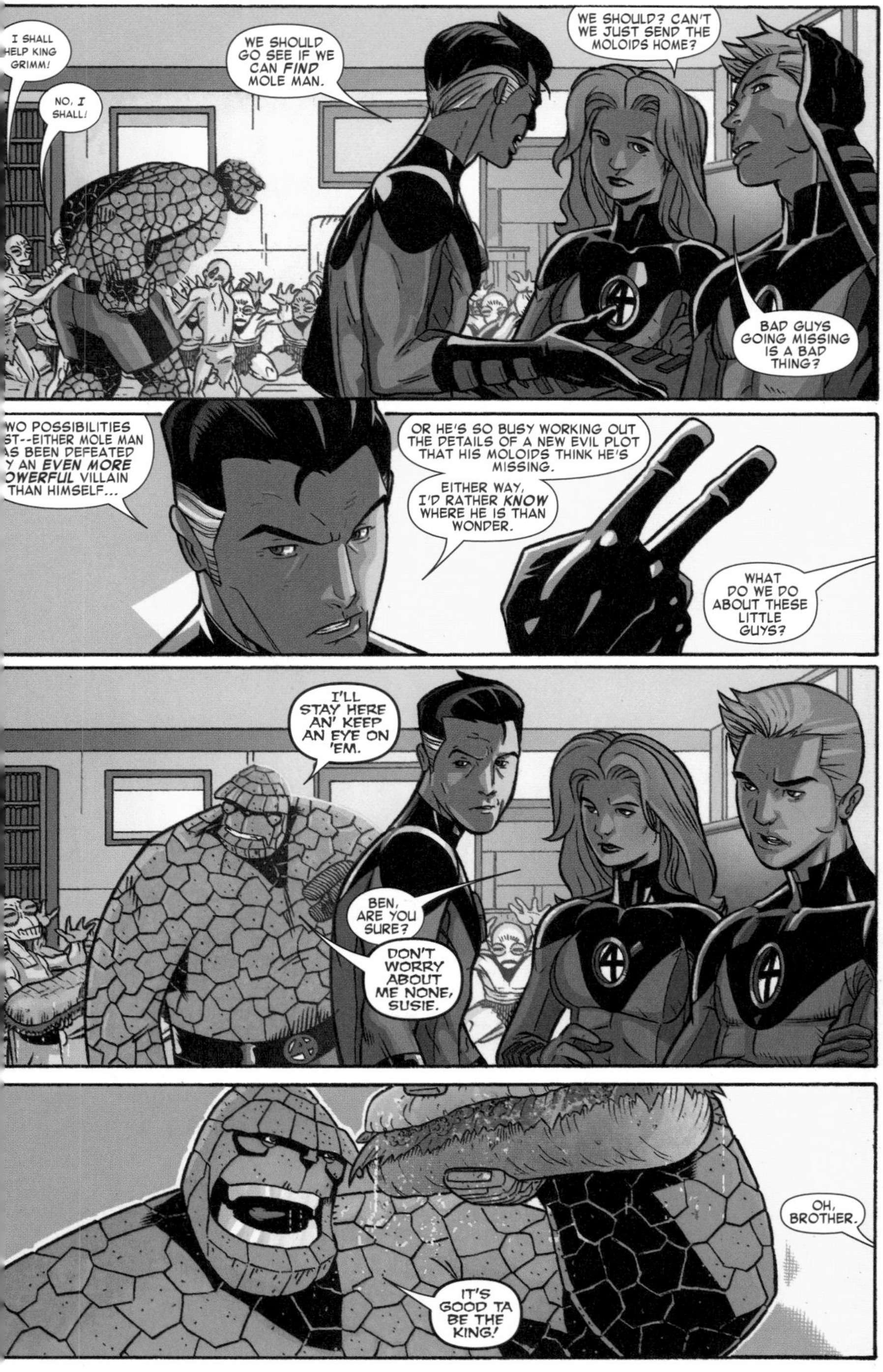
I SHALL HELP KING GRIMM!
NO, *I* SHALL!
WE SHOULD GO SEE IF WE CAN *FIND* MOLE MAN.
WE SHOULD? CAN'T WE JUST SEND THE MOLOIDS HOME?
BAD GUYS GOING MISSING IS A BAD THING?
WO POSSIBILITIES ST--EITHER MOLE MAN AS BEEN DEFEATED Y AN *EVEN MORE OWERFUL* VILLAIN THAN HIMSELF...
OR HE'S SO BUSY WORKING OUT THE DETAILS OF A NEW EVIL PLOT THAT HIS MOLOIDS THINK HE'S MISSING.
EITHER WAY, I'D RATHER *KNOW* WHERE HE IS THAN WONDER.
WHAT DO WE DO ABOUT THESE LITTLE GUYS?
I'LL STAY HERE AN' KEEP AN EYE ON 'EM.
BEN, ARE YOU SURE?
DON'T WORRY ABOUT ME NONE, SUSIE.
OH, BROTHER.
IT'S GOOD TA BE THE KING!

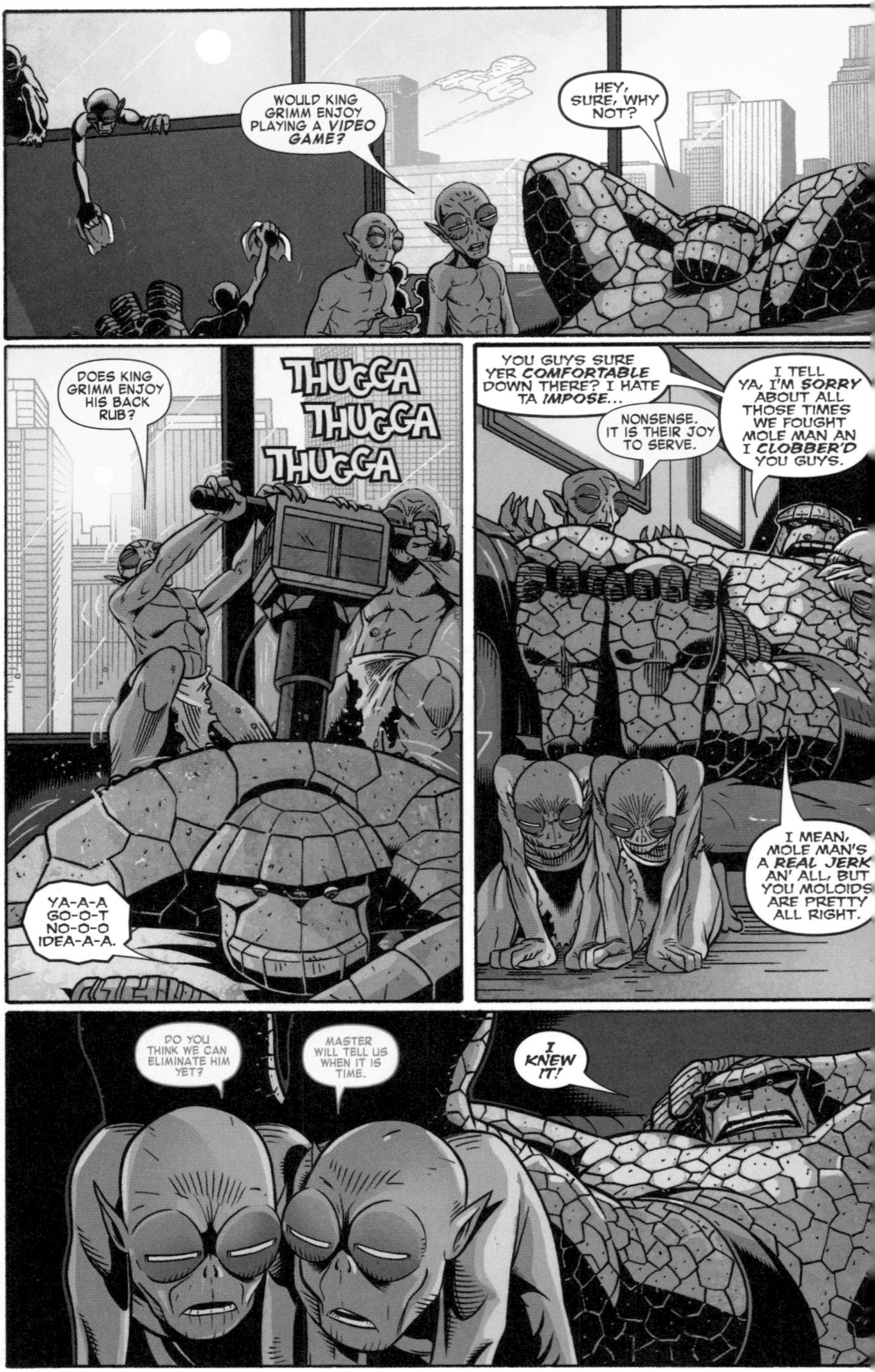

WOULD KING GRIMM ENJOY PLAYING A VIDEO GAME?
HEY, SURE, WHY NOT?
DOES KING GRIMM ENJOY HIS BACK RUB?
THUGGA THUGGA THUGGA
YA-A-A GO-O-T NO-O-O IDEA-A-A.
YOU GUYS SURE YER COMFORTABLE DOWN THERE? I HATE TA IMPOSE...
NONSENSE. IT IS THEIR JOY TO SERVE.
I TELL YA, I'M SORRY ABOUT ALL THOSE TIMES WE FOUGHT MOLE MAN AN I CLOBBER'D YOU GUYS.
I MEAN, MOLE MAN'S A REAL JERK AN' ALL, BUT YOU MOLOIDS ARE PRETTY ALL RIGHT.
DO YOU THINK WE CAN ELIMINATE HIM YET?
MASTER WILL TELL US WHEN IT IS TIME.
I KNEW IT!

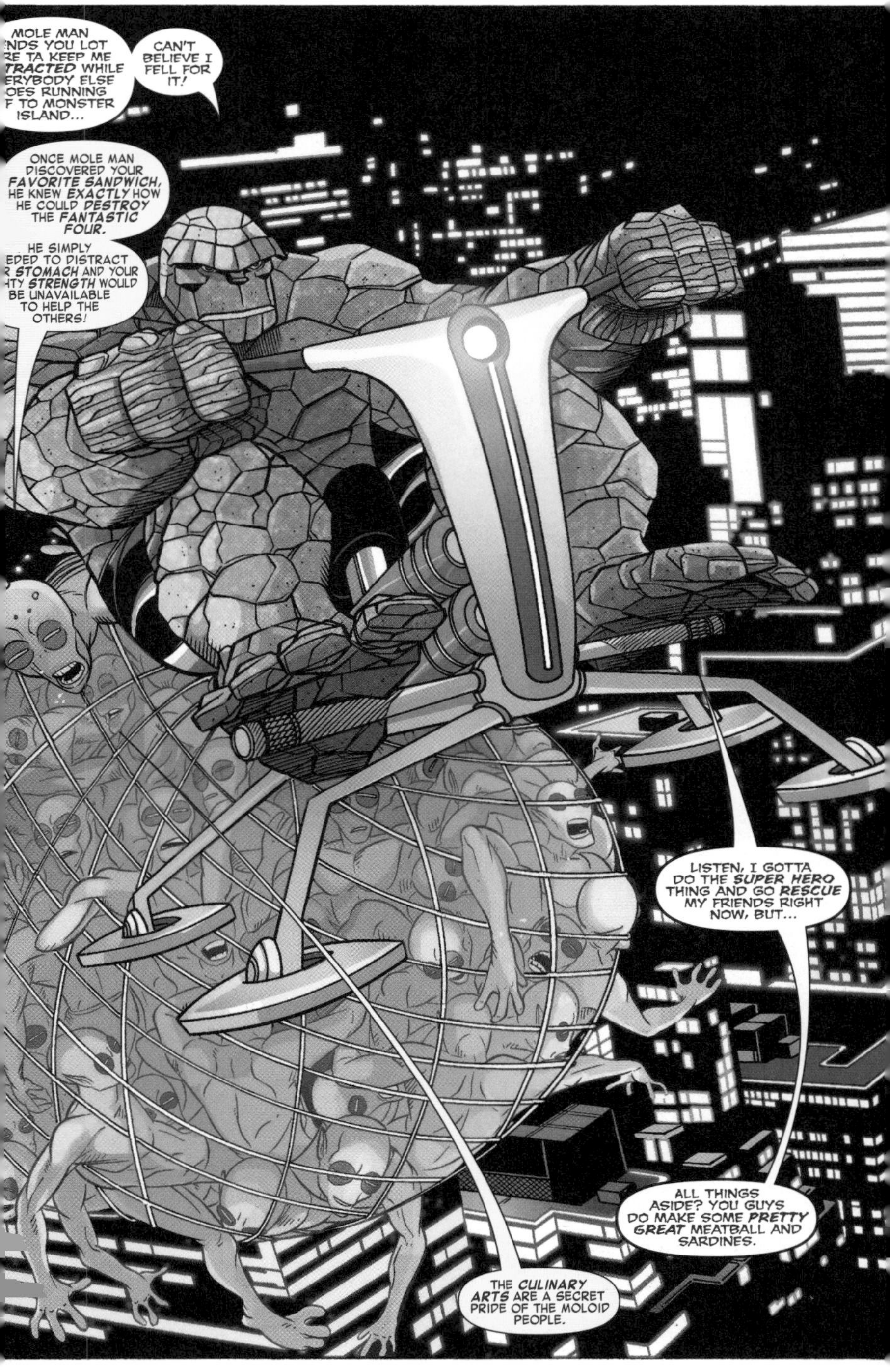

MOLE MAN ENDS YOU LOT RE TA KEEP ME TRACTED WHILE ERYBODY ELSE OES RUNNING F TO MONSTER ISLAND...
CAN'T BELIEVE I FELL FOR IT!
ONCE MOLE MAN DISCOVERED YOUR FAVORITE SANDWICH, HE KNEW EXACTLY HOW HE COULD DESTROY THE FANTASTIC FOUR.
HE SIMPLY EDED TO DISTRACT R STOMACH AND YOUR HTY STRENGTH WOULD BE UNAVAILABLE TO HELP THE OTHERS!
LISTEN, I GOTTA DO THE SUPER HERO THING AND GO RESCUE MY FRIENDS RIGHT NOW, BUT...
ALL THINGS ASIDE? YOU GUYS DO MAKE SOME PRETTY GREAT MEATBALL AND SARDINES.
THE CULINARY ARTS ARE A SECRET PRIDE OF THE MOLOID PEOPLE.

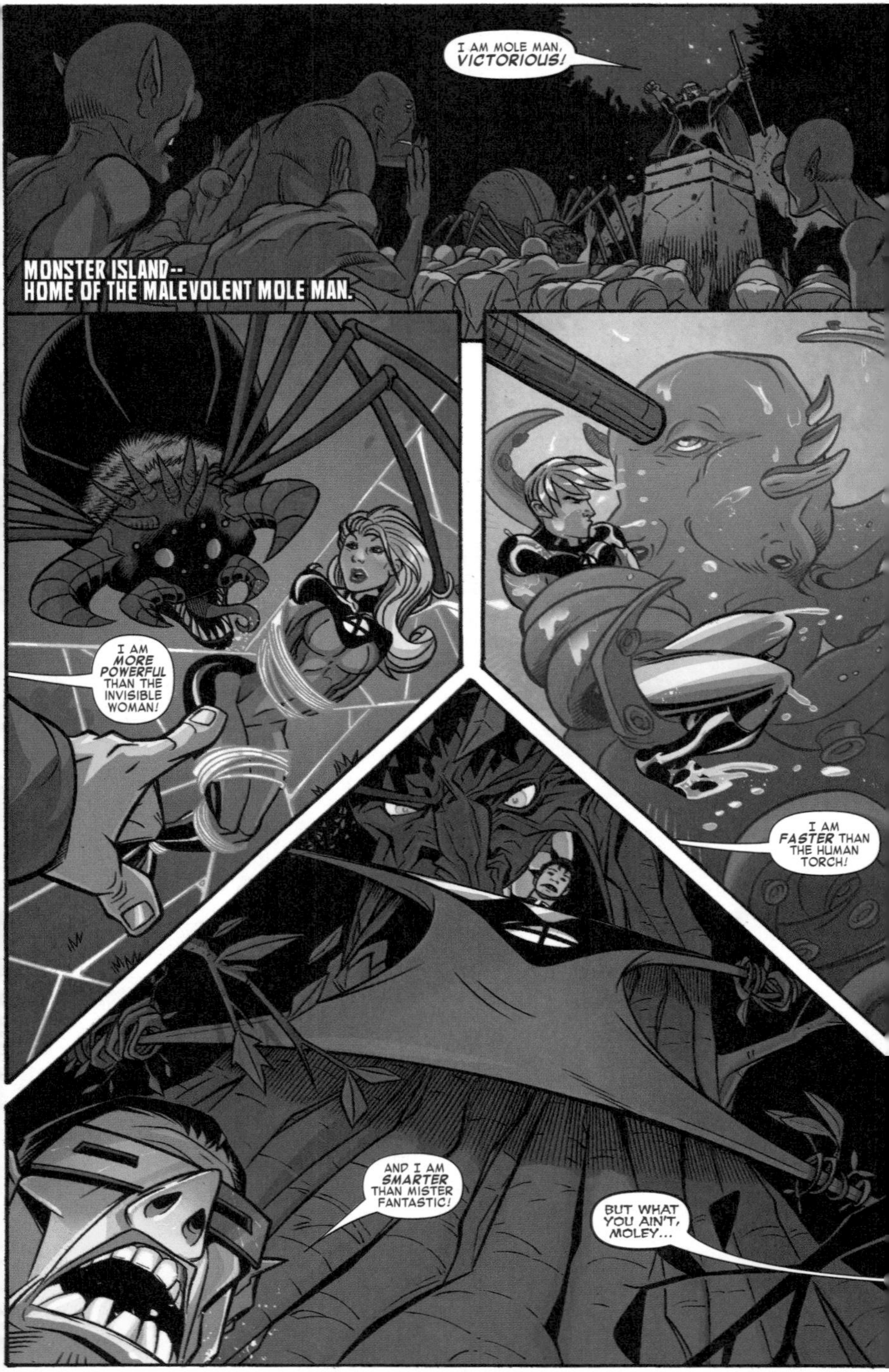

I AM MOLE MAN, VICTORIOUS!
MONSTER ISLAND-- HOME OF THE MALEVOLENT MOLE MAN.
I AM MORE POWERFUL THAN THE INVISIBLE WOMAN!
I AM FASTER THAN THE HUMAN TORCH!
AND I AM SMARTER THAN MISTER FANTASTIC!
BUT WHAT YOU AIN'T, MOLEY...

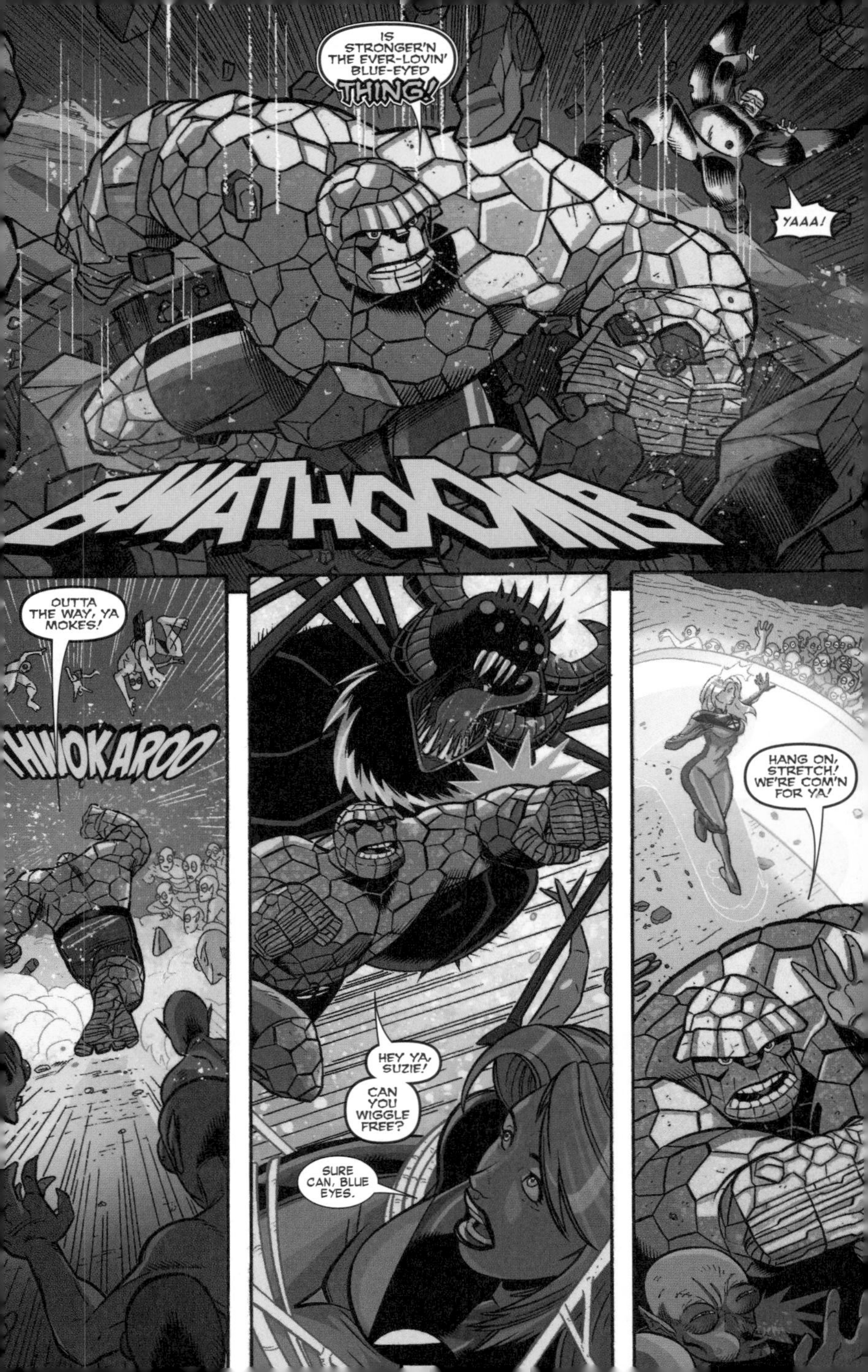
IS STRONGER'N THE EVER-LOVIN' BLUE-EYED THING!
YAAA!
BWATHOOMB
OUTTA THE WAY, YA MOKES!
THWOK AROO
HANG ON, STRETCH! WE'RE COM'N FOR YA!
HEY YA, SUZIE!
CAN YOU WIGGLE FREE?
SURE CAN, BLUE EYES.

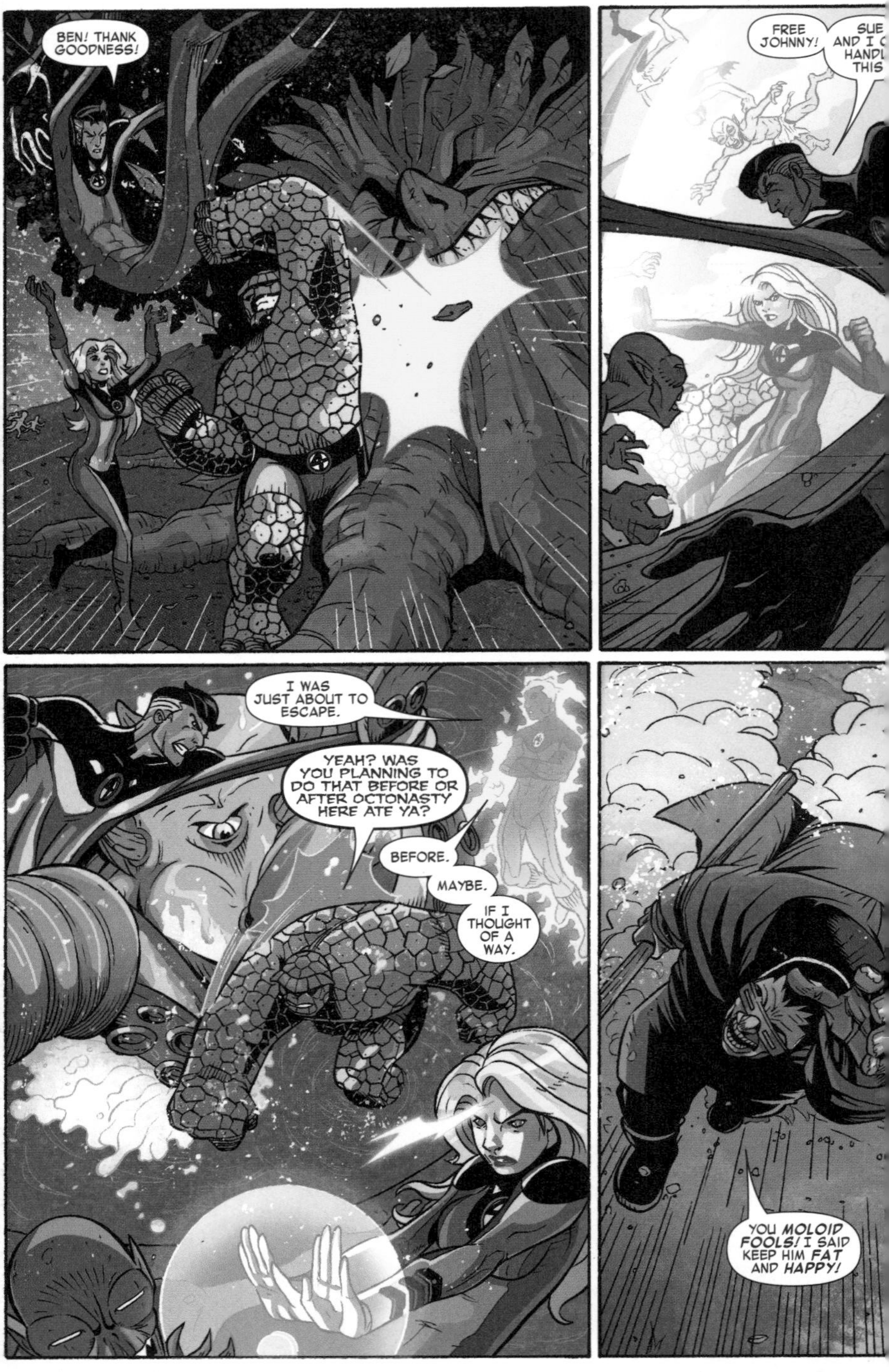
BEN! THANK GOODNESS!
FREE JOHNNY!
SUE AND I C HANDL THIS
I WAS JUST ABOUT TO ESCAPE.
YEAH? WAS YOU PLANNING TO DO THAT BEFORE OR AFTER OCTONASTY HERE ATE YA?
BEFORE.
MAYBE.
IF I THOUGHT OF A WAY.
YOU MOLOID FOOLS! I SAID KEEP HIM FAT AND HAPPY!

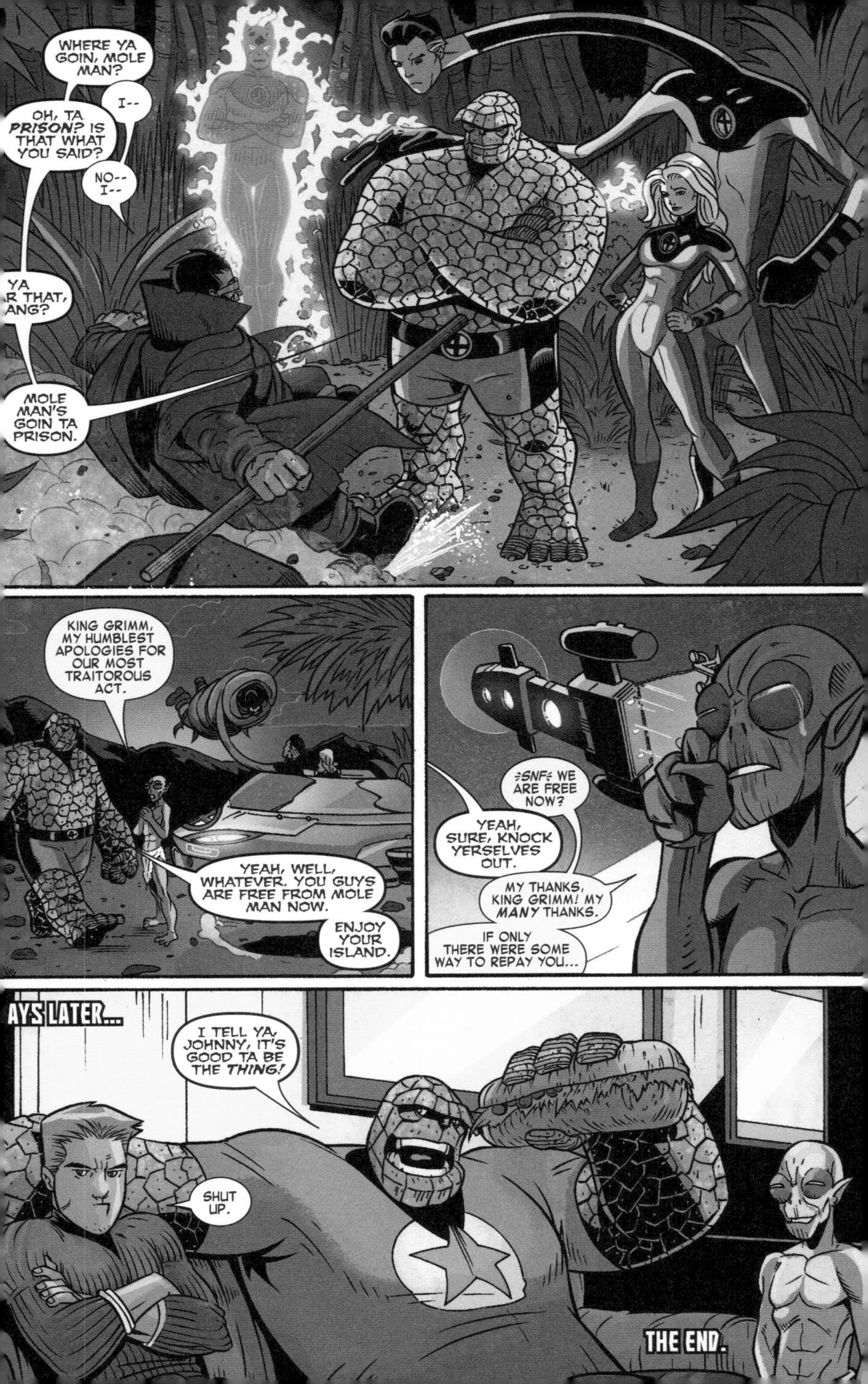
WHERE YA GOIN, MOLE MAN?
I--
OH, TA PRISON? IS THAT WHAT YOU SAID?
NO-- I--
YA R THAT, ANG?
MOLE MAN'S GOIN TA PRISON.
KING GRIMM, MY HUMBLEST APOLOGIES FOR OUR MOST TRAITOROUS ACT.
YEAH, WELL, WHATEVER. YOU GUYS ARE FREE FROM MOLE MAN NOW.
ENJOY YOUR ISLAND.
SNF WE ARE FREE NOW?
YEAH, SURE, KNOCK YERSELVES OUT.
MY THANKS, KING GRIMM! MY MANY THANKS.
IF ONLY THERE WERE SOME WAY TO REPAY YOU...
AYS LATER...
I TELL YA, JOHNNY, IT'S GOOD TA BE THE THING!
SHUT UP.
THE END.

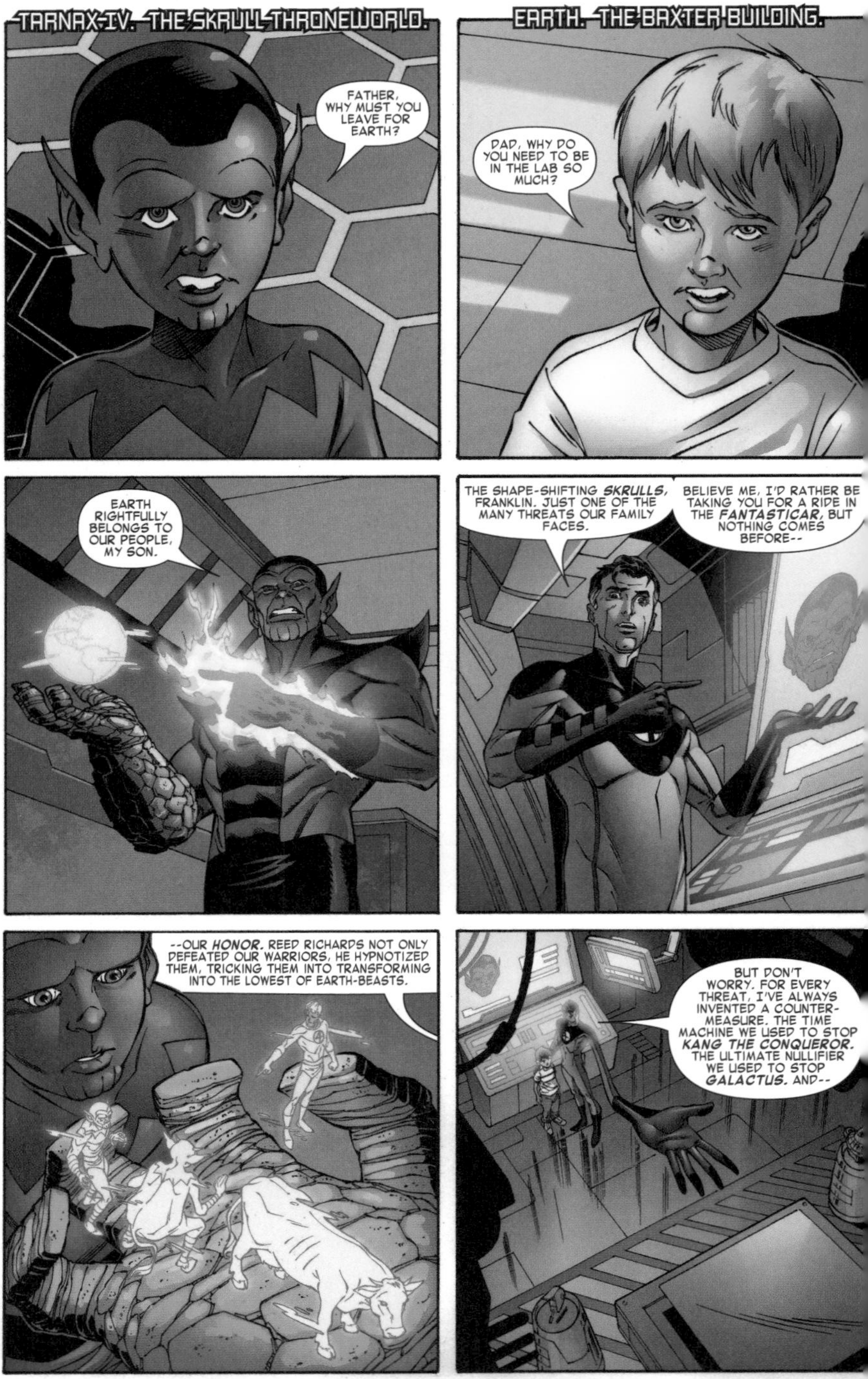
TARNAX-IV. THE SKRULL THRONEWORLD.
FATHER, WHY MUST YOU LEAVE FOR EARTH?
EARTH. THE BAXTER BUILDING.
DAD, WHY DO YOU NEED TO BE IN THE LAB SO MUCH?
EARTH RIGHTFULLY BELONGS TO OUR PEOPLE, MY SON.
THE SHAPE-SHIFTING SKRULLS, FRANKLIN. JUST ONE OF THE MANY THREATS OUR FAMILY FACES.
BELIEVE ME, I'D RATHER BE TAKING YOU FOR A RIDE IN THE FANTASTICAR, BUT NOTHING COMES BEFORE--
--OUR HONOR. REED RICHARDS NOT ONLY DEFEATED OUR WARRIORS, HE HYPNOTIZED THEM, TRICKING THEM INTO TRANSFORMING INTO THE LOWEST OF EARTH-BEASTS.
BUT DON'T WORRY. FOR EVERY THREAT, I'VE ALWAYS INVENTED A COUNTER-MEASURE. THE TIME MACHINE WE USED TO STOP KANG THE CONQUEROR. THE ULTIMATE NULLIFIER WE USED TO STOP GALACTUS. AND--

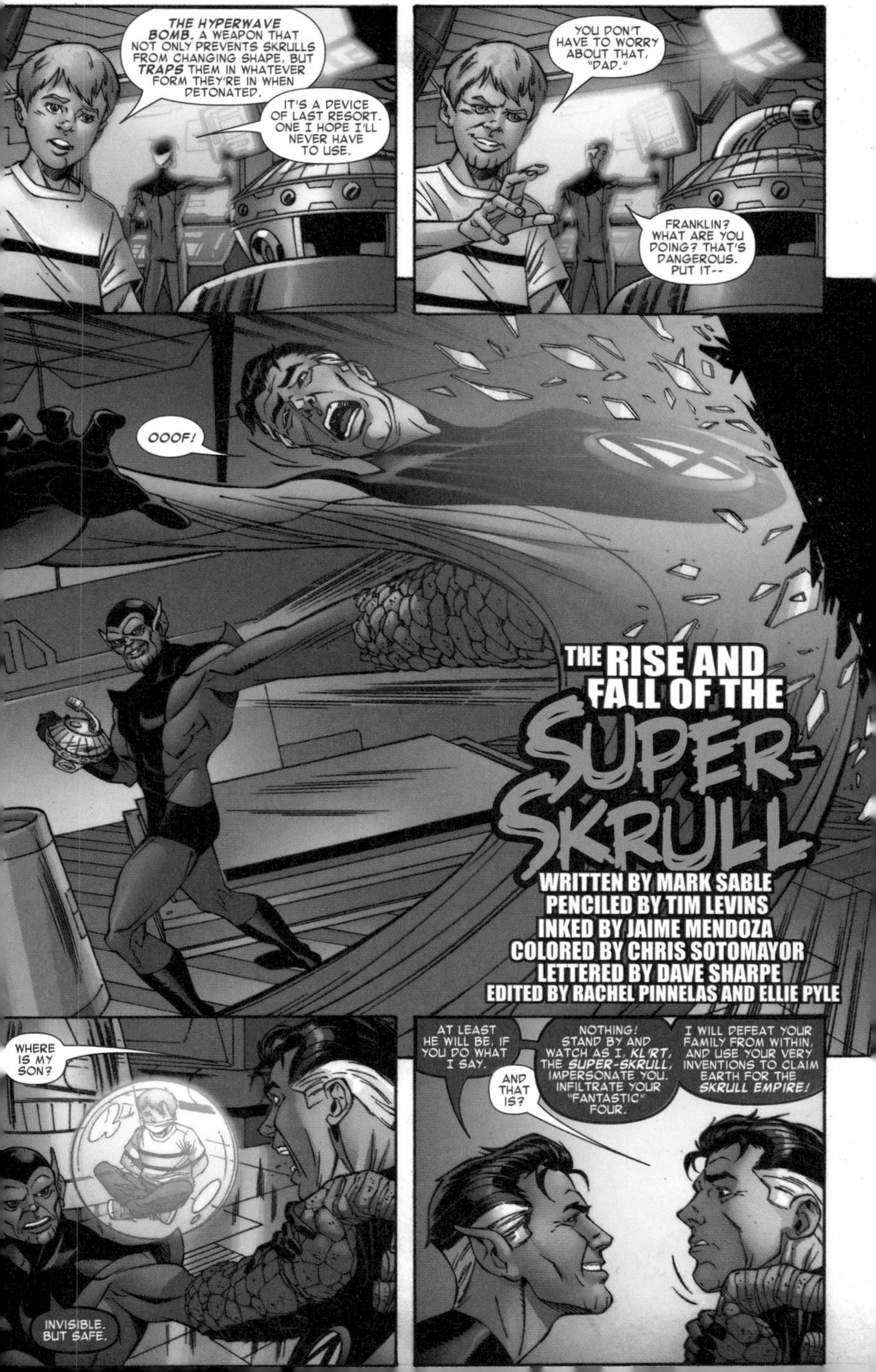
THE HYPERWAVE BOMB. A WEAPON THAT NOT ONLY PREVENTS SKRULLS FROM CHANGING SHAPE, BUT TRAPS THEM IN WHATEVER FORM THEY'RE IN WHEN DETONATED.
IT'S A DEVICE OF LAST RESORT. ONE I HOPE I'LL NEVER HAVE TO USE.
YOU DON'T HAVE TO WORRY ABOUT THAT, "DAD."
FRANKLIN? WHAT ARE YOU DOING? THAT'S DANGEROUS. PUT IT--
OOOF!
THE RISE AND FALL OF THE SUPER-SKRULL
WRITTEN BY MARK SABLE
PENCILED BY TIM LEVINS
INKED BY JAIME MENDOZA
COLORED BY CHRIS SOTOMAYOR
LETTERED BY DAVE SHARPE
EDITED BY RACHEL PINNELAS AND ELLIE PYLE
WHERE IS MY SON?
INVISIBLE. BUT SAFE.
AT LEAST HE WILL BE, IF YOU DO WHAT I SAY.
AND THAT IS?
NOTHING! STAND BY AND WATCH AS I, KL'RT, THE SUPER-SKRULL, IMPERSONATE YOU. INFILTRATE YOUR "FANTASTIC" FOUR.
I WILL DEFEAT YOUR FAMILY FROM WITHIN, AND USE YOUR VERY INVENTIONS TO CLAIM EARTH FOR THE SKRULL EMPIRE!

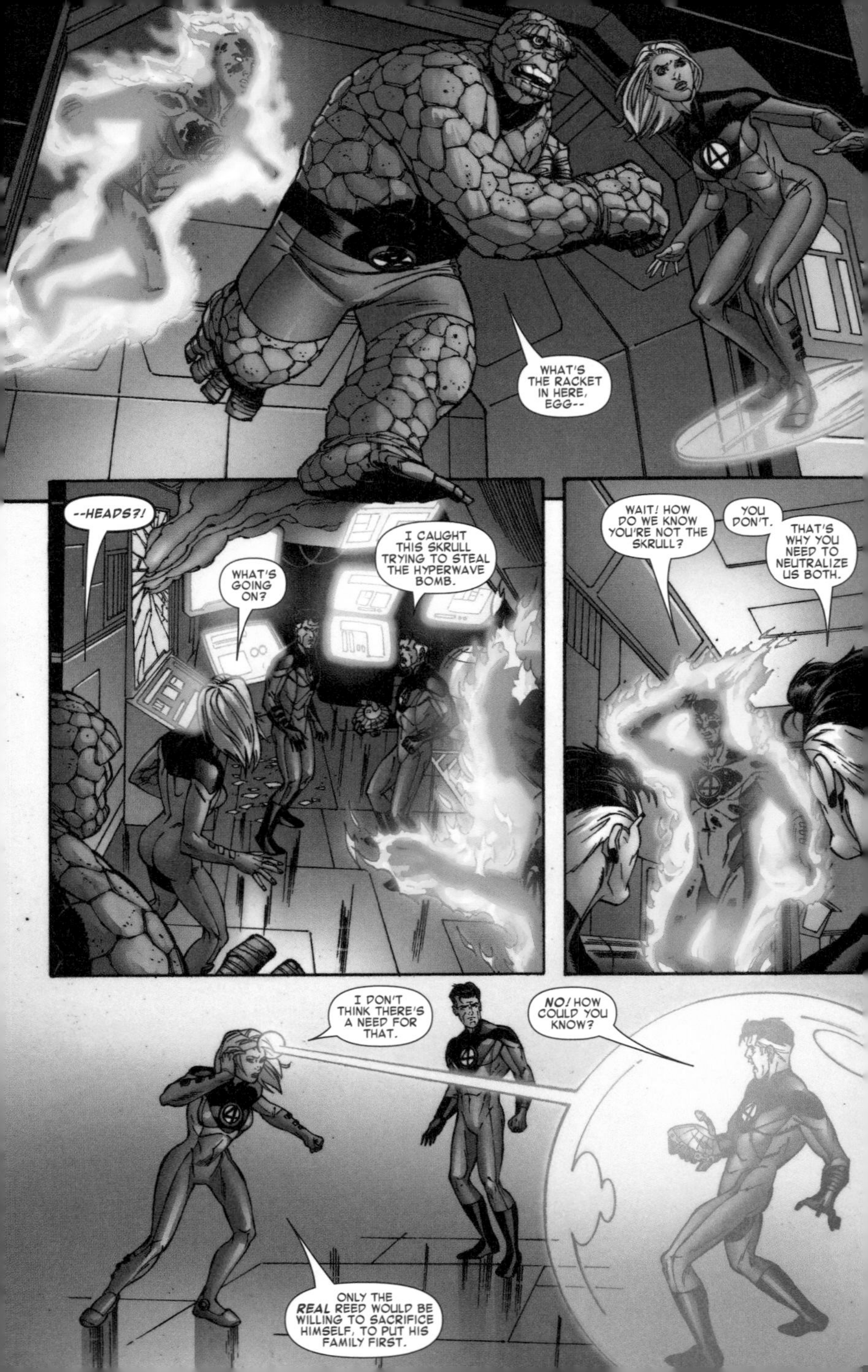
WHAT'S THE RACKET IN HERE, EGG--
--HEADS?!
WHAT'S GOING ON?
I CAUGHT THIS SKRULL TRYING TO STEAL THE HYPERWAVE BOMB.
WAIT! HOW DO WE KNOW YOU'RE NOT THE SKRULL?
YOU DON'T.
THAT'S WHY YOU NEED TO NEUTRALIZE US BOTH.
I DON'T THINK THERE'S A NEED FOR THAT.
NO! HOW COULD YOU KNOW?
ONLY THE REAL REED WOULD BE WILLING TO SACRIFICE HIMSELF, TO PUT HIS FAMILY FIRST.

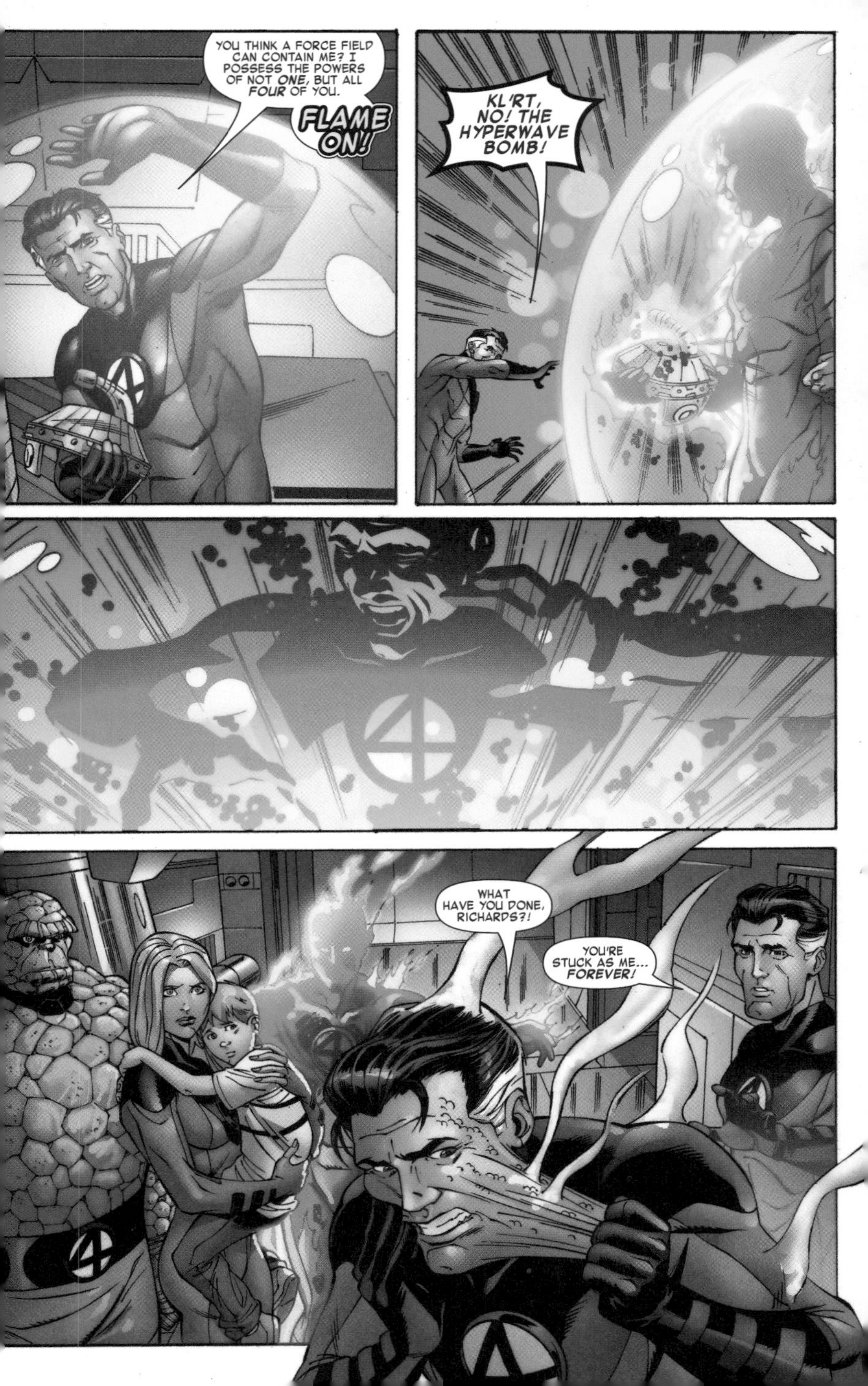
YOU THINK A FORCE FIELD CAN CONTAIN ME? I POSSESS THE POWERS OF NOT *ONE*, BUT ALL *FOUR* OF YOU.
FLAME ON!
KL'RT, NO! THE HYPERWAVE BOMB!
WHAT HAVE YOU DONE, RICHARDS?!
YOU'RE STUCK AS ME... *FOREVER!*

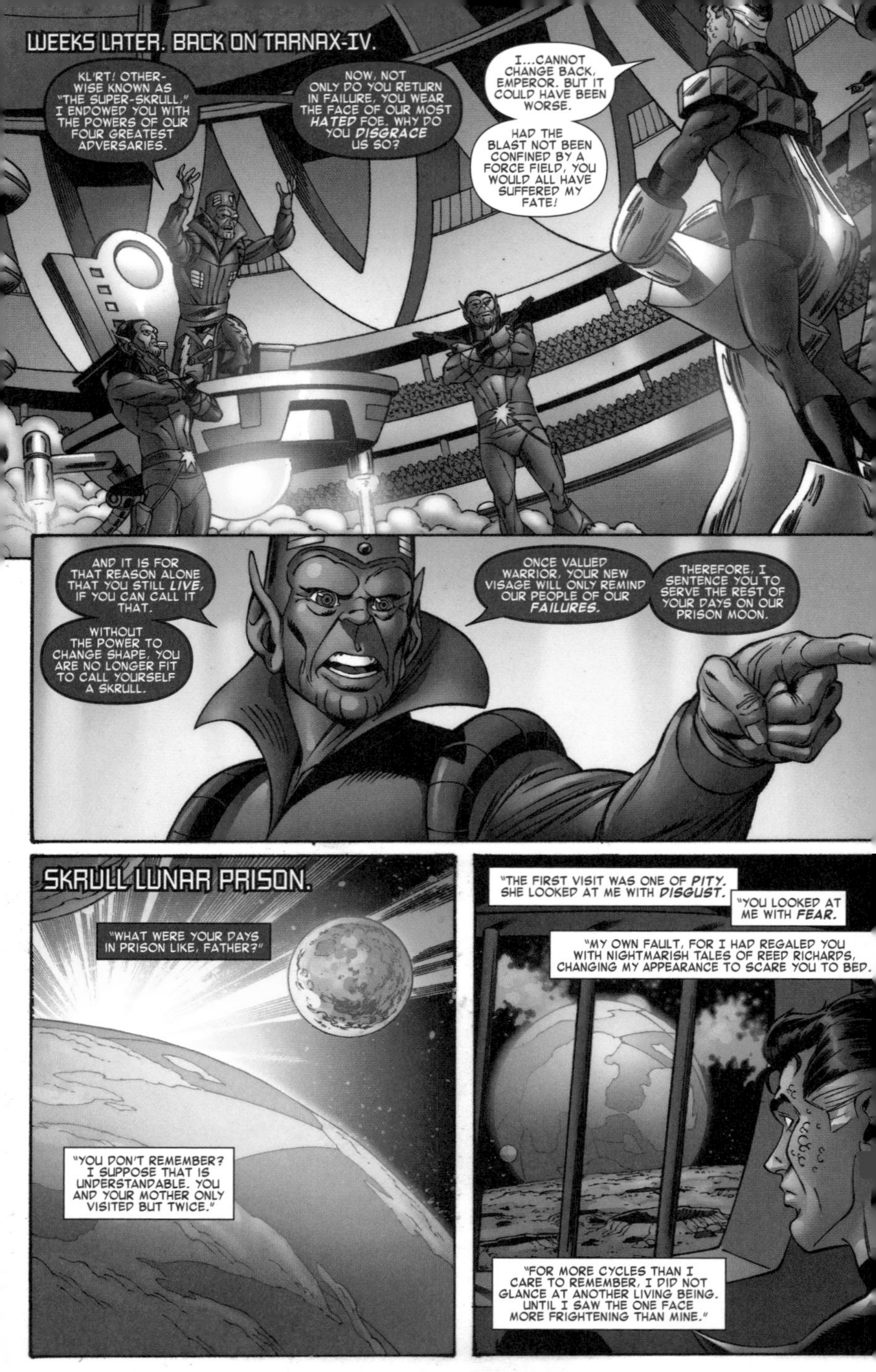
WEEKS LATER. BACK ON TARNAX-IV.
KL'RT! OTHER-WISE KNOWN AS "THE SUPER-SKRULL," I ENDOWED YOU WITH THE POWERS OF OUR FOUR GREATEST ADVERSARIES.
NOW, NOT ONLY DO YOU RETURN IN FAILURE, YOU WEAR THE FACE OF OUR MOST HATED FOE. WHY DO YOU DISGRACE US SO?
I...CANNOT CHANGE BACK, EMPEROR. BUT IT COULD HAVE BEEN WORSE.
HAD THE BLAST NOT BEEN CONFINED BY A FORCE FIELD, YOU WOULD ALL HAVE SUFFERED MY FATE!
AND IT IS FOR THAT REASON ALONE THAT YOU STILL LIVE, IF YOU CAN CALL IT THAT.
WITHOUT THE POWER TO CHANGE SHAPE, YOU ARE NO LONGER FIT TO CALL YOURSELF A SKRULL.
ONCE VALUED WARRIOR, YOUR NEW VISAGE WILL ONLY REMIND OUR PEOPLE OF OUR FAILURES.
THEREFORE, I SENTENCE YOU TO SERVE THE REST OF YOUR DAYS ON OUR PRISON MOON.
SKRULL LUNAR PRISON.
"WHAT WERE YOUR DAYS IN PRISON LIKE, FATHER?"
"YOU DON'T REMEMBER? I SUPPOSE THAT IS UNDERSTANDABLE. YOU AND YOUR MOTHER ONLY VISITED BUT TWICE."
"THE FIRST VISIT WAS ONE OF PITY. SHE LOOKED AT ME WITH DISGUST.
"YOU LOOKED AT ME WITH FEAR.
"MY OWN FAULT, FOR I HAD REGALED YOU WITH NIGHTMARISH TALES OF REED RICHARDS, CHANGING MY APPEARANCE TO SCARE YOU TO BED.
"FOR MORE CYCLES THAN I CARE TO REMEMBER, I DID NOT GLANCE AT ANOTHER LIVING BEING. UNTIL I SAW THE ONE FACE MORE FRIGHTENING THAN MINE."

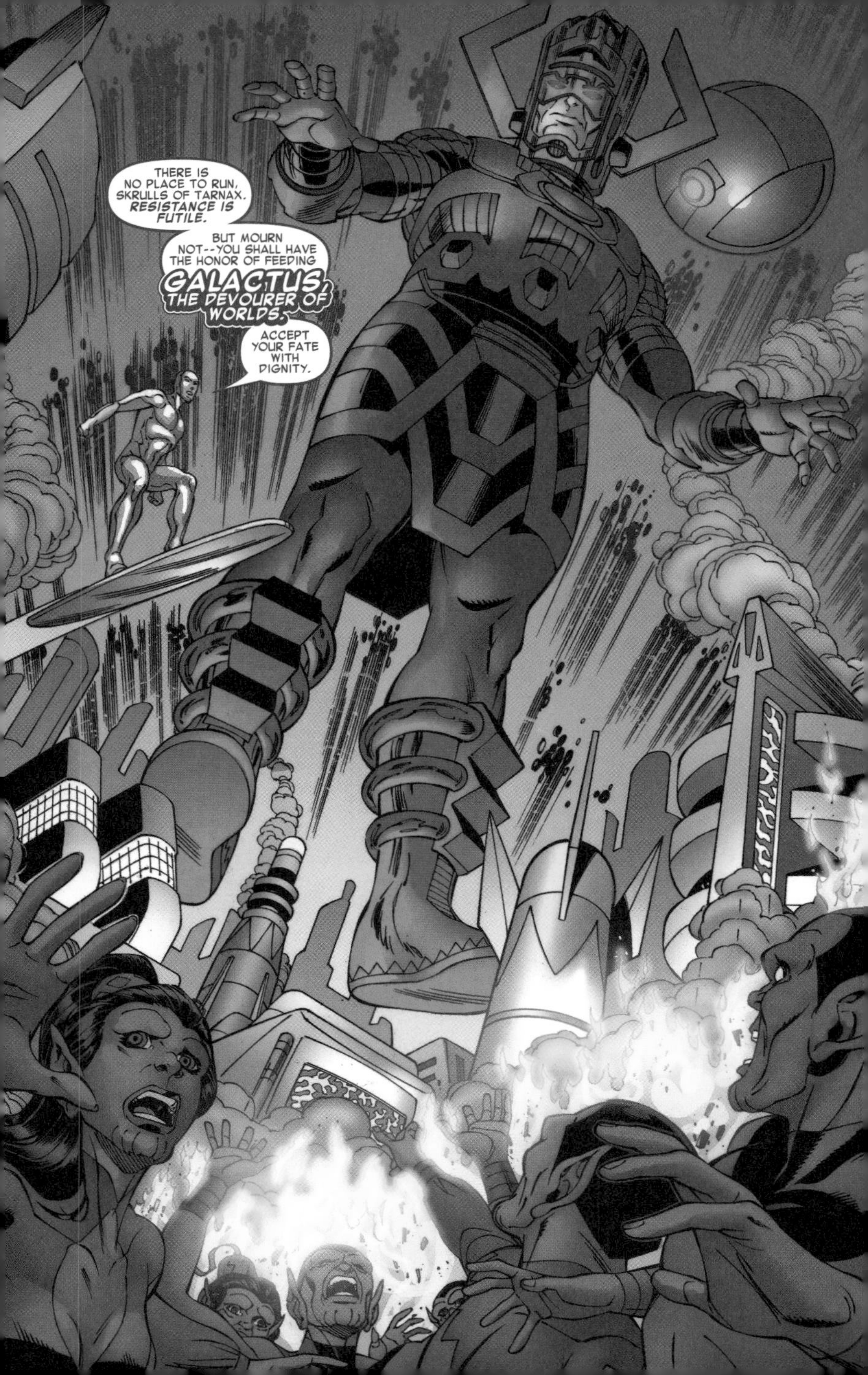
THERE IS NO PLACE TO RUN, SKRULLS OF TARNAX. RESISTANCE IS FUTILE.
BUT MOURN NOT--YOU SHALL HAVE THE HONOR OF FEEDING GALACTUS, THE DEVOURER OF WORLDS.
ACCEPT YOUR FATE WITH DIGNITY.

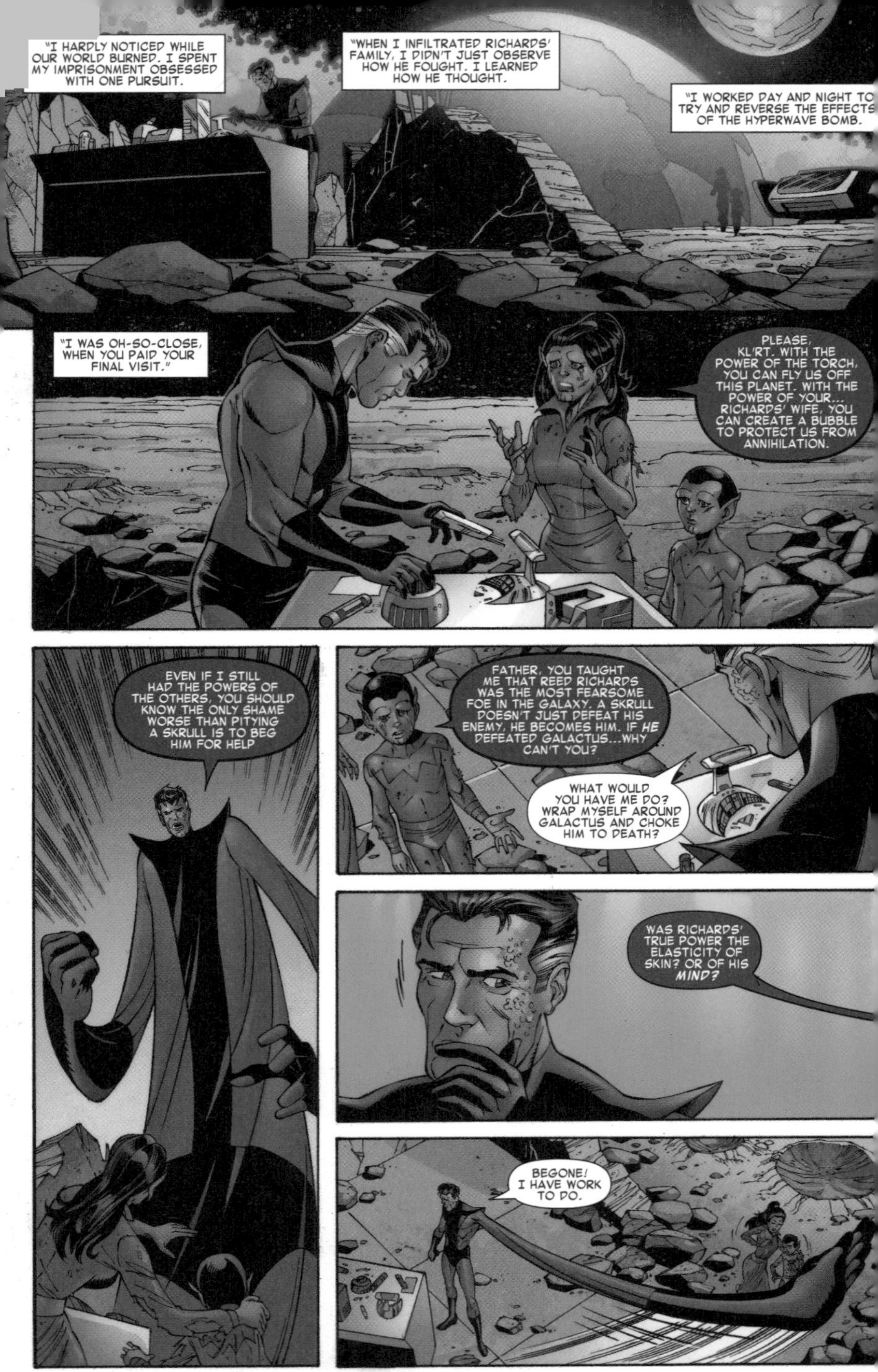
"I HARDLY NOTICED WHILE OUR WORLD BURNED. I SPENT MY IMPRISONMENT OBSESSED WITH ONE PURSUIT.
"WHEN I INFILTRATED RICHARDS' FAMILY, I DIDN'T JUST OBSERVE HOW HE FOUGHT. I LEARNED HOW HE THOUGHT.
"I WORKED DAY AND NIGHT TO TRY AND REVERSE THE EFFECTS OF THE HYPERWAVE BOMB.
"I WAS OH-SO-CLOSE, WHEN YOU PAID YOUR FINAL VISIT."
PLEASE, KL'RT. WITH THE POWER OF THE TORCH, YOU CAN FLY US OFF THIS PLANET. WITH THE POWER OF YOUR... RICHARDS' WIFE, YOU CAN CREATE A BUBBLE TO PROTECT US FROM ANNIHILATION.
EVEN IF I STILL HAD THE POWERS OF THE OTHERS, YOU SHOULD KNOW THE ONLY SHAME WORSE THAN PITYING A SKRULL IS TO BEG HIM FOR HELP
FATHER, YOU TAUGHT ME THAT REED RICHARDS WAS THE MOST FEARSOME FOE IN THE GALAXY. A SKRULL DOESN'T JUST DEFEAT HIS ENEMY, HE BECOMES HIM. IF *HE* DEFEATED GALACTUS...WHY CAN'T YOU?
WHAT WOULD YOU HAVE ME DO? WRAP MYSELF AROUND GALACTUS AND CHOKE HIM TO DEATH?
WAS RICHARDS' TRUE POWER THE ELASTICITY OF SKIN? OR OF HIS *MIND?*
BEGONE! I HAVE WORK TO DO.

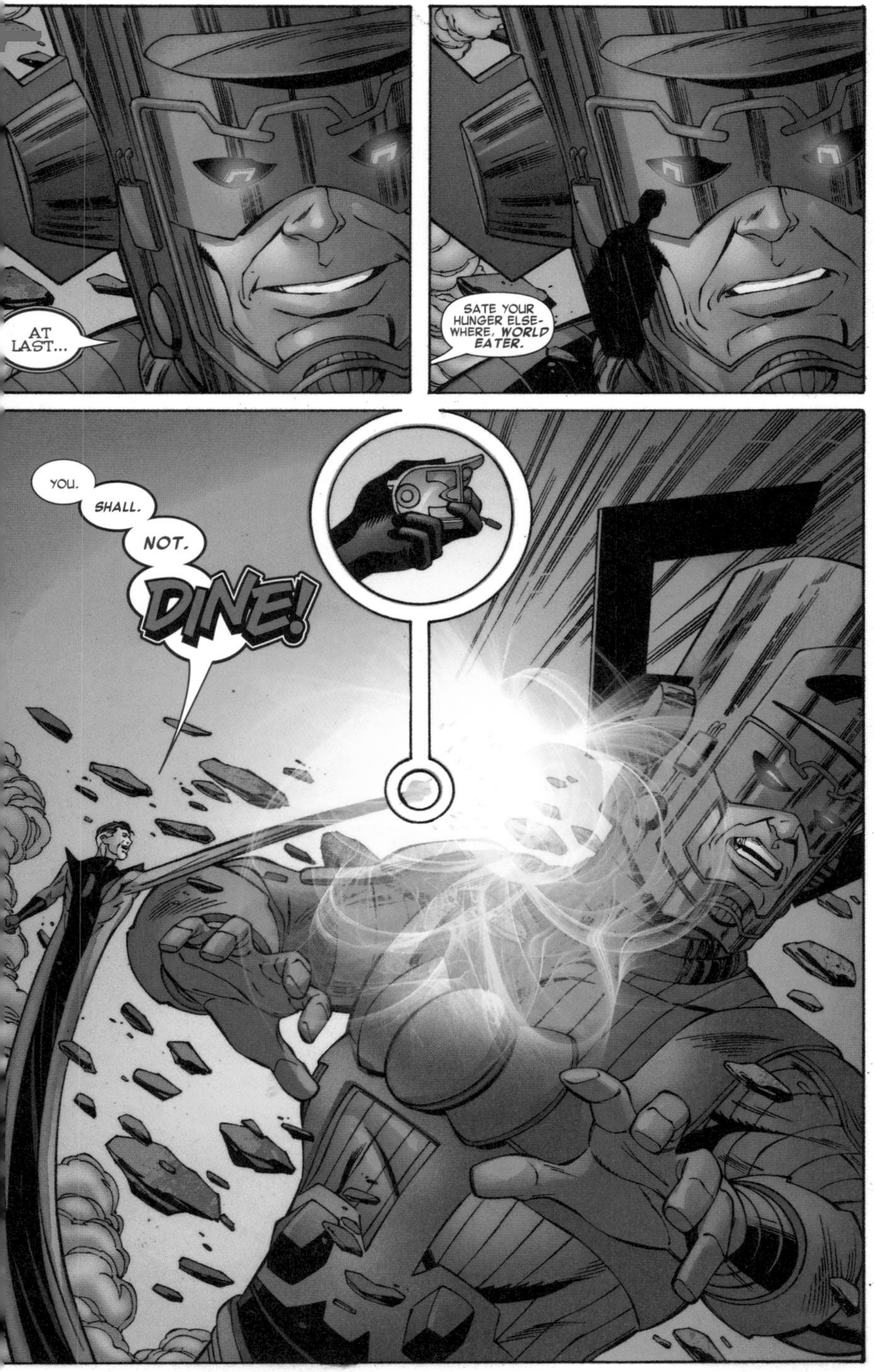
AT LAST...
SATE YOUR HUNGER ELSE-WHERE, WORLD EATER.
YOU.
SHALL.
NOT.
DINE!

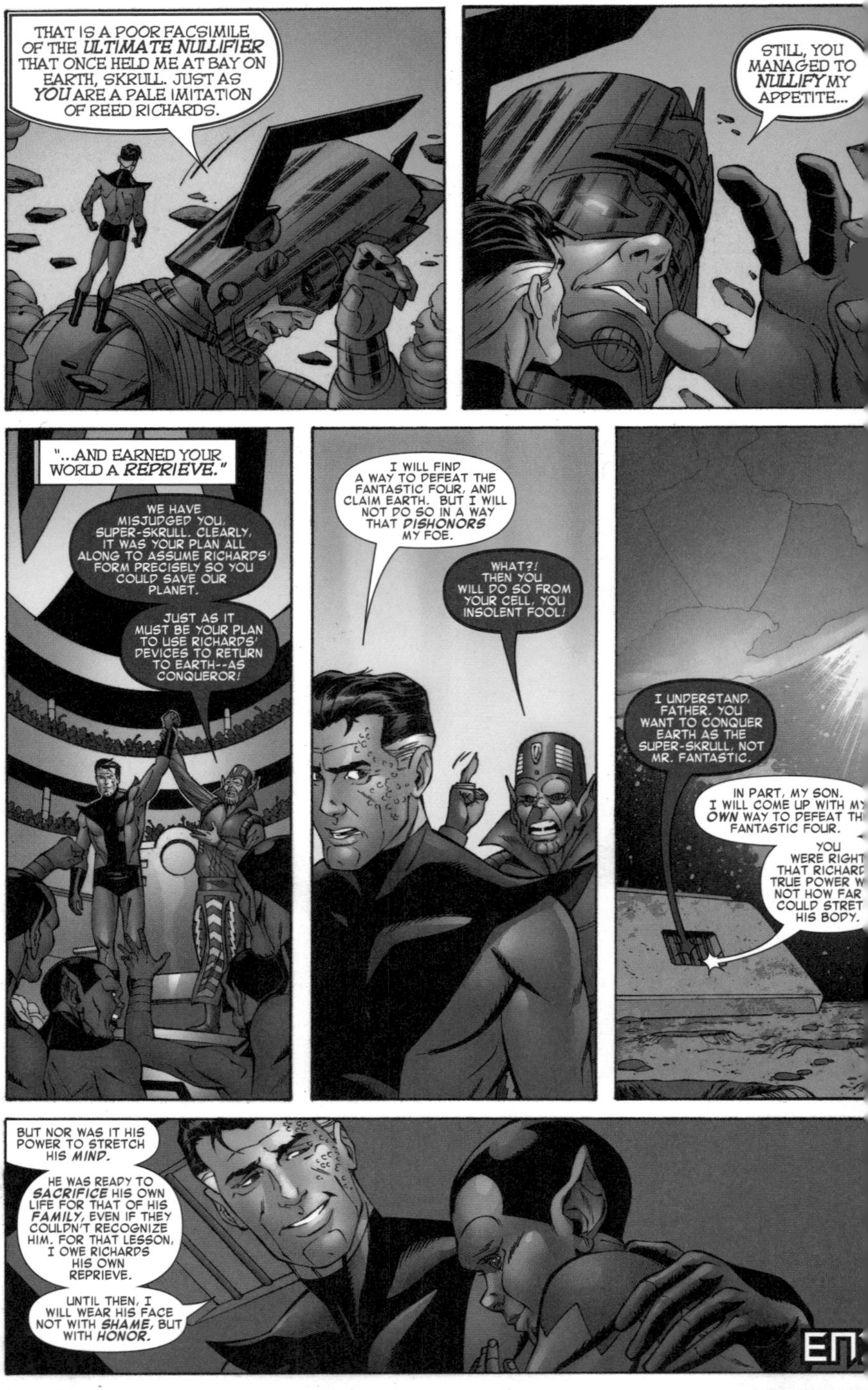
THAT IS A POOR FACSIMILE OF THE ULTIMATE NULLIFIER THAT ONCE HELD ME AT BAY ON EARTH, SKRULL. JUST AS YOU ARE A PALE IMITATION OF REED RICHARDS.
STILL, YOU MANAGED TO NULLIFY MY APPETITE...
"...AND EARNED YOUR WORLD A REPRIEVE."
WE HAVE MISJUDGED YOU, SUPER-SKRULL. CLEARLY, IT WAS YOUR PLAN ALL ALONG TO ASSUME RICHARDS' FORM PRECISELY SO YOU COULD SAVE OUR PLANET.
JUST AS IT MUST BE YOUR PLAN TO USE RICHARDS' DEVICES TO RETURN TO EARTH--AS CONQUEROR!
I WILL FIND A WAY TO DEFEAT THE FANTASTIC FOUR, AND CLAIM EARTH. BUT I WILL NOT DO SO IN A WAY THAT DISHONORS MY FOE.
WHAT?! THEN YOU WILL DO SO FROM YOUR CELL, YOU INSOLENT FOOL!
I UNDERSTAND, FATHER. YOU WANT TO CONQUER EARTH AS THE SUPER-SKRULL, NOT MR. FANTASTIC.
IN PART, MY SON. I WILL COME UP WITH M OWN WAY TO DEFEAT TH FANTASTIC FOUR.
YOU WERE RIGHT THAT RICHAR TRUE POWER W NOT HOW FAR COULD STRET HIS BODY.
BUT NOR WAS IT HIS POWER TO STRETCH HIS MIND.
HE WAS READY TO SACRIFICE HIS OWN LIFE FOR THAT OF HIS FAMILY, EVEN IF THEY COULDN'T RECOGNIZE HIM. FOR THAT LESSON, I OWE RICHARDS HIS OWN REPRIEVE.
UNTIL THEN, I WILL WEAR HIS FACE NOT WITH SHAME, BUT WITH HONOR.
EN

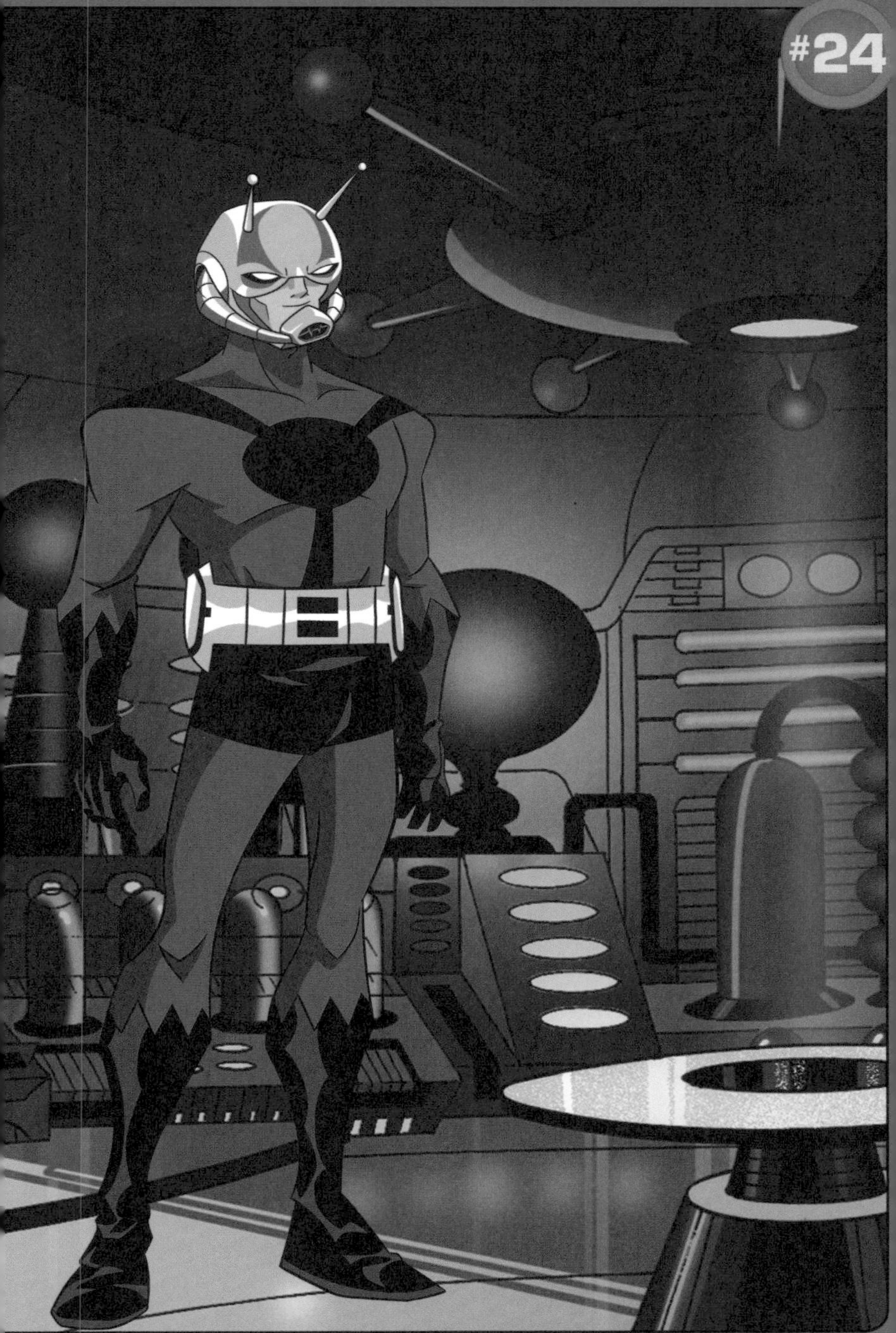
#24

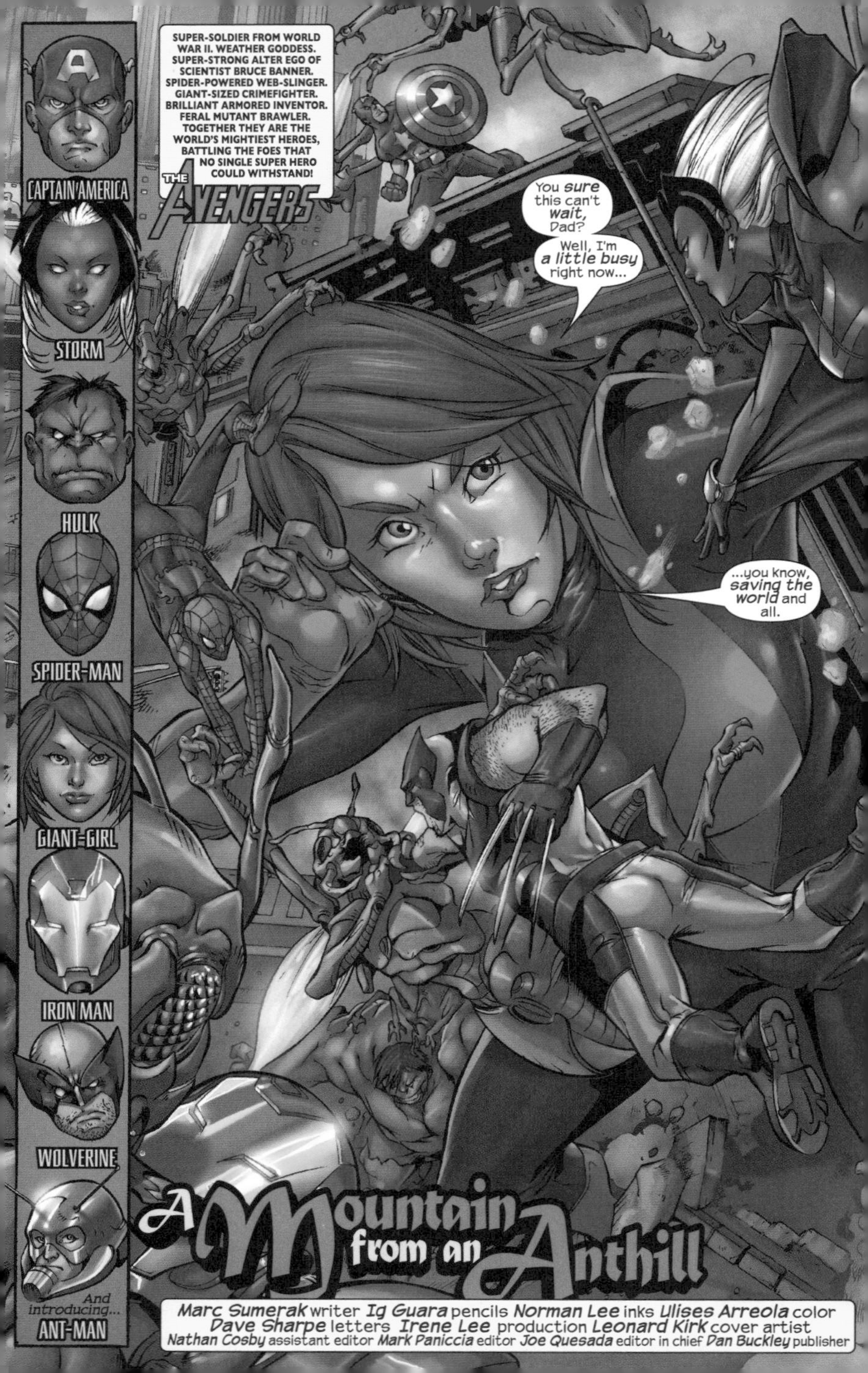

SUPER-SOLDIER FROM WORLD WAR II. WEATHER GODDESS. SUPER-STRONG ALTER EGO OF SCIENTIST BRUCE BANNER. SPIDER-POWERED WEB-SLINGER. GIANT-SIZED CRIMEFIGHTER. BRILLIANT ARMORED INVENTOR. FERAL MUTANT BRAWLER. TOGETHER THEY ARE THE WORLD'S MIGHTIEST HEROES, BATTLING THE FOES THAT NO SINGLE SUPER HERO COULD WITHSTAND!
THE AVENGERS
CAPTAIN AMERICA
STORM
HULK
SPIDER-MAN
GIANT-GIRL
IRON MAN
WOLVERINE
And introducing... ANT-MAN
You sure this can't wait, Dad?
Well, I'm a little busy right now...
...you know, saving the world and all.
A Mountain from an Anthill
Marc Sumerak writer Ig Guara pencils Norman Lee inks Ulises Arreola color
Dave Sharpe letters Irene Lee production Leonard Kirk cover artist
Nathan Cosby assistant editor Mark Paniccia editor Joe Quesada editor in chief Dan Buckley publisher

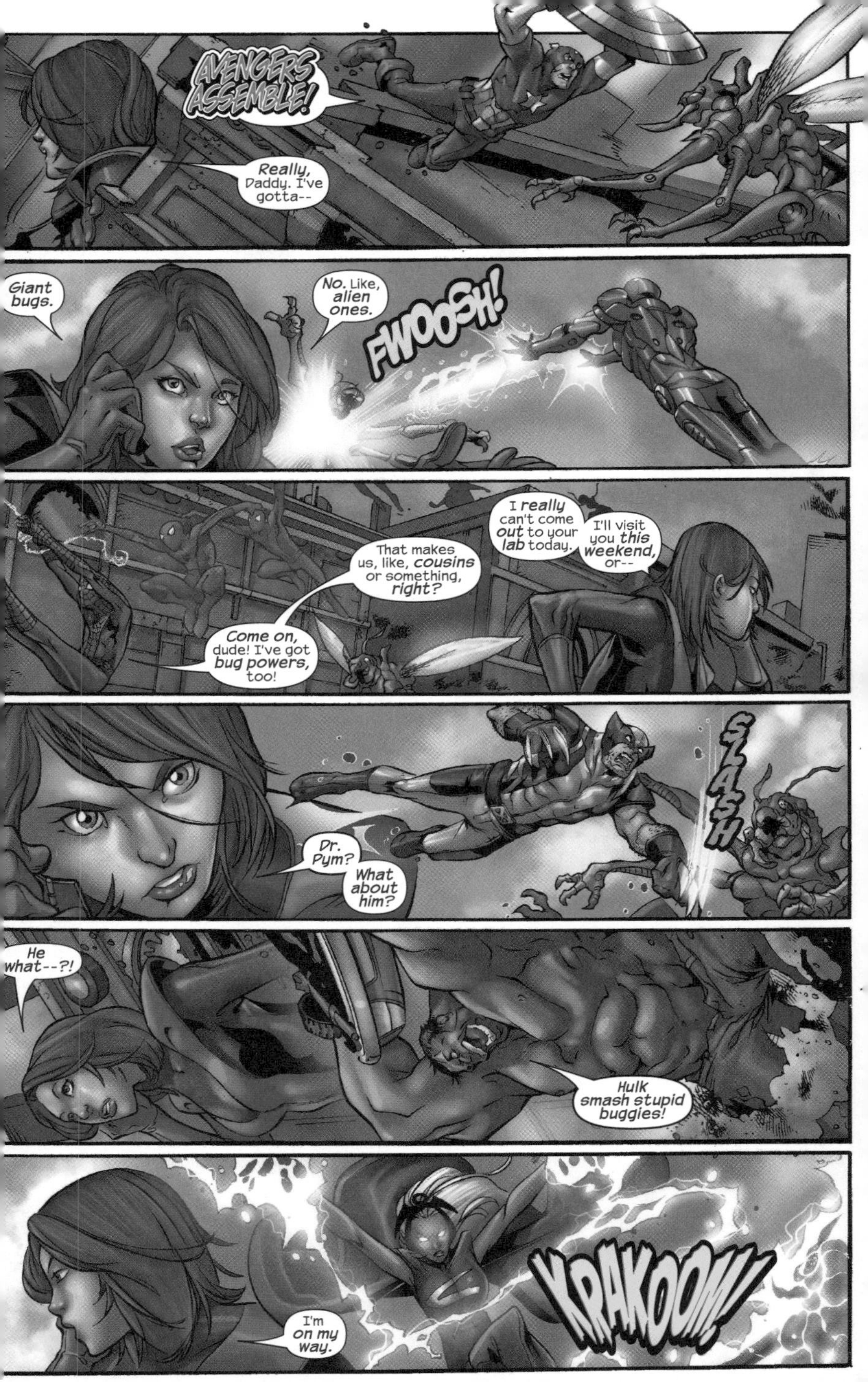
AVENGERS ASSEMBLE!
Really, Daddy. I've gotta--
Giant bugs.
No. Like, alien ones.
FWOOSH!
I really can't come out to your lab today.
I'll visit you this weekend, or--
That makes us, like, cousins or something, right?
Come on, dude! I've got bug powers, too!
SLASH
Dr. Pym? What about him?
He what--?!
Hulk smash stupid buggies!
I'm on my way.
KRAKOOM!

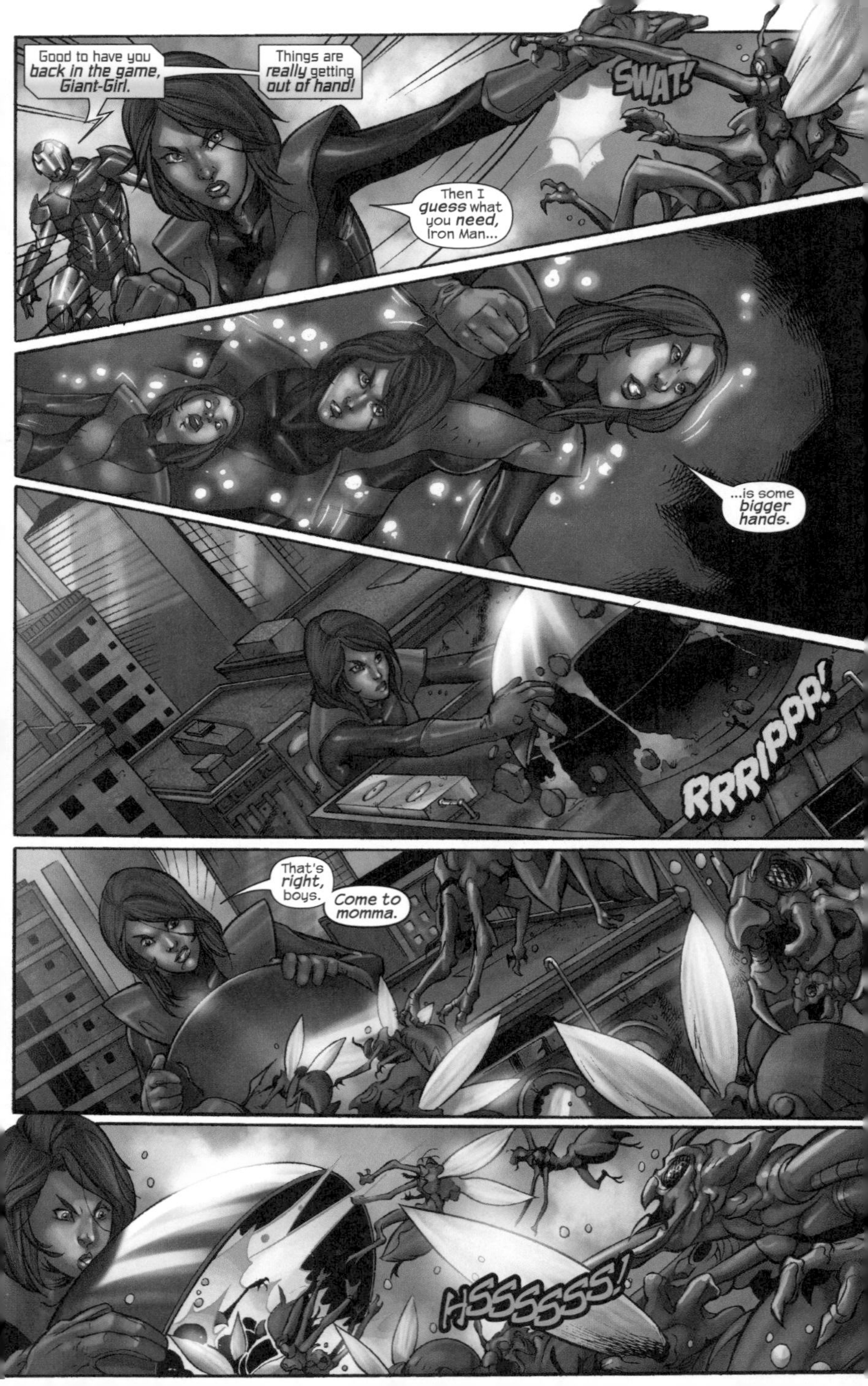

Good to have you back in the game, Giant-Girl.
Things are really getting out of hand!
SWAT!
Then I guess what you need, Iron Man...
...is some bigger hands.
RRRIPPP!
That's right, boys.
Come to momma.
HSSSSSS!

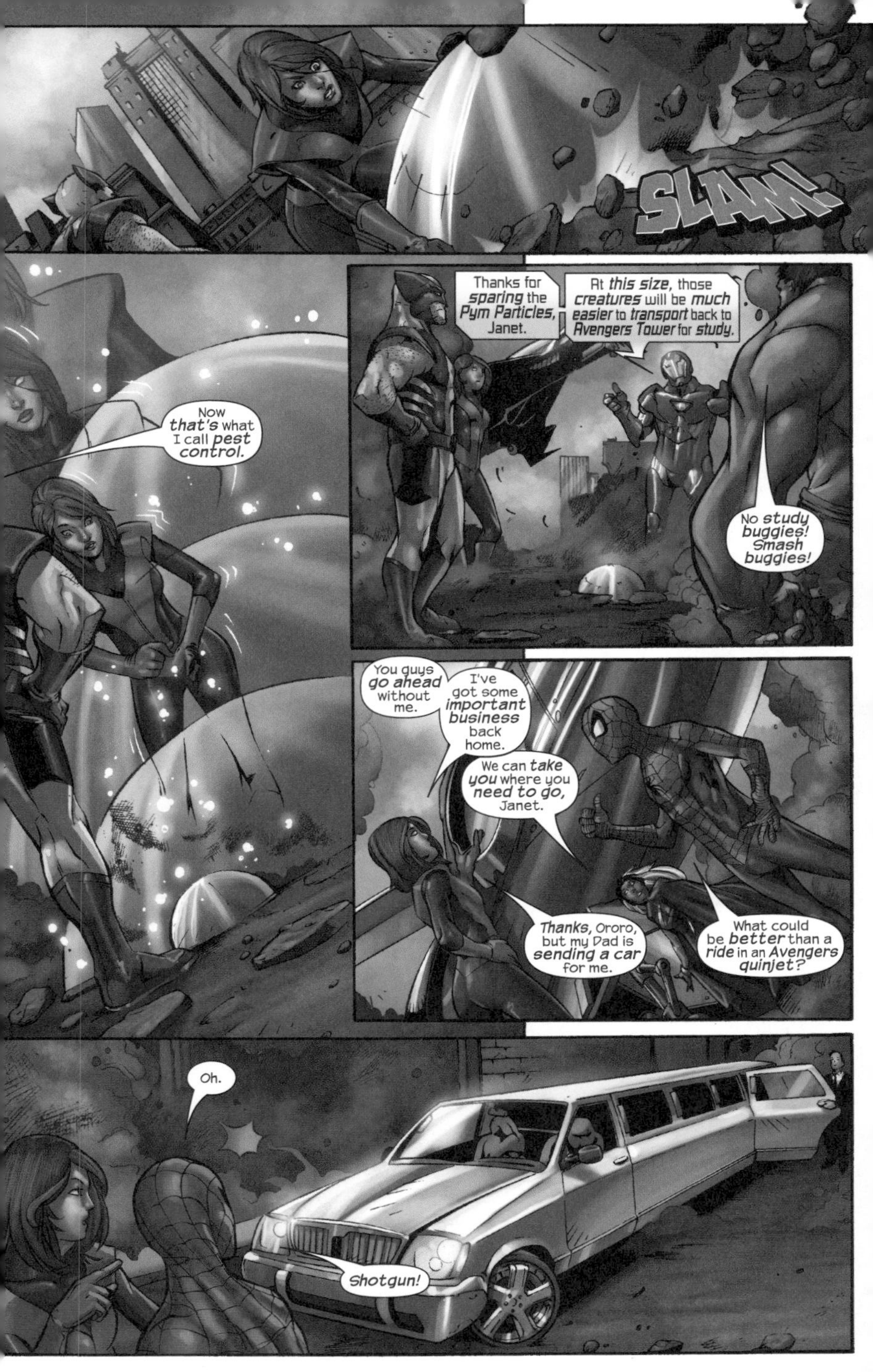
SLAM!
Now that's what I call pest control.
Thanks for sparing the Pym Particles, Janet.
At this size, those creatures will be much easier to transport back to Avengers Tower for study.
No study buggies! Smash buggies!
You guys go ahead without me.
I've got some important business back home.
We can take you where you need to go, Janet.
Thanks, Ororo, but my Dad is sending a car for me.
What could be better than a ride in an Avengers quinjet?
Oh.
Shotgun!

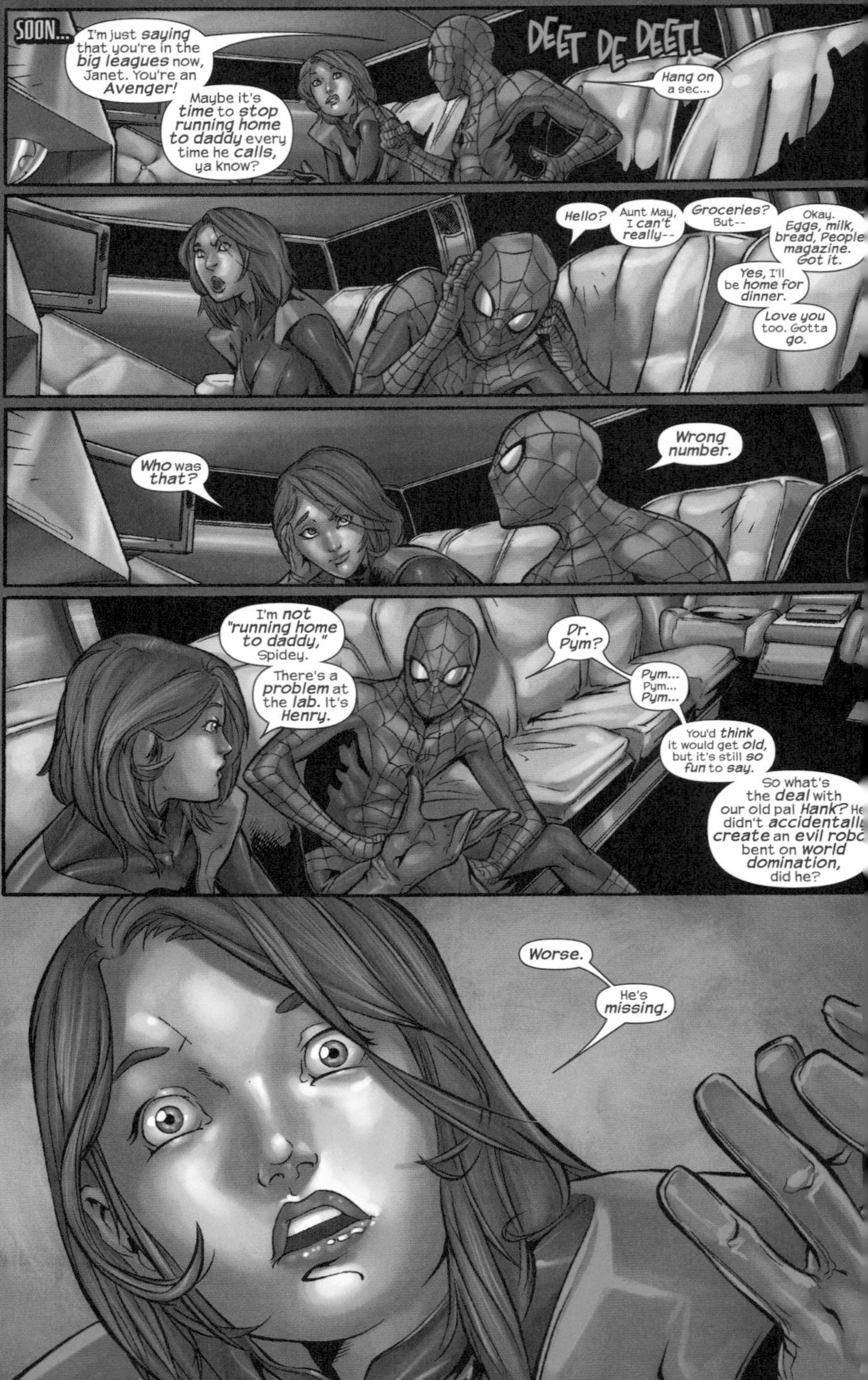
SOON...
I'm just saying that you're in the big leagues now, Janet. You're an Avenger!
Maybe it's time to stop running home to daddy every time he calls, ya know?
DEET DE DEET!
Hang on a sec...
Hello?
Aunt May, I can't really--
Groceries? But--
Okay. Eggs, milk, bread, People magazine. Got it.
Yes, I'll be home for dinner.
Love you too. Gotta go.
Who was that?
Wrong number.
I'm not "running home to daddy," Spidey.
There's a problem at the lab. It's Henry.
Dr. Pym?
Pym... Pym... Pym...
You'd think it would get old, but it's still so fun to say.
So what's the deal with our old pal Hank? He didn't accidentally create an evil robo bent on world domination, did he?
Worse.
He's missing.

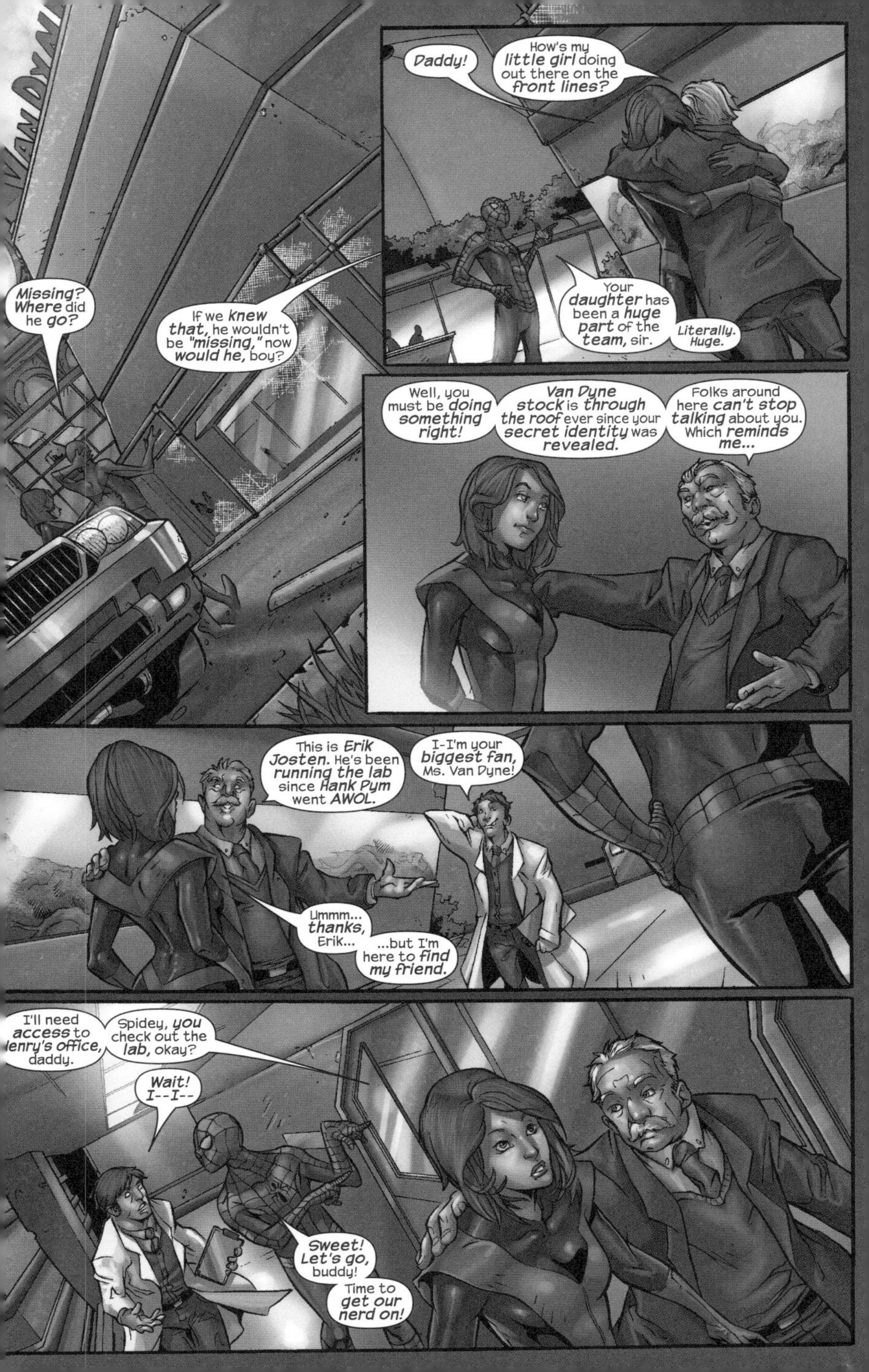

VAN DYNE
Missing? Where did he go?
If we knew that, he wouldn't be "missing," now would he, boy?
Daddy!
How's my little girl doing out there on the front lines?
Your daughter has been a huge part of the team, sir.
Literally. Huge.
Well, you must be doing something right!
Van Dyne stock is through the roof ever since your secret identity was revealed.
Folks around here can't stop talking about you. Which reminds me...
This is Erik Josten. He's been running the lab since Hank Pym went AWOL.
I-I'm your biggest fan, Ms. Van Dyne!
Ummm... thanks, Erik...
...but I'm here to find my friend.
I'll need access to Henry's office, daddy.
Spidey, you check out the lab, okay?
Wait! I--I--
Sweet! Let's go, buddy!
Time to get our nerd on!

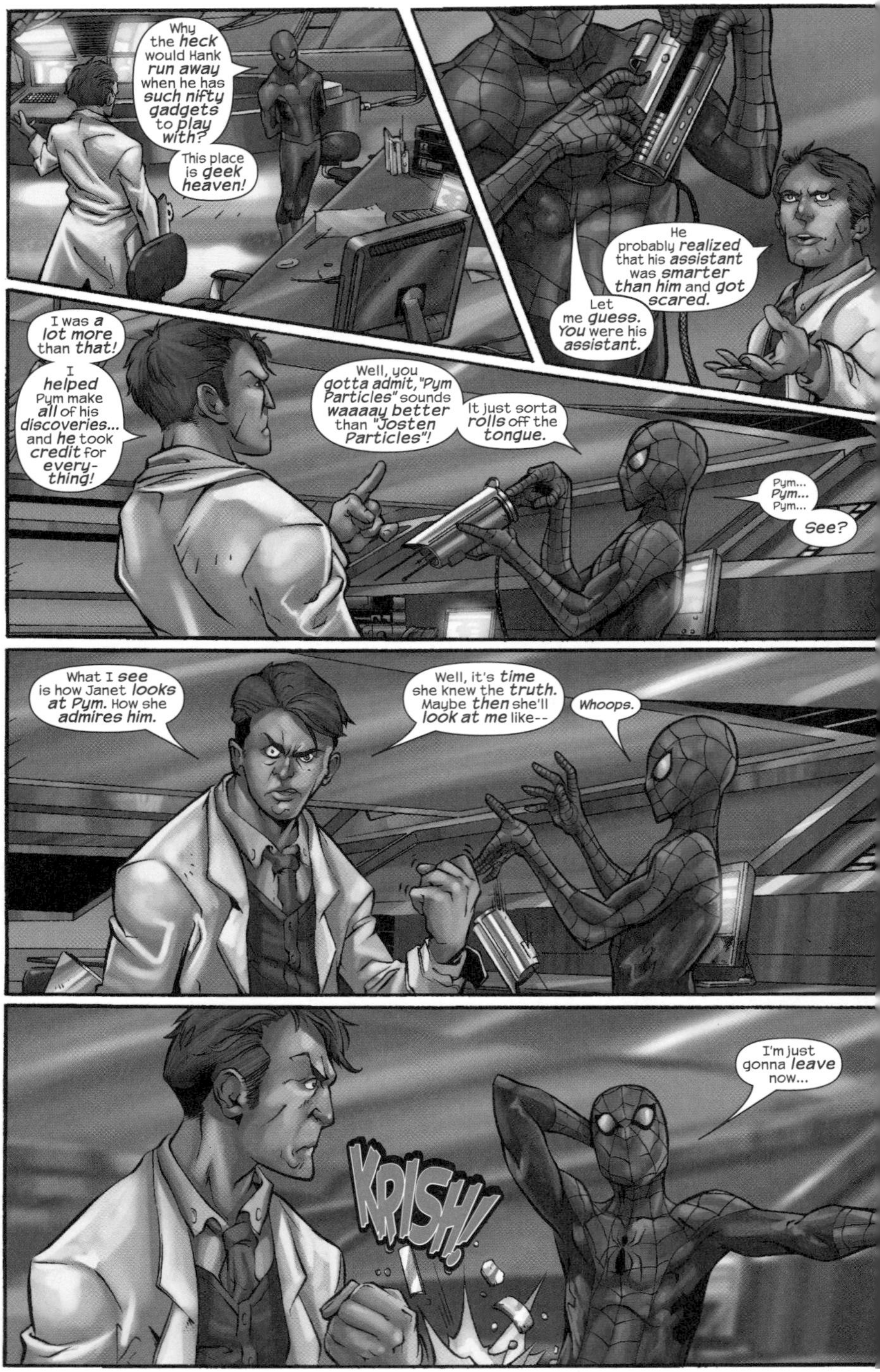
Why the heck would Hank run away when he has such nifty gadgets to play with?
This place is geek heaven!
He probably realized that his assistant was smarter than him and got scared.
Let me guess. You were his assistant.
I was a lot more than that!
I helped Pym make all of his discoveries... and he took credit for every-thing!
Well, you gotta admit, "Pym Particles" sounds waaaay better than "Josten Particles"!
It just sorta rolls off the tongue.
Pym... Pym... Pym...
See?
What I see is how Janet looks at Pym. How she admires him.
Well, it's time she knew the truth. Maybe then she'll look at me like--
Whoops.
KRISH!
I'm just gonna leave now...

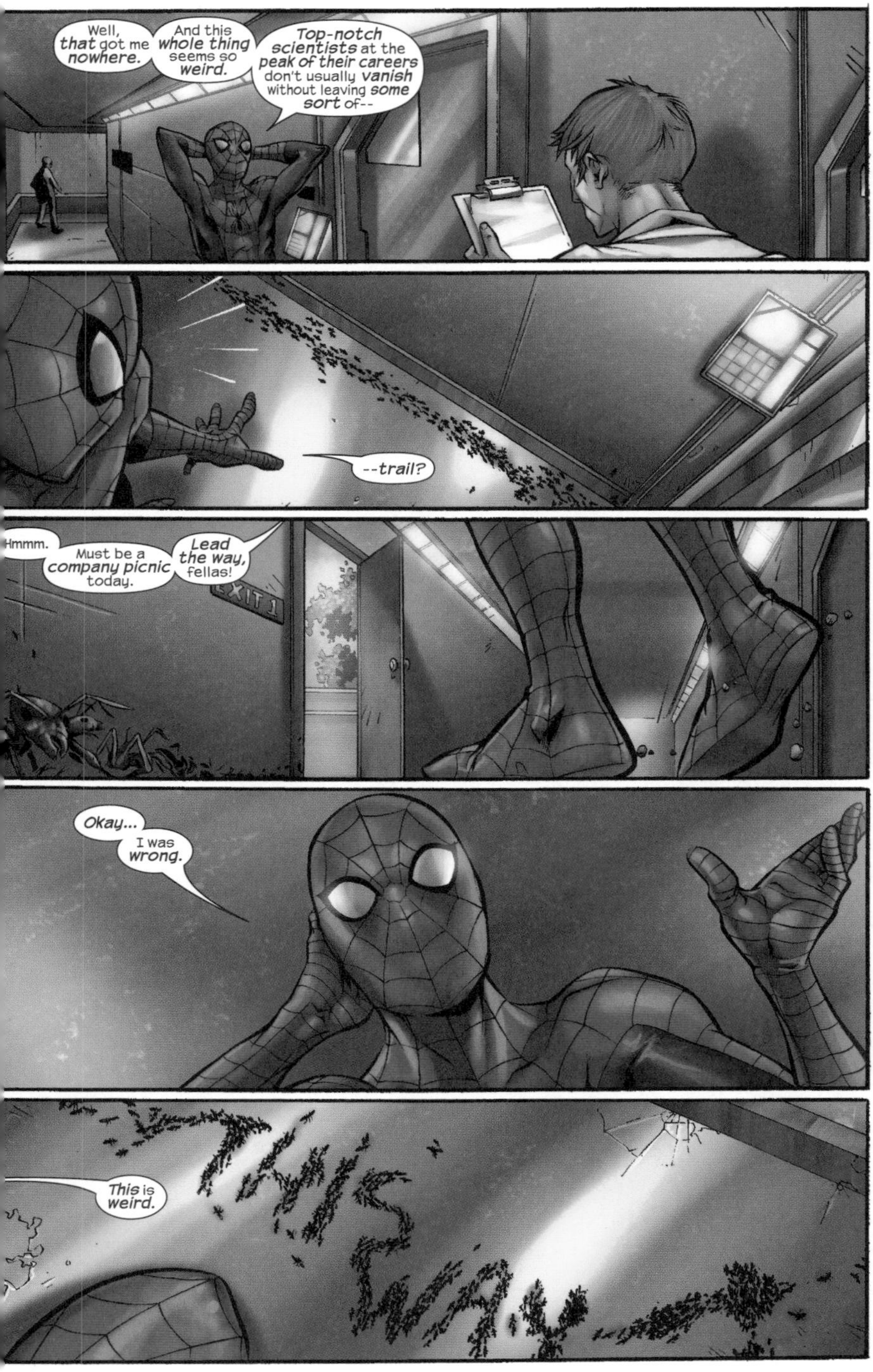
Well, that got me nowhere.
And this whole thing seems so weird.
Top-notch scientists at the peak of their careers don't usually vanish without leaving some sort of--
--trail?
Hmmm.
Must be a company picnic today.
Lead the way, fellas!
EXIT 1
Okay... I was wrong.
This is weird.
THIS WAY

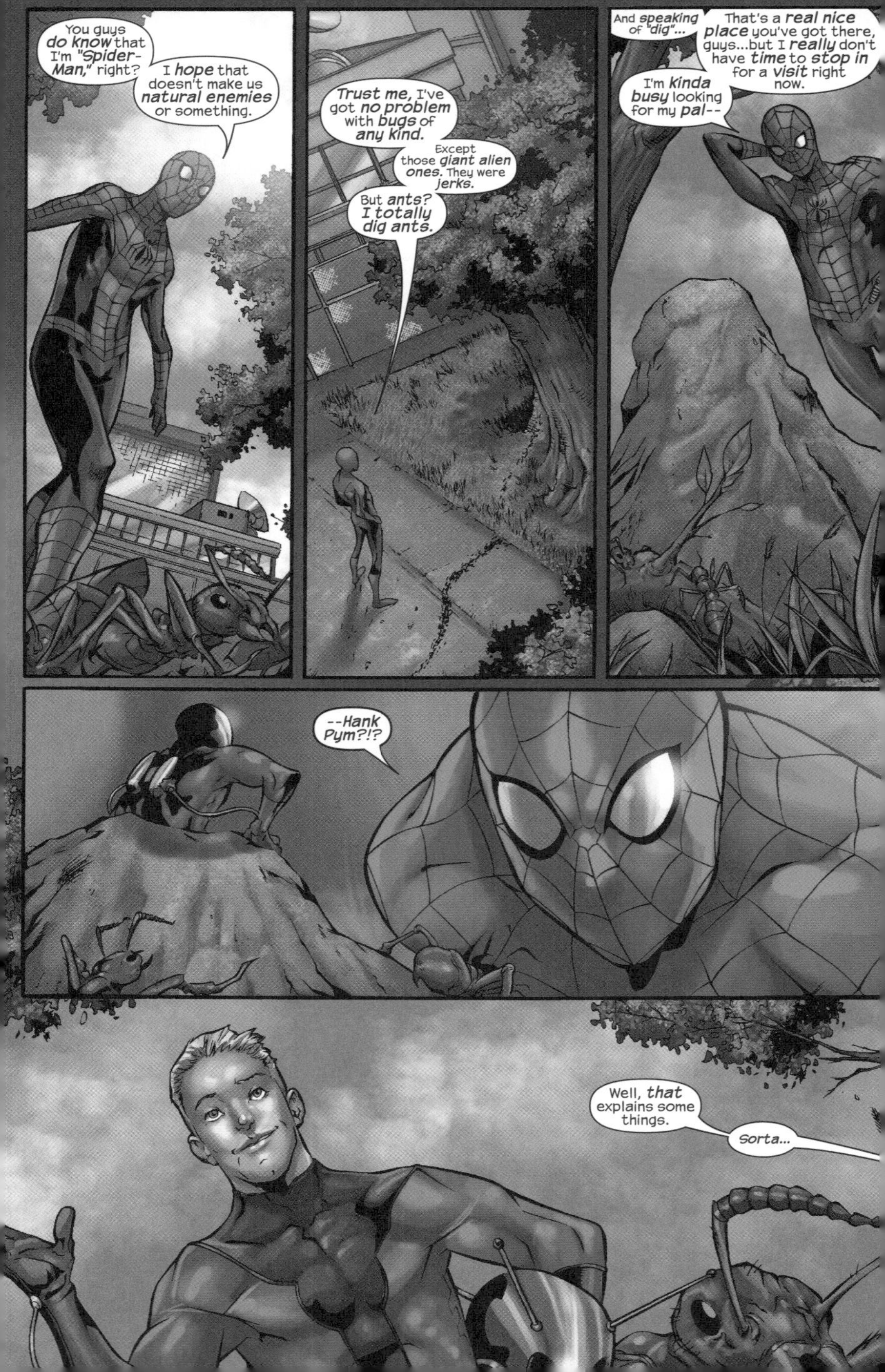

You guys do know that I'm "Spider-Man," right?
I hope that doesn't make us natural enemies or something.
Trust me, I've got no problem with bugs of any kind.
Except those giant alien ones. They were jerks.
But ants? I totally dig ants.
And speaking of "dig"...
That's a real nice place you've got there, guys...but I really don't have time to stop in for a visit right now.
I'm kinda busy looking for my pal--
--Hank Pym?!?
Well, that explains some things.
Sorta...

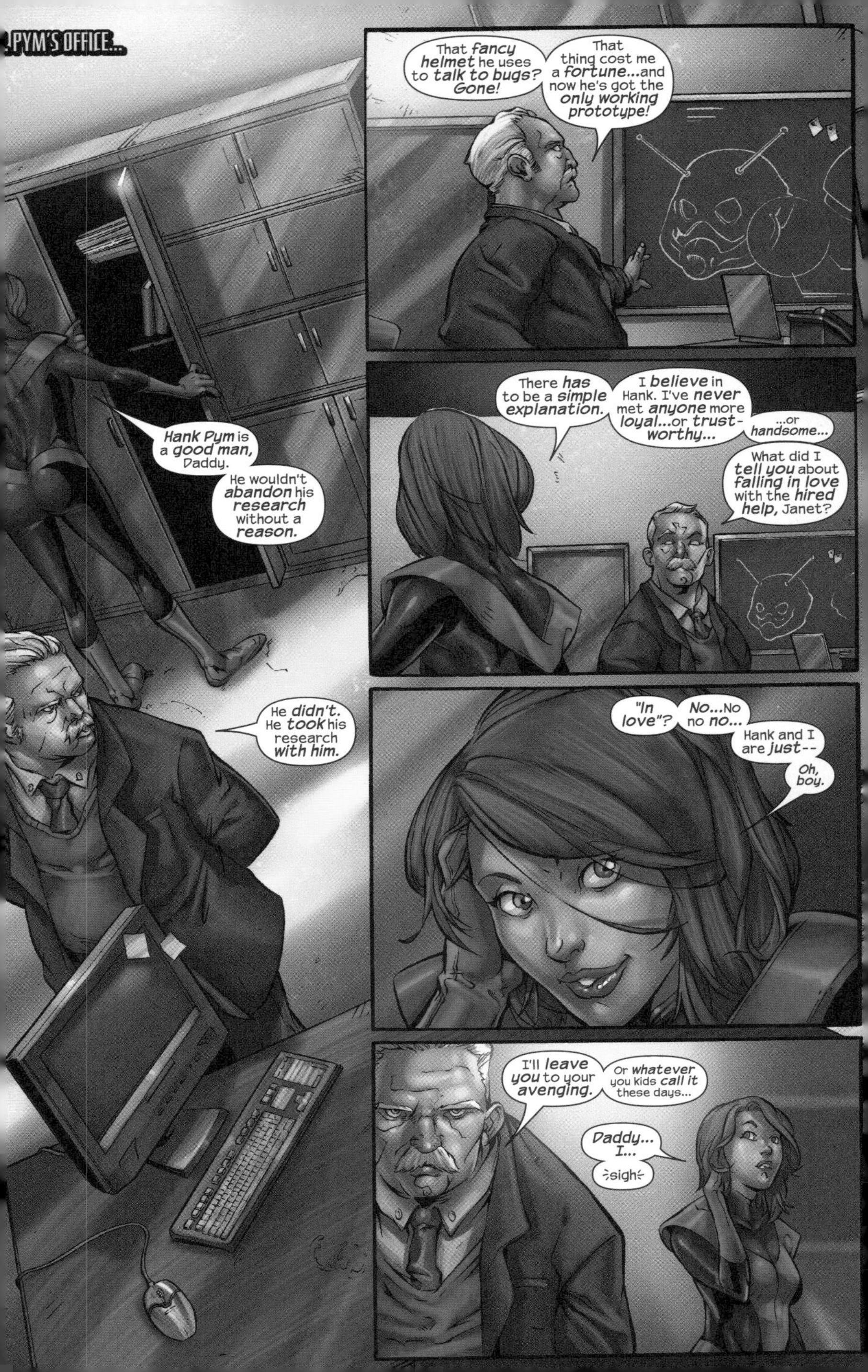
...PYM'S OFFICE...
That fancy helmet he uses to talk to bugs? Gone!
That thing cost me a fortune...and now he's got the only working prototype!
Hank Pym is a good man, Daddy.
He wouldn't abandon his research without a reason.
There has to be a simple explanation.
I believe in Hank. I've never met anyone more loyal...or trust-worthy...
...or handsome...
What did I tell you about falling in love with the hired help, Janet?
He didn't. He took his research with him.
"In love"?
No...No no no...
Hank and I are just--
Oh, boy.
I'll leave you to your avenging.
Or whatever you kids call it these days...
Daddy... I...
sigh

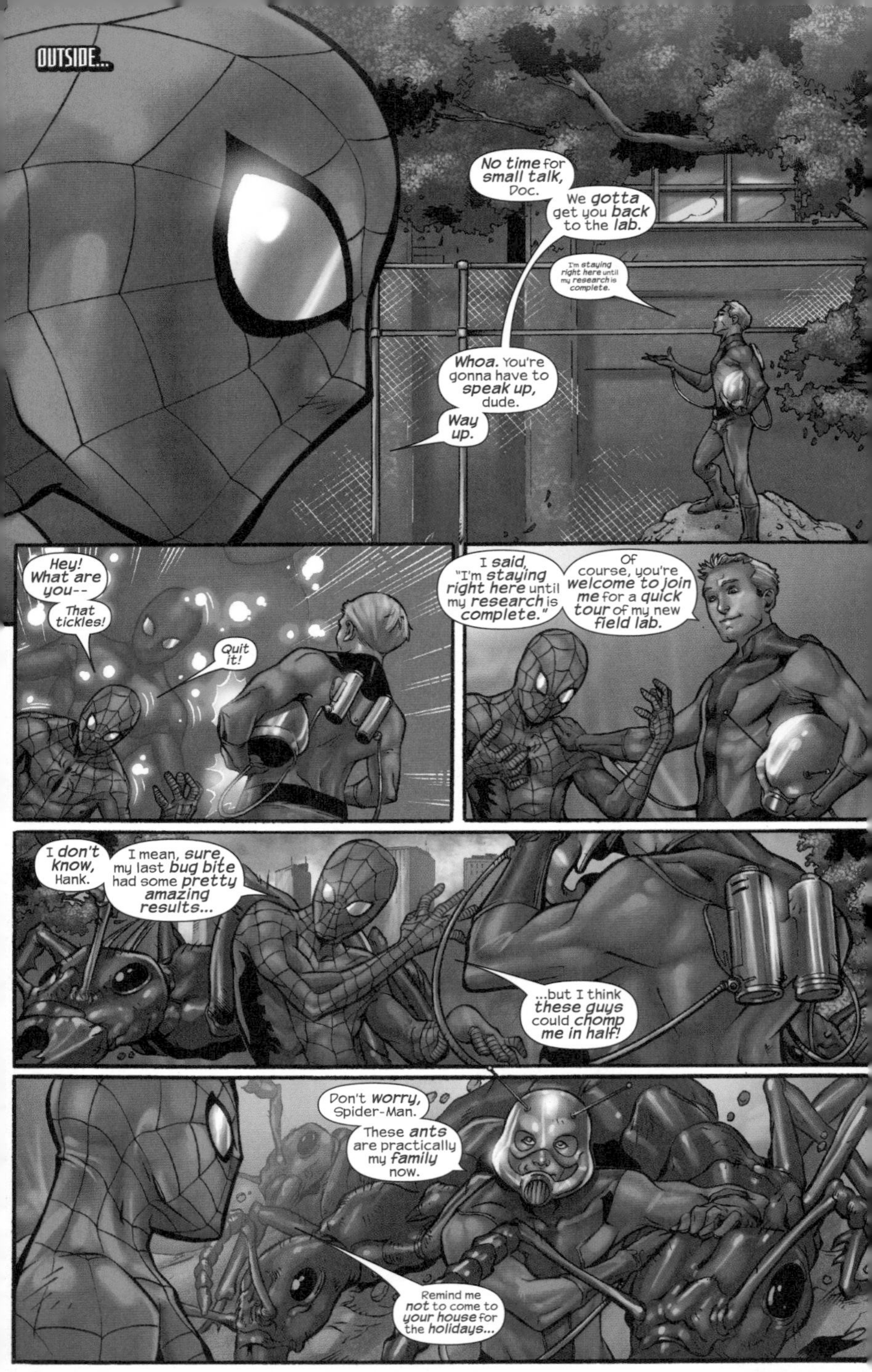

OUTSIDE...
No time for small talk, Doc.
We gotta get you back to the lab.
I'm staying right here until my research is complete.
Whoa. You're gonna have to speak up, dude.
Way up.
Hey! What are you--
That tickles!
Quit it!
I said, "I'm staying right here until my research is complete."
Of course, you're welcome to join me for a quick tour of my new field lab.
I don't know, Hank.
I mean, sure, my last bug bite had some pretty amazing results...
...but I think these guys could chomp me in half!
Don't worry, Spider-Man.
These ants are practically my family now.
Remind me not to come to your house for the holidays...

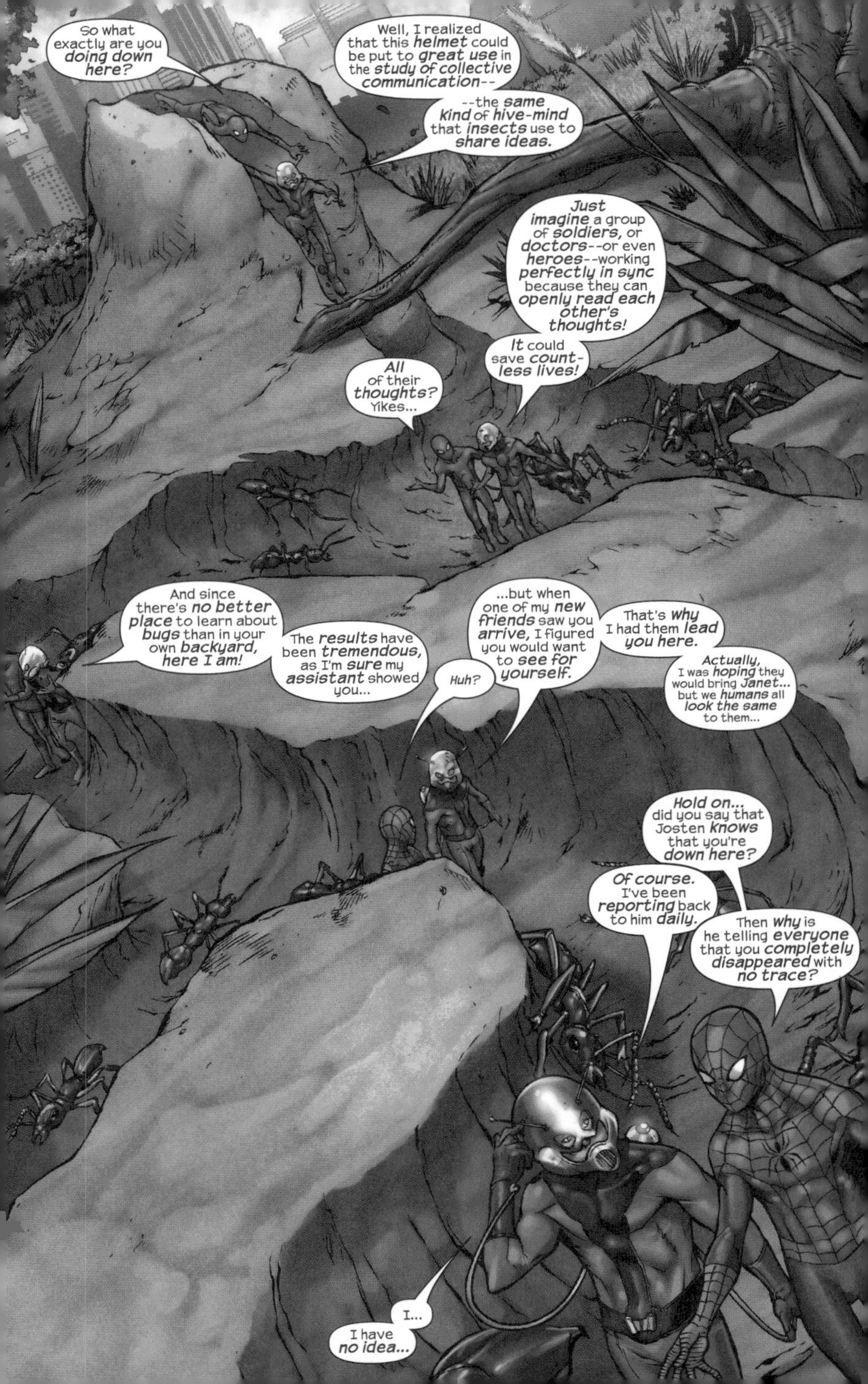
So what exactly are you doing down here?
Well, I realized that this helmet could be put to great use in the study of collective communication--
--the same kind of hive-mind that insects use to share ideas.
Just imagine a group of soldiers, or doctors--or even heroes--working perfectly in sync because they can openly read each other's thoughts!
It could save count-less lives!
All of their thoughts? Yikes...
And since there's no better place to learn about bugs than in your own backyard, here I am!
The results have been tremendous, as I'm sure my assistant showed you...
...but when one of my new friends saw you arrive, I figured you would want to see for yourself.
Huh?
That's why I had them lead you here.
Actually, I was hoping they would bring Janet... but we humans all look the same to them...
Hold on... did you say that Josten knows that you're down here?
Of course. I've been reporting back to him daily.
Then why is he telling everyone that you completely disappeared with no trace?
I... I have no idea...

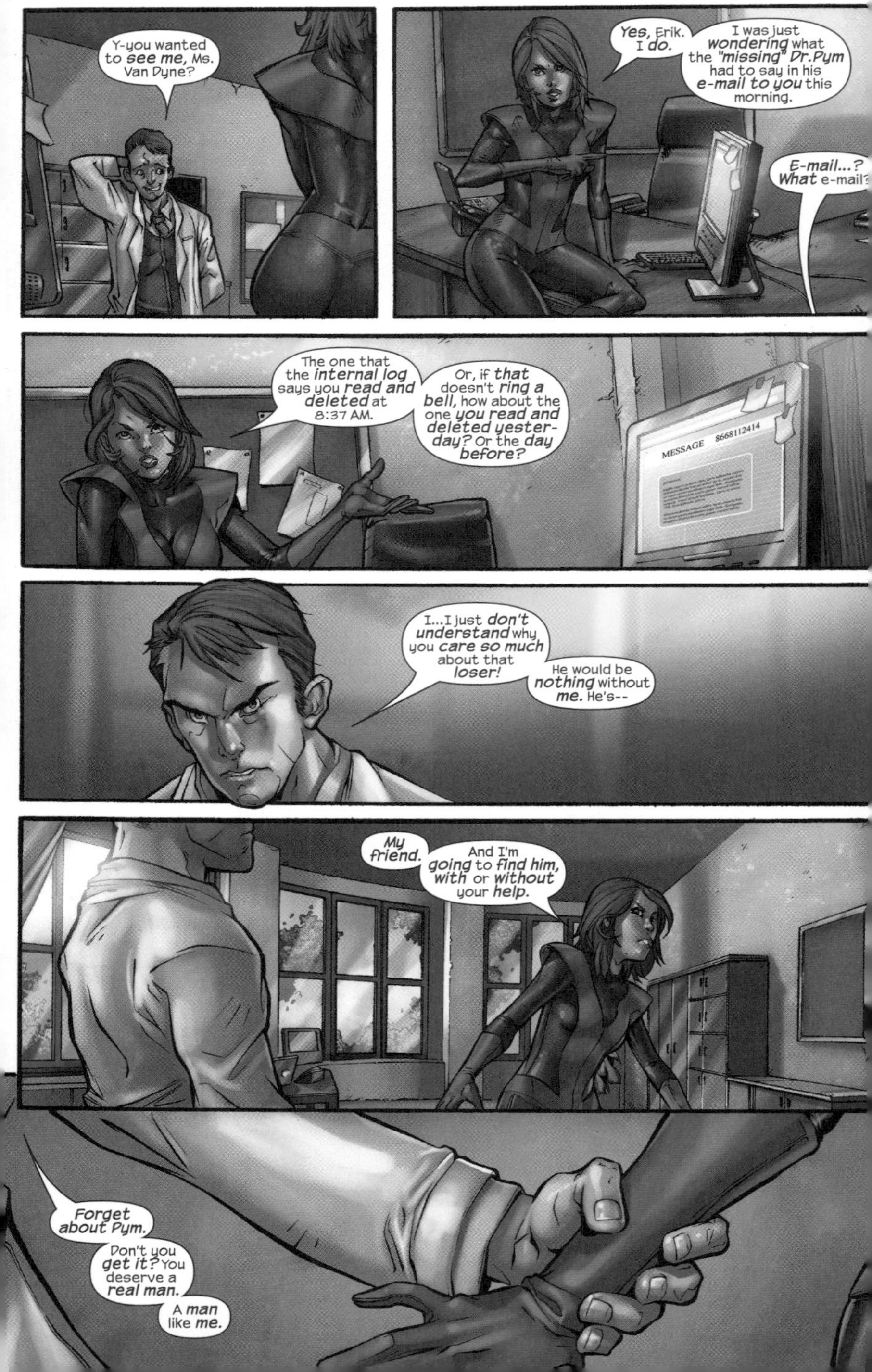

Y-you wanted to see me, Ms. Van Dyne?
Yes, Erik. I do.
I was just wondering what the "missing" Dr. Pym had to say in his e-mail to you this morning.
E-mail...? What e-mail?
The one that the internal log says you read and deleted at 8:37 AM.
Or, if that doesn't ring a bell, how about the one you read and deleted yesterday? Or the day before?
MESSAGE 8668112414
I...I just don't understand why you care so much about that loser!
He would be nothing without me. He's--
My friend.
And I'm going to find him, with or without your help.
Forget about Pym.
Don't you get it? You deserve a real man.
A man like me.

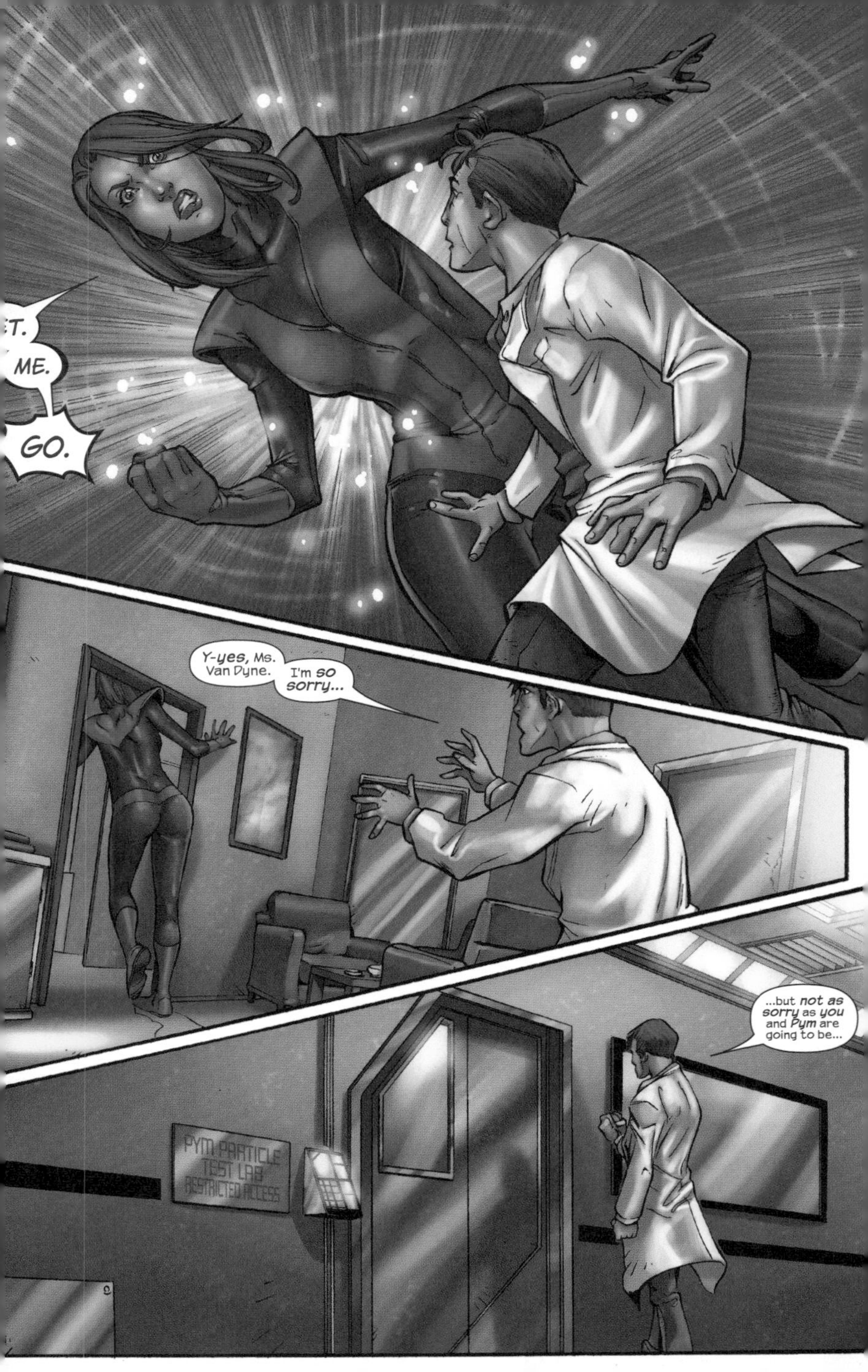

ET.
ME.
GO.
Y-yes, Ms. Van Dyne.
I'm so sorry...
...but not as sorry as you and Pym are going to be...
PYM PARTICLE TEST LAB RESTRICTED ACCESS

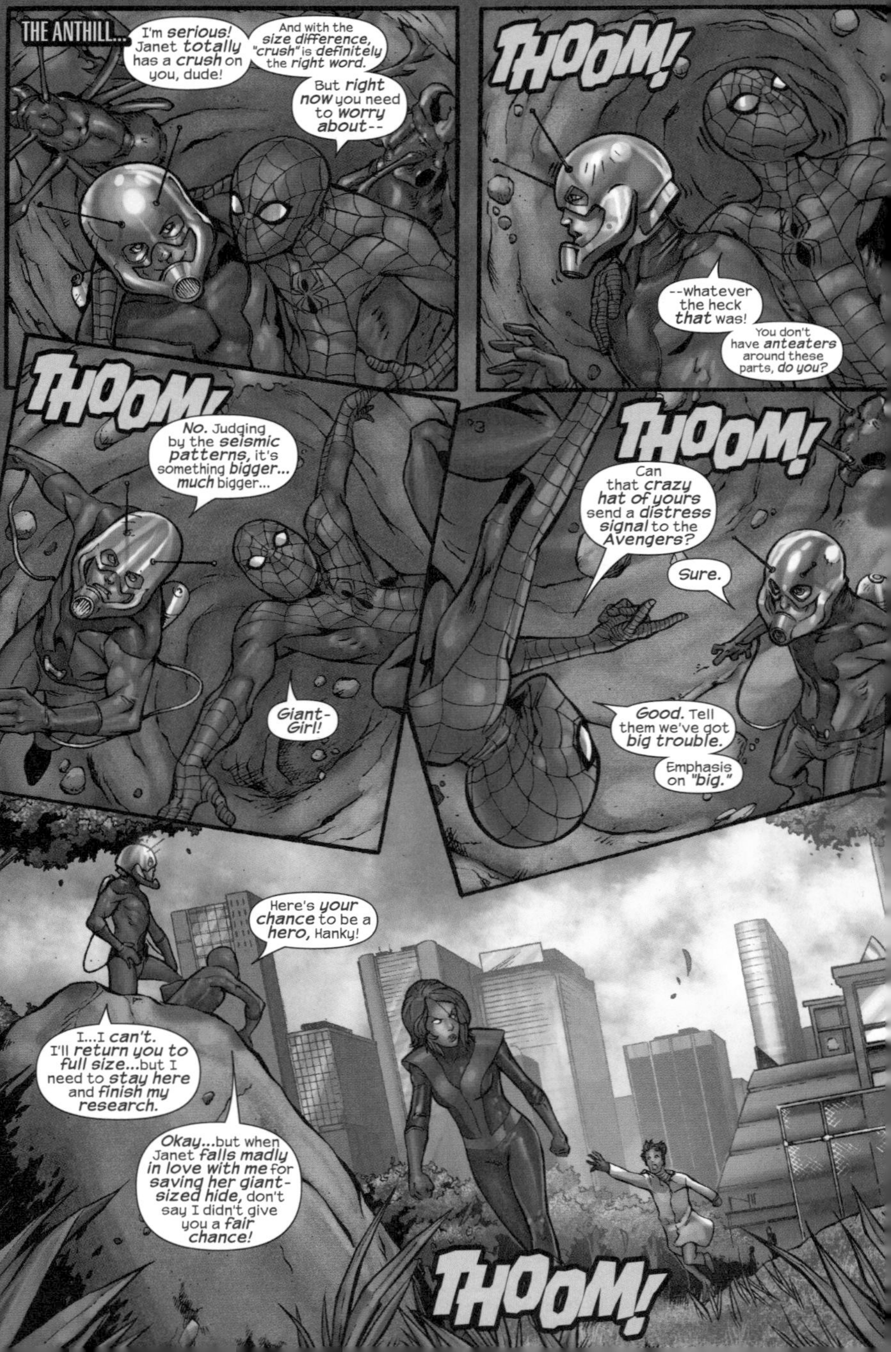
THE ANTHILL...
I'm serious! Janet totally has a crush on you, dude!
And with the size difference, "crush" is definitely the right word.
But right now you need to worry about--
THOOM!
--whatever the heck that was!
You don't have anteaters around these parts, do you?
THOOM!
No. Judging by the seismic patterns, it's something bigger... much bigger...
Giant-Girl!
THOOM!
Can that crazy hat of yours send a distress signal to the Avengers?
Sure.
Good. Tell them we've got big trouble.
Emphasis on "big."
Here's your chance to be a hero, Hanky!
I...I can't. I'll return you to full size...but I need to stay here and finish my research.
Okay...but when Janet falls madly in love with me for saving her giant-sized hide, don't say I didn't give you a fair chance!
THOOM!

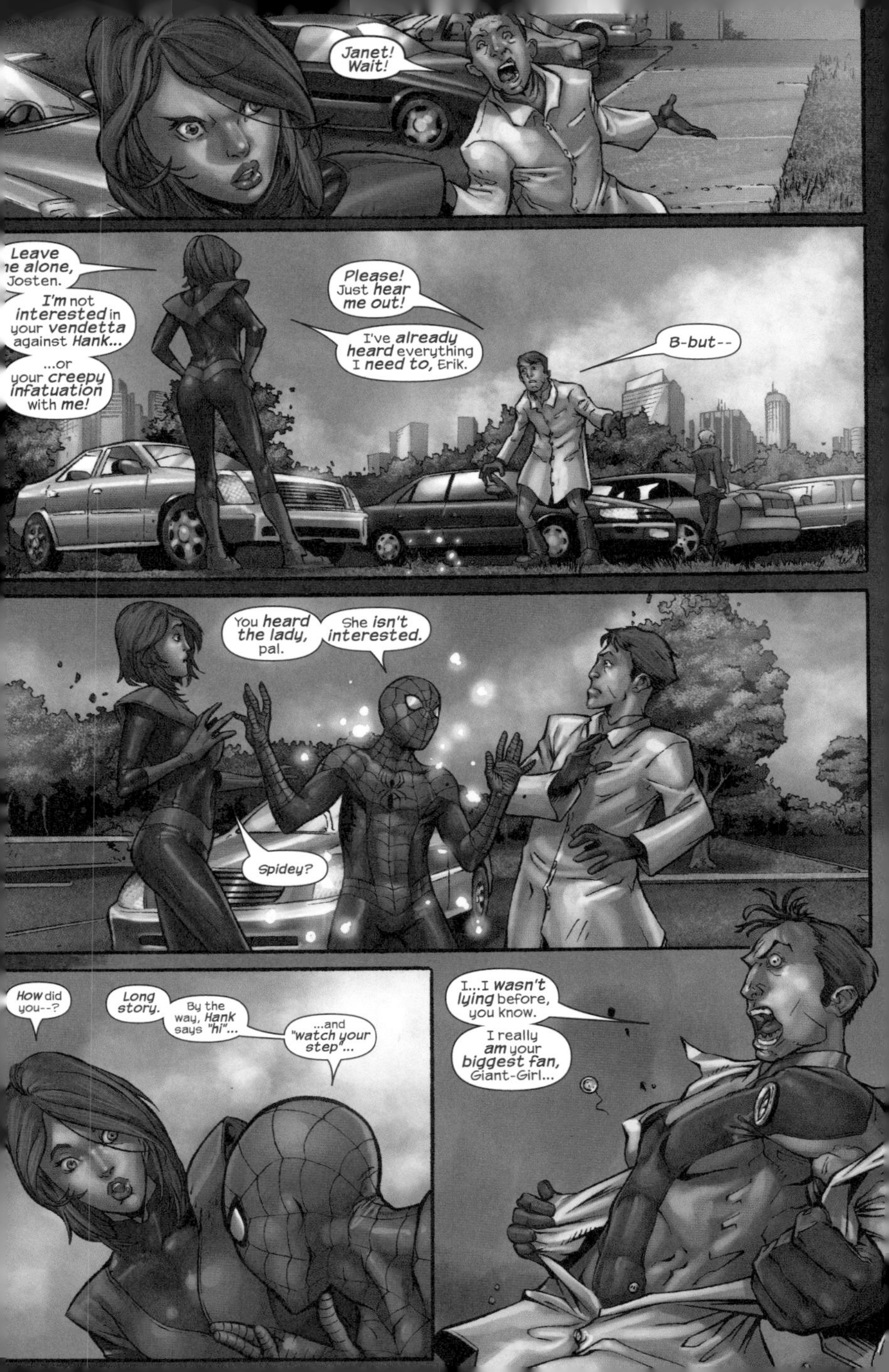

Janet! Wait!
Leave me alone, Josten.
I'm not interested in your vendetta against Hank...
...or your creepy infatuation with me!
Please! Just hear me out!
I've already heard everything I need to, Erik.
B-but--
You heard the lady, pal.
She isn't interested.
Spidey?
How did you--?
Long story.
By the way, Hank says "hi"...
...and "watch your step"...
I...I wasn't lying before, you know.
I really am your biggest fan, Giant-Girl...

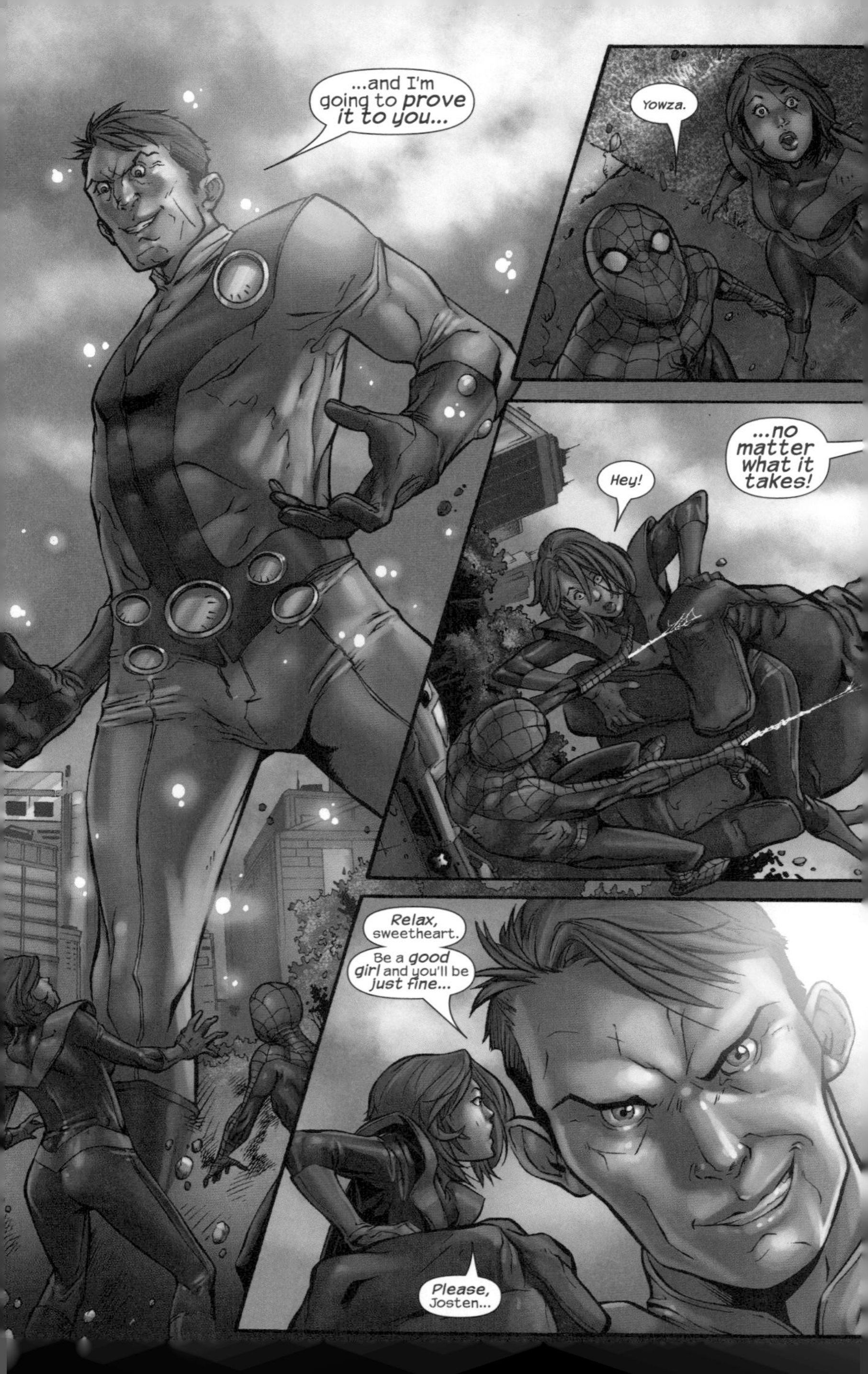
...and I'm going to prove it to you...
Yowza.
...no matter what it takes!
Hey!
Relax, sweetheart.
Be a good girl and you'll be just fine...
Please, Josten...

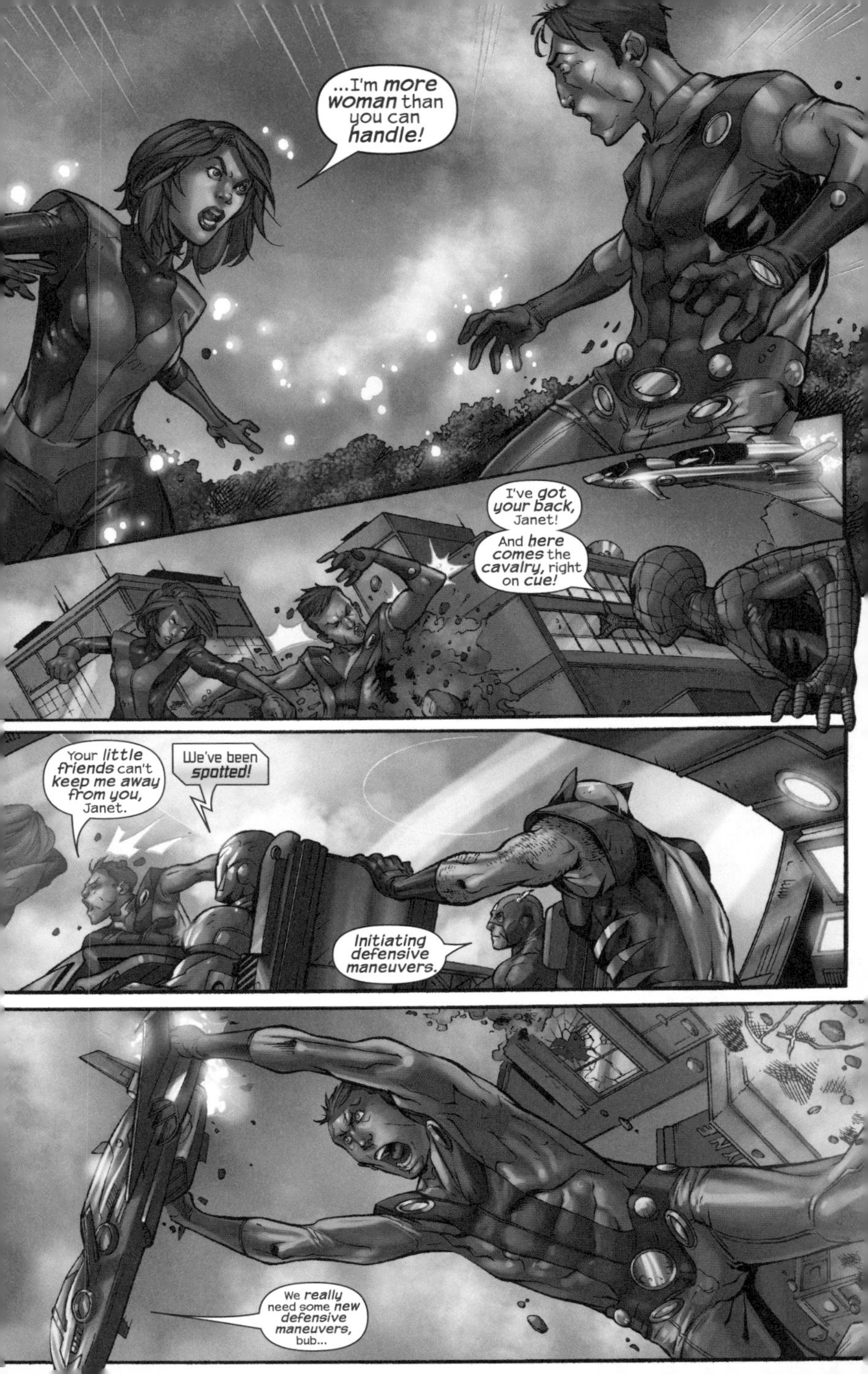
...I'm more woman than you can handle!
I've got your back, Janet!
And here comes the cavalry, right on cue!
Your little friends can't keep me away from you, Janet.
We've been spotted!
Initiating defensive maneuvers.
We really need some new defensive maneuvers, bub...

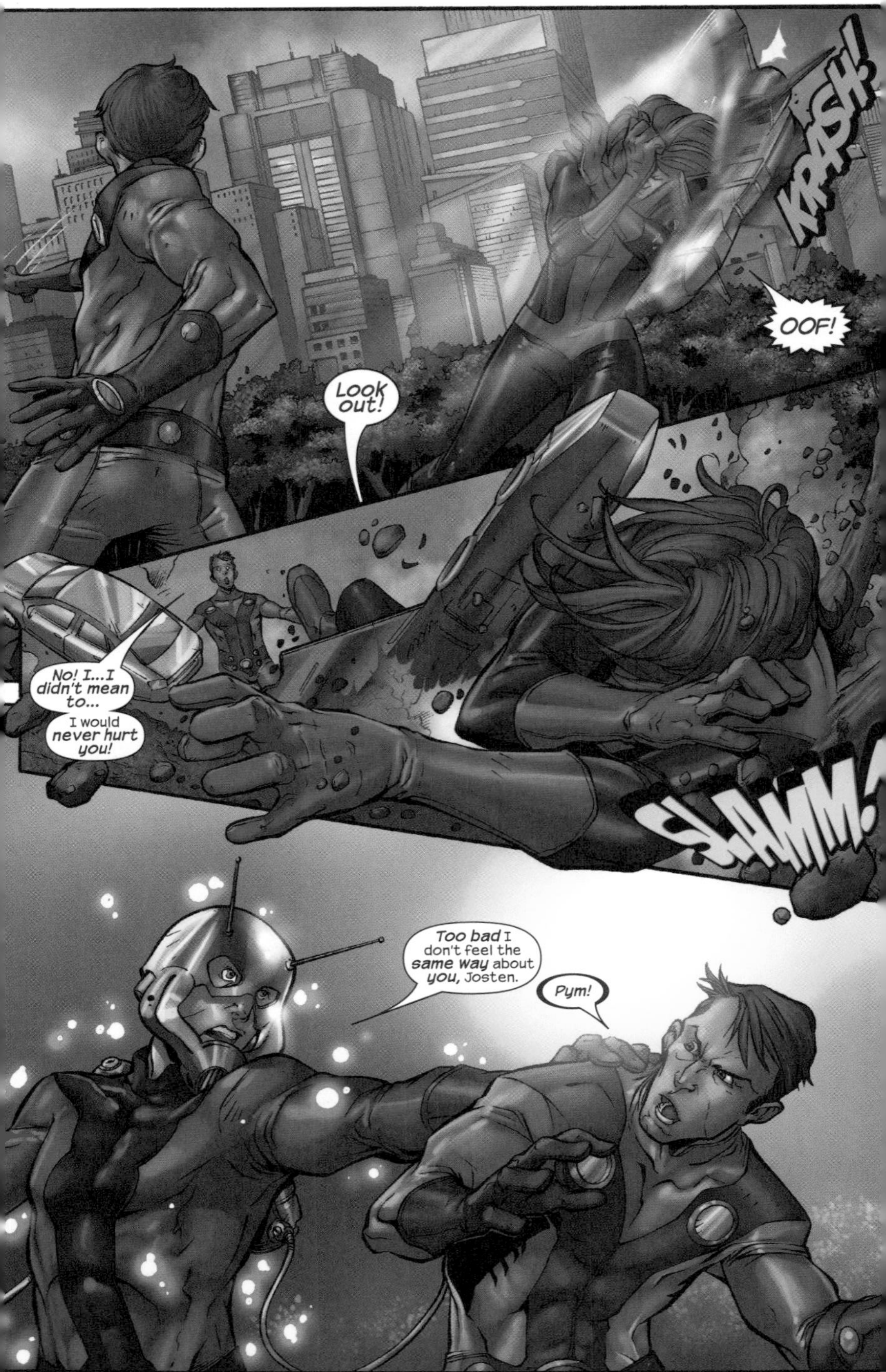
KRASH!
OOF!
Look out!
No! I...I didn't mean to...
I would never hurt you!
SLAMM!
Too bad I don't feel the same way about you, Josten.
Pym!

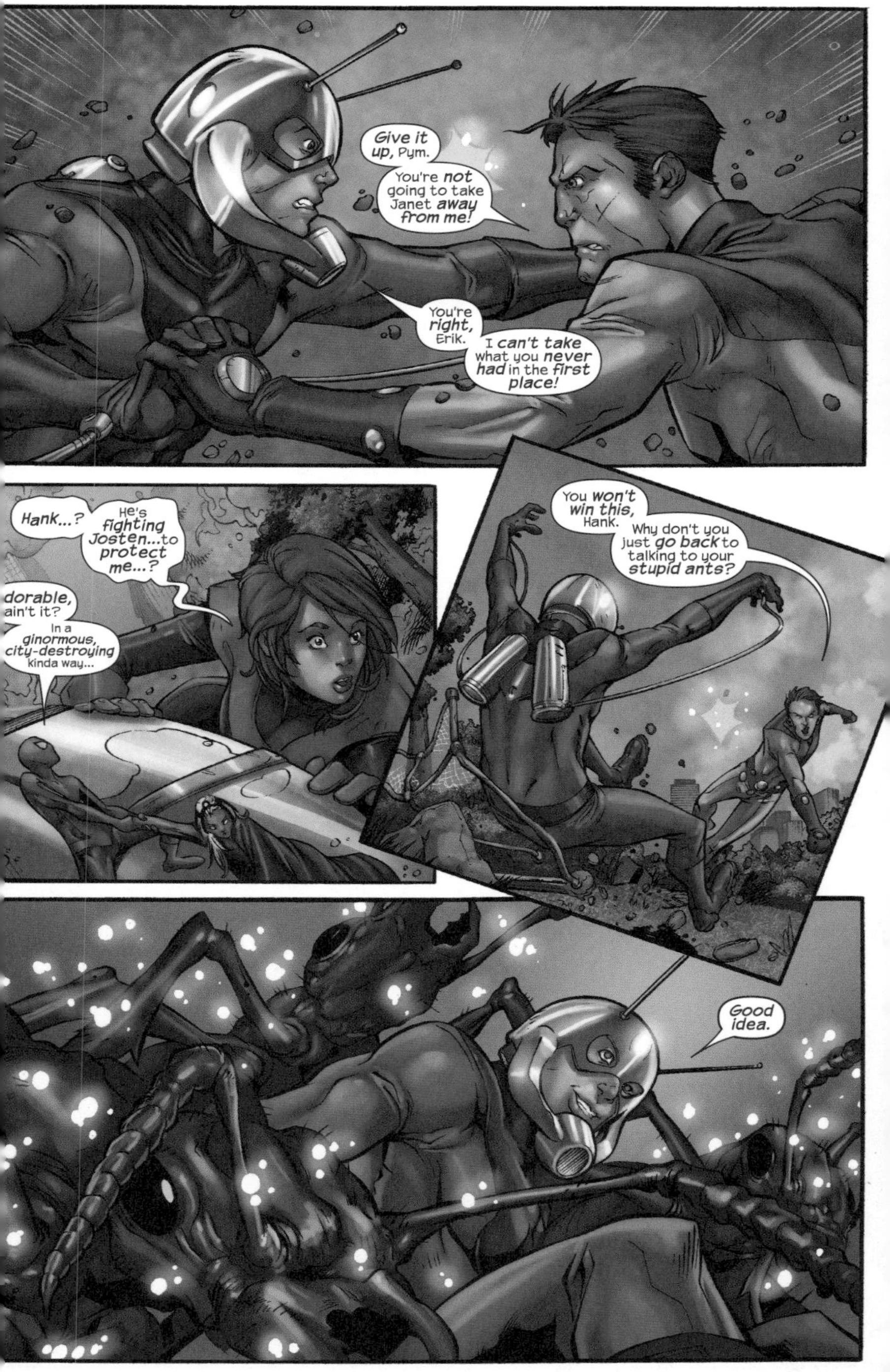
Give it up, Pym.
You're not going to take Janet away from me!
You're right, Erik.
I can't take what you never had in the first place!
Hank...?
He's fighting Josten...to protect me...?
dorable, ain't it?
In a ginormous, city-destroying kinda way...
You won't win this, Hank.
Why don't you just go back to talking to your stupid ants?
Good idea.

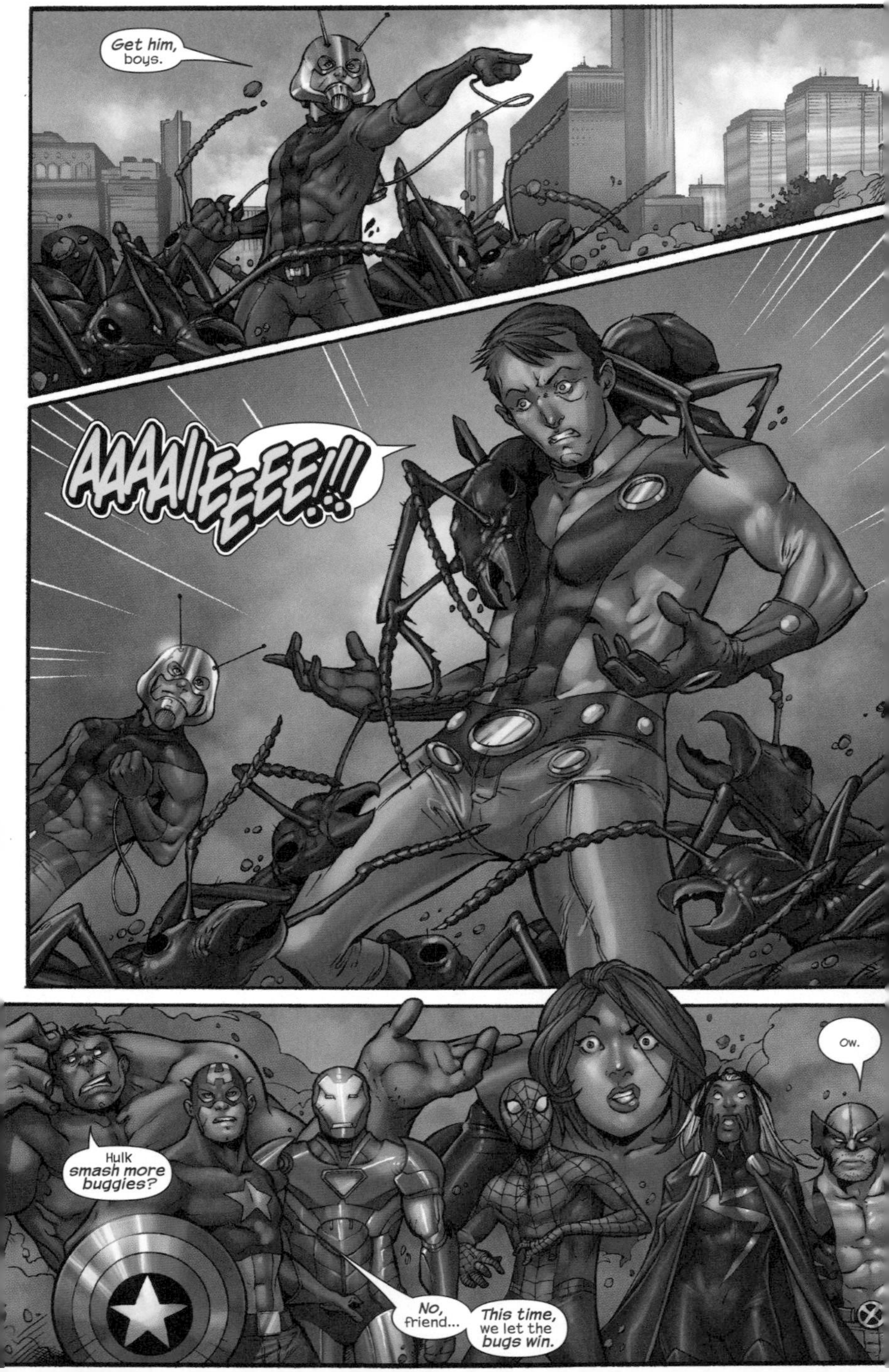
Get him, boys.
AAAAIIEEEEE!!!
Hulk smash more buggies?
No, friend...
This time, we let the bugs win.
Ow.

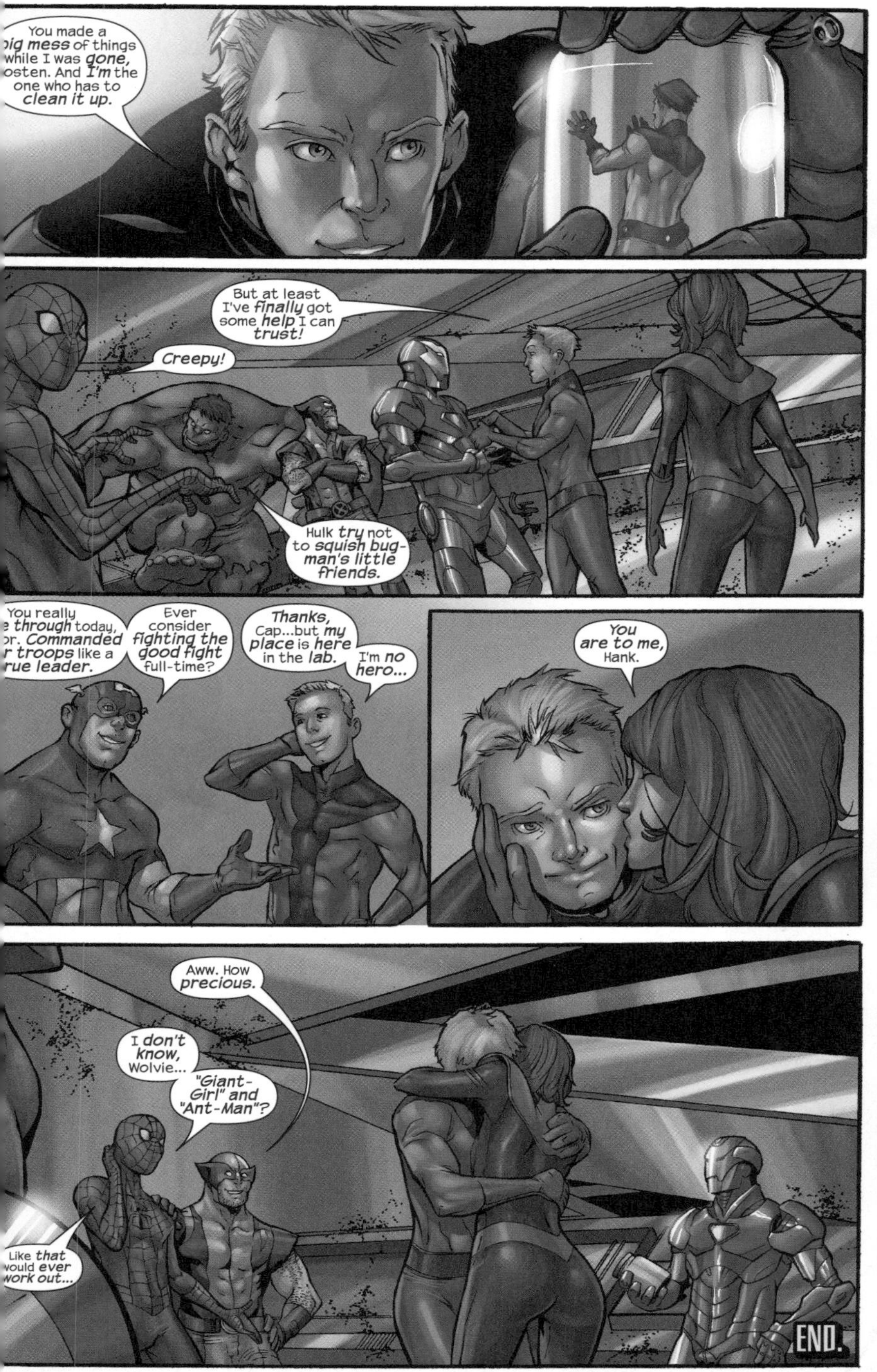

You made a big mess of things while I was gone, osten. And I'm the one who has to clean it up.
But at least I've finally got some help I can trust!
Creepy!
Hulk try not to squish bug-man's little friends.
You really through today, or. Commanded r troops like a rue leader.
Ever consider fighting the good fight full-time?
Thanks, Cap...but my place is here in the lab.
I'm no hero...
You are to me, Hank.
Aww. How precious.
I don't know, Wolvie...
"Giant-Girl" and "Ant-Man"?
Like that would ever work out...
END.